MADAME CHARLES MOULTON

IN THE
COURTS OF MEMORY
1858–1875

FROM CONTEMPORARY LETTERS

BY

L. DE HEGERMANN–LINDENCRONE

ILLUSTRATED WITH
PORTRAITS, FACSIMILES, ETC

HARPER & BROTHERS PUBLISHERS
NEW YORK AND LONDON
MCMXII

E–N

ILLUSTRATIONS

ILLUSTRATIONS

PREFACE

THESE letters, written by me in my younger days to a dear and indulgent mother and aunt, were returned to me after their death. In writing them I allowed myself to go into the smallest details, even the most insignificant ones, as I was sure that they would be welcome and appreciated by those to whom they were addressed. They were certainly not intended to be made public.

If I have decided, after much hesitation, to publish these letters, it is because many of my friends, having read them, have urged me to do so, thinking that they might be of interest, inasmuch as they refer to some important events of the past, and especially to people of the musical world whose names and renown are not yet forgotten.

LILLIE DE HEGERMANN-LINDENCRONE.

BERLIN, *July, 1912.*

NOTE

MADAME DE HEGERMANN-LINDENCRONE, the writer of these letters, which give so vivid a picture of the brilliant court of the last Napoleon, is the wife of the present Danish Minister to Germany. She was formerly Miss Lillie Greenough, of Cambridge, Massachusetts, where she lived with her grandfather, Judge Fay, in the fine old Fay mansion, now the property of Radcliffe College.

As a child Miss Greenough developed the remarkable voice which later was to make her well known, and when only fifteen years of age her mother took her to London to study under Garcia. Two years later Miss Greenough became the wife of Charles Moulton, the son of a well-known American banker, who had been a resident in Paris since the days of Louis Philippe. As Madame Charles Moulton, the charming American became an appreciated guest at the court of Napoleon III. The Paris papers of the days of the Second Empire are filled with the praises of her personal attractions and exquisite singing.

After nine years of gaiety in the gayest city in the world came the war of 1870 and the Commune. Upon the fall of the Empire, Mrs. Moulton returned to America, where Mr. Moulton died, and a few years afterward she married M. de Hegermann-Lindencrone, at that time Danish Minister to the United States, and later

NOTE

successively his country's representative at Stockholm, Rome, and Paris.

Few persons of her day have known so many of those whom the world has counted great. Among her friends have been not only the ruling monarchs of several countries, and the most distinguished men and women of their courts, but almost all the really important figures in the world of music of the past half-century, among them Wagner, Liszt, Auber, Gounod, and Rossini. And of many of these great men the letters give us glimpses of the most fascinatingly intimate sort.

IN THE COURTS OF MEMORY

IN THE COURTS OF MEMORY

CAMBRIDGE, *1856*.

DEAR M.,—You say in your last letter, "Do tell me something about your school." If I only had the time, I could write volumes about my school, and especially about my teachers.

To begin with, Professor Agassiz gives us lectures on zoölogy, geology, and all other ologies, and draws pictures on the blackboard of trilobites and different fossils, which is very amusing. We call him "Father Nature," and we all adore him and try to imitate his funny Swiss accent.

Professor Pierce, who is, you know, the greatest mathematician in the world, teaches us mathematics and has an awful time of it; we must be very stupid, for the more he explains, the less we seem to understand, and when he gets on the rule of three we almost faint from dizziness. If he would only explain the rule of one! The Harvard students say that his book on mathematics is so intricate that not one of them can solve the problems.

We learn history and mythology from Professor Felton, who is very near-sighted, wears broad-brimmed

I

spectacles, and shakes his curly locks at us when he thinks we are frivolous. He was rather nonplussed the other day, when Louise Child read out loud in the mythology lesson something about "Jupiter and ten." "What," cried Mr. Felton, "what are you reading? You mean 'Jupiter and Io,' don't you?" "It says ten here," she answered.

Young Mr. Agassiz teaches us German and French; we read Balzac's *Les Chouans* and Schiller's *Wallenstein*.

Our Italian teacher, Luigi Monti, is a refugee from Italy, and has a sad and mysterious look in his black eyes; he can hardly speak English, so we have things pretty much our own way during the lessons, for he cannot correct us. One of the girls, translating *capelli neri*, said "black hats," and he never saw the mistake, though we were all dying of laughter.

No one takes lessons in Greek from long-bearded, fierce-eyed Professor Evangelinus Apostolides Sophocles, so he is left in peace. He does not come more than once a week anyway, and then only to say it is no use his coming at all.

Cousin James Lowell replaces Mr. Longfellow the days he can't come. He reads selections of "literary treasures," as he calls them, and on which he discourses at length. He seems very dull and solemn when he is in school; not at all as he is at home. When he comes in of an afternoon and reads his poems to aunty and to an admiring circle of cousins and sisters-in-law, they all roar with laughter, particularly when he reads them with a Yankee accent. He has such a rippling little giggle while reading, that it is impossible not to laugh.

2

The other day he said to me, "Cousin Lillie, I will take you out for a walk in recess." I said, "Nothing I should like better, but I can't go." "Why not?" said he. "Because I must go and be a beggar." "What do you mean?" he asked. "I mean that there is a duet that Mrs. Agassiz favors just now, from Meyerbeer's 'Le Prophète,' where she is beggar number one and I am beggar number two." He laughed. "You are a lucky little beggar, anyway. I envy you." "Envy me? I thought you would pity me," I said. "No, I do not pity you, I envy you being a beggar with a voice!"

I consider myself a victim. In recess, when the other girls walk in Quincy Street and eat their apples, Mrs. Agassiz lures me into the parlor and makes me sing duets with her and her sister, Miss Carey. I hear the girls filing out of the door, while I am caged behind the piano, singing, "Hear Me, Norma," wishing Norma and her twins in Jericho.

There are about fourteen pupils now; we go every morning at nine o'clock and stay till two o'clock. We climb up the three stories in the Agassiz house and wait for our teachers, who never are on time. Sometimes school does not begin for half an hour.

Mrs. Agassiz comes in, and we all get up to say good morning to her. As there is nothing else left for her to teach, she teaches us manners. She looks us over, and holds up a warning finger smilingly. She is so sweet and gentle.

I don't wonder that you think it extraordinary that all these fine teachers, who are the best in Harvard College, should teach us; but the reason is, that the

Agassiz's have built a new house and find it difficult
to pay for it, so their friends have promised to help
them to start this school, and by lending their names
they have put it on its legs, so to speak.

The other day I was awfully mortified. Mr. Longfellow, who teaches us literature, explained all about
rhythm, measures, and the feet used in poetry. The
idea of poetry having feet seemed so ridiculous that I
thought out a beautiful joke, which I expected would
amuse the school immensely; so when he said to me
in the lesson, "Miss Greenough, can you tell me what
blank verse is?" I answered promptly and boldly,
"Blank verse is like a blank-book; there is nothing in it,
not even feet," and looked around for admiration, but
only saw disapproval written everywhere, and Mr.
Longfellow, looking very grave, passed on to the next
girl. I never felt so ashamed in my life.

Mr. Longfellow, on passing our house, told aunty
that he was coming in the afternoon, to speak to
me; aunty was worried and so was I, but when he
came I happened to be singing Schubert's "Dein ist
mein Herz," one of aunty's songs, and he said, "Go
on. Please don't stop." When I had finished he
said:

"I came to scold you for your flippancy this morning,
but you have only to sing to take the words out of my
mouth, and to be forgiven."

"And I hope you will forget," I said, penitently.

"I have already forgotten," he answered, affectionately. "How can one be angry with a dear little bird?
But don't try again to be so witty."

"Never again, I promise you."

4

THE FAY HOUSE, CAMBRIDGE, MASSACHUSETTS

"That's the dear girl you are, and 'Dein ist mein Herz'!" He stooped down and kissed me.

I burst into tears, and kissed his hand. This is to show you what a dear, kind man Mr. Longfellow is.

CAMBRIDGE, *June, 1857.*

If you were here, dear mama, I would sing, "Oh, Wake and Call Me Early, Call Me Early, Mother Dear," for I am to dance the quadrille on the "Green" on Class Day. To be asked by a Harvard graduate to be one of the four girls to dance is a great compliment. All the college windows are full of people gazing at you, and just think of the other girls, who are filled with envy fuller than the windows!

Aunty is "pestered" (as she calls it) to death by people wanting me to sing for their charities. Every one has a pet charity, which it seems must be attended to just at this time, and they clamor for help from me, and aunty has not the courage to say "no." Therefore, about once a week I am dressed in the white muslin and the black shoes, which is my gala get-up, and a carriage is sent for me. Then aunty and I are driven to the Concert Hall, where, when my turn comes, I go on the platform and sing, "Casta Diva," "Ah, non Credea," etc., and if I am encored then I sing, "Coming Thro' the Rye."

I am sure every one says that it is a shame to make me sing, but they make me sing, all the same. I enjoy the applause and the excitement—who would not? What I do *not* enjoy is being obliged to sing in church every Sunday. Dr. Hoppin has persuaded aunty to

2   5

let me help in the choir; that is, to sing the Anthem and the "Te Deum," but it amounts to my doing about all the singing. Don't you think this is cruel? However, there is one hymn I love to sing, and that is, "Shout the Glad Tidings, Exultingly Sing." I put my whole heart and soul in this, and soon find myself shouting the "glad tidings" all alone, my companions having left me in the lurch.

We laughed very much at aunty's efforts in the Antislavery movement (just now at its height), when all Massachusetts has risen up with a bound in order to prove that the blacks are as good as the whites (if not better), and should have all their privileges. She, wishing to demonstrate this point, introduced Joshua Green, a little colored boy (the washerwoman's son), into the Sunday-school class. The general indignation among the white boys did not dismay her, as she hoped that Joshua would come up to the mark. The answer to the first question in the catechism (what is your name?), he knew, and answered boldly, "Joshua Green." But the second question, "Who made you?" was the stumbling-block. He sometimes answered, "Father," and sometimes, "Mother." Aunty, being afraid that he would answer, "Miss Fay," had him come to the house during the week, where she could din into him that it was God who made him and all creation. "Now, Joshua, when Dr. Hoppin says to you, 'Who made you?' you must answer, 'God, who made everything on earth and in heaven'—you understand?" "Yes, ma'am," and repeated the phrase until aunty thought him ripe to appear at Sunday-school, which he did on the following Sunday. You may imagine aunty's consternation when Dr. Hoppin asked Joshua, "Who made you?" and Joshua looked at aunty with a broad grin, showing all his teeth, and said, "Lor', Miss Fay, I forget who you said it was." This was aunty's last effort to teach the blacks. She repeated this episode to Mr. Phillips Brooks, who, in return, told her an amusing story of a colored man who had been converted to the Catholic religion, and went one day to confession (he seems not to have been very sure about this function). The priest said to him, "Israel, what have you to confess? Have you been perfectly honest since the last time? No thefts?"

"No, sir."

"None at all? Stolen no chickens?"

"No, sir."

"No watermelons?"

"No, sir."

"No eggs?"

"No, sir."

"No turkeys?"

"No, sir; not one."

Then the priest gave absolution. Outside the church Israel found the companions whom he had left waiting for him.

"Well, how did you get on?" they asked.

"Bully!" answered Israel. "But if he'd said ducks he'd have got me."

Cousin James Lowell said: "See how a negro appreciates the advantages of the confession."

DEAR L.,—A family council was held yesterday, and it is now quite decided that mama is to take me

7

to Europe, and that I shall study singing with the best masters. We will first go to New York for a visit of ten days with Mr. and Mrs. Cooley. I shall see New York and hear a little music; and then we start for Europe on the 17th in the *Commodore Vanderbilt*.

NEW YORK.

DEAR AUNT,—We have now been here a week, and I feel ashamed that I have not written to you before, but I have been doing a great deal. The Cooleys have a gorgeous house in Fifth Avenue, furnished with every luxury one can imagine. The sitting-room, dining-room, library, and a conservatory next to the billiard-room, are down-stairs; up-stairs are the drawing-rooms (first, second, and third), which open into a marble-floored Pompeian room, with a fountain. Then comes mama's and my bed-room, with bath-room attached. On the third floor the family have their apartment. We have been many times to the opera, and heard an Italian tenor, called Brignoli, whom people are crazy over. He has a lovely voice and sings in "Trovatore." Last night, when he sang "Di quella pira," people's enthusiasm knew no bounds. They stood up and shouted, and ladies waved their handkerchiefs; he had to repeat it three times, and each time people got wilder. Nina and I clapped till our gloves were in pieces and our arms actually ached.

A Frenchman by the name of Musard has brought over a French orchestra, and is playing French music at the opera-house. People are wild over him also. Madame La Grange, who they say is a fine lady in her own country, is singing in "The Huguenots." She has rather a thin voice, but vocalizes beautifully. Nina and I weep over the hard fate of Valentine, who has to be present when her husband is conspiring against the Huguenots, knowing that her lover is listening behind the curtain and can't get away. The priests come in and bless the conspiracy, all the conspirators holding their swords forward to be blessed. This music is really too splendid for words, and we enjoy it intensely.

Mr. Bancroft, the celebrated historian, invited us to dinner, and after dinner they asked me to sing. I had to accompany myself. Every one pretended that they were enchanted. Just for fun, at the end I sang, "Three Little Kittens Took Off Their Mittens, to Eat a Christmas Pie," and one lady (would you believe it?) said she wept tears of joy, and had cold shivers down her back. When I sang, "For We Have Found Our Mittens," there was, she said, such a jubilant ring in my voice that her heart leaped for joy.

Mr. Bancroft sent me the next day a volume of Bryant's poems, with the dedication, "To Miss Lillie Greenough, in souvenir of a never-forgetable evening." I made so many acquaintances, and received so many invitations, that if we should stay much longer here there would be nothing left of me to take to Europe.

I will write as soon as we arrive on the other side. On whatever side I am, I am always your loving niece, who thinks that there is no one in the wide world to compare to you, that no one is as clever as you, that no one can sing like you, and that there never was any one who can hold a candle to you. There!

IN THE COURTS OF MEMORY

DEAR AUNT,—At last we have arrived at our journey's end, and we are happy to have got out of and away from the steamer, where we have been cooped up for the last weeks. However, we had a very gay time during those weeks, and some very sprightly companions. Among them a runaway couple; he was a Mr. Aulick Palmer, but I don't know who she was. One could have learned it easily enough for the asking, as they were delighted to talk about themselves and their elopement, and how they did it. It was their favorite topic of conversation. I was intensely interested in them; I had never been so near a romance in my life. They had been married one hour when they came on board; she told her parents that she was going out shopping, and then, after the marriage, wrote a note to them to say that she was married and off to Europe, adding that she was not sorry for what she had done. He is a handsome man, tall and dark; she is a jolly, buxom blonde, with a charming smile which shows all her thirty and something teeth, and makes her red, thick lips uncurl. I thought, for such a newly married couple, they were not at all sentimental, which I should have supposed natural. She became sea-sick directly, and he called attention to her as she lay stretched out on a bench looking dreadfully green in the face: "We are a sick couple—home-sick, love-sick, and sea-sick."

The captain, who thought himself a wag but who forgot every morning what he had wagged about the day before, would say for his daily greeting, "Wie [as the Germans say] befinden sie sich?" He thought the pun on sea-sick was awfully funny, and would laugh uproariously. He said to Mr. Palmer, "Why are you not like a melon?" We all guessed. One person said, "Because he was not meloncholic [Aulick]." But all the guesses were wrong. "No," said the captain, "it is because the melon can't elope, and you can." He thought himself very funny, and was rather put out that we did not think him so, and went on repeating the joke to every one on the boat *ad nauseam*.

LONDON, *1859.*

DEAREST A.,—We arrived here, as we intended, on the 27th. . . . We easily found Garcia's address, and drove there without delay. I was very anxious to see the "greatest singing master in the world," and there he was standing before me, looking very much as I had imagined him; but not like any one I had ever seen before. He has grayish hair and a black mustache, expressive big eyes, and such a fascinating smile! Mama said, having heard of his great reputation, she wished that he would consent to give me a *few* lessons. He smiled, and answered that, if I would kindly sing something for him, he could better judge how much teaching I required. I replied—I was so sure of myself—that, if he would accompany "Qui la voce," I would sing that. "Ha, ha!" he cried, with a certain sarcasm. "By all means let us have that," and sat down before the piano while I spread out the music before him. I sang, and thought I sang very well; but he just looked up into my face with a very quizzical expression, and said, "How

11

long have you been singing, Mademoiselle?" Mama
answered for me before I could speak, "She has sung,
Monsieur, since she was a very small child."

He was not at all impressed by this, but said, "I
thought so." Then he continued, "You say you would
like to take some lessons of me?" I was becoming very
humble, and said, meekly, that I hoped he would give
me some. "Well, Mademoiselle, you have a very
wonderful voice, but you have not the remotest idea
how to sing." What a come-down! I, who thought
I had only to open my mouth to be admired, and only
needed a *few* finishing touches to make me perfect,
to be told that I had "not the remotest idea how to
sing"!

Mama and I both gasped for breath, and I could
have cried for disappointment as well as mortification.
However, I felt he was right, and, strange to say, mama
felt so too. He said, "Take six months' rest and don't
sing a single note, then come back to me." When he
saw the crestfallen look on my face, he added, kindly,
"Then we shall see something wonderful."

We leave for Dresden this evening. . . . Love to all.

Your humble

LILLIE.

LONDON, *May, 1860.*

DEAR A.,—I have not written since we left the kind
V. Rensselaers in Dresden. Mama must have given
you all the details of our life there. . . . I hope, now that
I have studied French, German, and Italian like a good
little girl for six months and not "sung a single note,"

that I may venture to present myself before the great Garcia again.

I can't imagine that I am the same person who has (it seems to me years ago) sung before large, distinguished, and enthusiastic audiences, has been a little belle, in a way, in Cambridge, has had serenades from the Harvard Glee Club (poor aunty! routed out of your sleep in the middle of the night to listen to them), inspired poetry, and danced on "the Green" on Class Day. I felt as if I ought to put on pantalettes and wear my hair down my back. I look now upon myself as a real *Backfisch*, as the Germans call very young girls, and that is simply what I am; and I feel that I ought never to have been allowed to sport about in those fascinating clear waters which reflected no shadows, now that I must go back to the millpond and learn to swim.

I have been already three weeks studying hard with Garcia, who is not only a wonderful teacher, but is a wonderful personality. I simply worship him, though he is very severe and pulls me up directly I "slipshod," as he calls it; and so far I have literally sung nothing but scales. He says that a scale must be like a beautiful row of pearls: each note like a pearl, perfect in roundness and color.

This is so easy to say, but very difficult to accomplish. Stone-breaking on the highroad is nothing to it. I come home tired out from my lessons, only to begin singing scales again. I tell mama I feel like a fish with the scales being taken off him.

Four hours by myself and two lessons a week will soon reduce your poor niece to *a scaleton*. Ah! please forgive this. . . .

No question of a song yet. "Qui la voce" seems 'way back in the Middle Ages. Garcia says, "If, when your voice is well oiled [that is what he calls the scaling process], you are not intelligent enough to sing a song by yourself, then you had better knit stockings for the poor."

"Then," I answered, "I had better begin at once to learn to knit stockings."

"Not quite yet," he laughed. "Wait till I have finished with you." More than once he has said, "Your voice reminds me of my sister Marie's [meaning Malibran]; but she had no brains to speak of, whereas you have, and you ought to be thankful for it."

I murmured that I was glad he thought so, and, if I really had some brains, I should be thankful; but I was not quite sure that I had. "Trust me to tell you if you have not," said he.

I trusted him, indeed, for I knew very well that he would not let the occasion slip had he anything of that sort to say.

LONDON, *July, 1860.*

DEAR A.,—Still hard at work. I wonder at mama's patience and endurance. To hear scales, cadenzas, and trills from morning till night must be terribly wearing on the nerves. I said as much to the master, and he consented to give me "Bel raggio," of "Semiramide." It is as good as an exercise, anyway, because it is nothing but cadenzas. Then he allowed me to sing "Una voce poco fa." I told him that mama had put on a pound of flesh since I was permitted to roam in these fresh pastures. This made him laugh. After he had seen that I had "brains enough" to sing these songs according to his august liking, he said, "Now we will try 'Voi che sapete,' of Mozart."

Garcia has not the ghost of a voice; but he has the most enchanting way of singing mezzo-voce, and occasionally says, "Sing this so," and sings the phrase for me. It sounds delightfully when he does it; but I do not think he would have liked me to "sing it so," and would probably swear a gentle little Spanish swear under his garlicky breath, because (I say it, though I hate to) the dear master eats garlic—pounds of it, I fear—and his voice is highly scented when it cracks, which it often does.

He once said, "You may imitate my way of singing, but don't imitate my crack."

"Oh," I said, "I love to hear you sing. I don't even hear the crack."

"Ah," he sighed, "if it had not been for that crack I should be in the opera now."

"I am glad," I answered, "that you are not there; for then you would not be here, teaching me." I think this pleased him.

Sometimes he is very nervous. Once, when I was singing "Voi che sapete," the tears rolled down his cheeks, and another time, when he was showing me how to sing it "so," I burst into tears, and the poor man had to order his servant to bring me some sherry to restore my nerves. There is one phrase in this song which I never can hear sung, or never can sing myself, without emotion.

The season is getting so late mama thinks we ought to leave London, especially as Garcia is taking his vacation; and we are going in a few days to Paris.

Garcia has given us a letter to his sister, Madame Viardot (of whom he said she had brains but no voice). He wrote: "I send you my pupil. Do all you can to persuade her to go on the stage. She has it in her."

But Madame Viardot may "do all she can"; I will never go on the stage.

If "it" is in me, it must work out some other way.

PARIS, *May, 1861.*

DEAR A.,—Mother will have written to you of my engagement to Charles Moulton. I wish you would come and see me married, and that I could present all my future family to the most lovable of aunts.

I think I shall have everything to make me happy. In the first place, my fiancé is very musical, composes charming things, and plays delightfully on the piano; my future mother-in-law is a dear old lady, musical and universally talented; my future father-in-law is a *bona-fide* American, a dear quixotic old gentleman who speaks the most awful French. Although he has lived in Paris for forty years, he has never conquered the pronunciation of the French language, but has invented a unique dialect of his own. Every word that can be pronounced in English he pronounces in English, as well as all numbers. For instance, a phrase such as *La guerre de mille huit cent quinze était une démonstration de la liberté nationale* would sound like this: "La gur de 1815 (in English) était une demonstration (in English) de la liberty national." It is almost impossible to understand

16

him; but he will read for hours unabashed, not only to us, the drowsy and inattentive members of his family, but to the most fastidious and illustrious Frenchmen. There are two brothers and a sweet little sister. I shall have a beautiful home, or rather homes, because they have not only a handsome hotel in Paris, but an ideal country place (Petit Val) and a villa in Dinard.

Good-by. Greet all the united family from me, and tell them not to worry over my future, as you wrote they were doing. I have renounced forever the pomps and allurements of the stage, and I trust the leaves on the genealogical tree will cease their trembling, and that the Fays, my ancestors, will not trouble themselves to turn in their graves, as you threatened they would if I did anything to disgrace them.

CHÂTEAU DE PETIT VAL, *June, 1862.*

DEAREST A.,—I wish I could give you an idea of Petit Val and our life as lived by me. Petit Val is about twelve miles from Paris, and was built for the Marquis de Marigny, whose portrait still hangs in the salon—the brother of Madame de Pompadour—by the same architect who built and laid out the park of Petit Trianon.

There is an avenue of tall poplar-trees leading from Petit Val straight to Choisy-le-Roi, where Madame de Pompadour lived, a distance of ten miles.

Like Petit Trianon, Petit Val has little lakes with shady trees bordering them; it has grottos, waterfalls, winding paths, magnificent greenhouses, fountains, a *rivière*, pavilions, aviaries, terraces, *charmilles, berceaux, enfin tout!* One feels like saying, "Mein Liebchen,

17

was willst du mehr?" as the poet Heine says. The park is surrounded by a *saut de loup* (a sunken wall about twenty feet high like "la Muette" in Paris). There is no need of putting up sign-boards with "No trespassing here," as no one could scale the walls of the *saut de loup;* so we feel very safe, especially when the five iron gates are locked. Beyond the park are the *chasse*, the farm, the vineyards, and the *potager*. We are so near Paris that we have many visitors. The drive out here is a pleasant one, going through Vincennes, Charenton, Alfort, etc., and one can get here in about an hour. Duke de Morny, the Duke de Persigny and the Rothschild family, Prince de Sagan, and different diplomats, not to speak of our numerous American friends who are thankful for a breath of fresh air, are frequent guests. The nearest château to us is Montalon, where Madame de Sévigné used to live, and from which she wrote some of her letters. If she ever wrote a tiresome one, it must surely have been from here, as the damp and moldy house, covered with creeping vines and overgrown with ivy, surrounded by melancholy cypress and poplar trees, which shut out the view, could scarcely have inspired her with brilliant ideas.

Petit Val's *potager* is known far and wide for the best peaches and pears in France, and the gardener takes all the prizes in the shows: if the prizes are in money, he pockets them; if they are diplomas, he allows us to keep them. He is a rare old scamp.

When Mr. Moulton bought the place he had the right to call himself "De Petit Val," and he could have—if he had wished to—been "Moulton de Petit Val." But he turned up his American nose at such cheap nobility as this; still he was obliged, much against his will, to conform to the obligations which belonged to the estate. For instance, he had to give so many bushels of potatoes to the curé, so many bushels of grain to the doctor, so many bushels of vegetables to the post-master, and to them all so many casks of the awful wine we produce on the estate, known in the vernacular as "*le petit bleu.*"

When this sour wine is in the golden period of effer-vescing, any sick child in the village ticketed by the doctor can be brought to the wine-presses and dipped in. If labeled "*trés malade,*" he is dipped in twice. Don't you think that this is a dreadful custom? I think that it is awful to put such an article as this on the market; but then we know that if a person has tasted it once they never do it again. We try to grow green corn here; but it degenerates unless the seed is brought every year from America. This year, not hav-ing been renewed, the corn is a failure; but the American melons ripen here in perfection, and rivalize successfully with the big French melons. The other day an am-bassador ate so many of them that he begged us to let him stay all night. We were quite anxious about him, as he had an audience with the Emperor the next morn-ing; but he managed it somehow.

An important member of the family I must not for-get! the governess, Mademoiselle Wissembourg, who is very much of a personage. After she has given my sister-in-law and myself our French lessons (for I still go on studying), she gives the cook his orders, gives out the linen, writes the letters, smooths away all annoy-ances, pays the bills, and keeps the accounts, which she does in an oriental sort of way, with such fantastic summings-up that my poor father-in-law is often on the verge of distraction.

Our stables are well garnished; there are eleven horses (my pair included), fourteen carriages, three coachmen, and no end of stable-boys. My coachman, who was one of the "anciens zouaves"—so renowned for their bravery—generally has cramps when he is told that I am going to drive myself to Paris. And when I drive those twelve miles I do it in double-quick time with Medjé and Hilda, my two "limousin" horses. No wonder Louis offers up a prayer to the saints before starting, and sits, holding with both hands on to his little seat back of me, with an expression on his face of "O Lord, what is going to happen?"

PARIS, *January, 1863.*

DEAREST MAMA,—I have been expecting letters from you and home for a long time, but nothing has come yet.

The coldest day that Paris has ever known, since goodness knows when, has suddenly burst upon us, and skating is just dawning on the Parisians.

The ice on the little lake of Suresnes has frozen *d'emblée*, and I was crazy to go there and skate. We had stayed late in the country, having spent Christmas *en famille*, and only returned to Paris a few days ago. I had just received the skates you sent me for my Christmas present, and I was wild to try them. What beauties they are! My old ones, with their screws and their innumerable straps, seem horribly complicated and clumsy. As you advised, I had very tight-fitting boots

20

with low heels made for them. I drove out to the Bois with baby and his *nounou*, and to gain time put on my skates in the carriage, and when I arrived, I walked down to the lake. I never saw such splendid ice (and I have seen many ices). No tardy layers, no treacherous holes, just one even mirror of marble. Imagine my surprise at not seeing a person on the ice; but there were masses of spectators gathered on the edge of the lake looking at it. The Emperor and the Empress were there. I knew them by sight; but the only one I knew personally was Prince Joachim Murat, our neighbor in the country. He married Elizabeth Wagram, and they lived with her parents at Gros-Bois, near Petit Val.

Therefore, I stood unknown and unnoticed. I ventured one foot on the indiscreet, reflecting surface, then the other; and while the assembled crowd gazed at me in amazement, I made the tour of the lake on my skates.

My experience of seven years on Fresh Pond did not fail me, and I skimmed over the flawless ice on the outer edge, like a bird with close-fitting wings; indeed, I felt like one. The ice was so clear that one could see the grass and stones at the bottom.

This was an exhilarating moment!

When I returned to the starting-place I saw that no one had dared to follow my example, and as an act of (I hardly dare to write it) silly *bravoura* I took baby out of the nurse's arms, and with him gurgling and chuckling with delight, his little head on my shoulder, I skated around with him. *Only once!* Don't scold me! I felt directly what a wicked thing I was doing,

for, if there had been a stone or a branch frozen in the
ice, I might have fallen, and then—what might not
have happened! But as long as I was alone and sure
of my skates I was not afraid. I saw some of the more
courageous skaters beginning to invade the ice, and I
flew back, thoroughly ashamed of myself, and delivered
my rosy burden into the arms of its nurse, who stood
aghast, like a frozen Niobe, with wide eyes, watching
me, the foolish mother. I sent them back to Paris in
the coupé, begging my husband to come and fetch me.
I was vain enough to wish him to see me in my glory.

Prince Murat came up to speak to me. As we saw
the Emperor, who was on skates, coming toward us,
Prince Murat said, "Here comes the Emperor to speak
to you." I felt dreadfully frightened, for I was not
sure—it being the first time I had ever spoken to a sovereign—what was the proper manner to address him. I
knew I must say "Sire," and "votre Majesté"; but when
and how often I did not know. His Majesty held in his
hand a short stick with an iron point, such as are used
in climbing the Alps, and managed to propel himself
forward by little right-legged shunts, his left leg not
daring to do anything but slide, and stopped like an
engine nearing a station, puffing and out of breath.
Prince Murat moved aside, and his Majesty looked at
me, then at Prince Murat, who, in an introductory
manner, said, "This is Madame Moulton, your Majesty,
the daughter-in-law of our neighbor, whom you know."
"Ah!" said the Emperor, and, turning to me, he said,
"How beautifully you skate, Madame; it is wonderful
to look at you!"

I (frightened out of my wits) murmured that I had

EMPEROR NAPOLEON III

skated since I was eight years old. "One can only skate like that when one learns young," the Emperor said. And while I was wondering when I should say "Votre Majesté," he said, "Oserai - je demander à une patineuse si parfaite de patiner avec un humble patineur (Dare I ask such a perfect skater as you to skate with so humble a skater as myself)?"

He was a humble skater indeed! I answered that it would be a great honor to me. He then stretched out his hands, and I took them very much as I would have taken any one else's hands, and we ambled forth, I supporting and upholding the tottering steps of the monarch of the French nation. I felt that the eye of the nation was on me, and, indeed, it was, as much of the nation as happened to be there; but, proud as I was, I wished that some one would relieve me of this responsibility. Suppose his Majesty should fall! . . . Dreadful thought! The Emperor skated on silently, intent on balancing himself, and I, you may be sure, was intent on keeping him intent. He stumbled at every stroke; but as I was on his left side—the weak one—we got along very nicely, and we felt that we were being admired—*patineusement*. His hat fell off once (he skated in a tall hat), and I had to pick it up for him while he clung to my hand and lifted his other hand to put the hat on his head. In our course we came upon the Empress, and we slowed down neatly. She was being supported by two very "trembling" chamberlains, who almost knocked us down in their efforts to keep their balance. When we had come to anchor the Emperor said to the Empress, "This is Madame Moulton! Does she not skate beautifully?" I ought to have made a courtesy; but how could I—on skates?

The Empress was dressed in a more suitable style than the other ladies, who evidently were going on to some receptions (the idea of combining visiting and skating!), and had rather long dresses, high heels and hats. The Empress, though crinolined and high-heeled, had a short skirt. I had a short cloth dress bordered with fur and a little fur toque. The Empress looked very kindly at me and said something to the Emperor which escaped me. When—oh, when—should I say "Your Majesty"? But I forgot everything, gazing at the Empress, who appeared as a vision of beauty, with a bright color in her cheeks, her eyes sparkling with animation. The Emperor said to her, "Tu devrais patiner avec Madame (You ought to skate with Madame)," letting go my hands. With the sweetest smile she said to me, "Will *you* skate with *me?*" Of course I was only too enchanted. Could I uphold the throne in which her Majesty was strapped? I took her two hands, and we sped on our way as best we could. I had sometimes to dig my skates in the ice to prevent too much speed, and to keep us both on our legs, one pair of which were Imperial. "How strange!" said her Majesty, in a moment of breath-taking, "that I should have never seen you before, and yet, as the Emperor says, you live in Paris!"

I replied: "Your Majesty [at last I said it], I spent last winter in the country taking care of my health, and last summer I was in Dinard."

"Ah, je comprends," with a lovely smile, "and now?"

"Now, your Majesty [I was getting on nicely], I am

24

going to be presented to society in due form by my mother-in-law."

"You will then come to the Tuileries?"

"Of course, your Majesty [now I had complete court manners], I shall come there first. My mother-in-law will take the necessary steps,"

"But you will not need to go through all those steps," she said, smilingly, "now that we know you"; and added, most kindly, "To-morrow you must come and skate with us again."

After this little breathing spell we went off on another tour, and as all is well that ends better than you expect, I was thankful to bring her Majesty back safely. We were hailed with enthusiasm. Charles, coming back with the coupé, was duly complimented by both their Majesties on the prowess of his spouse. And so we drove home.

Here endeth the first chapter and my first appearance in Parisian society.

January, 1863.

DEAR M.,—We received the invitation for the first ball at the Tuileries before my mother-in-law had presented me to the Grande Maîtresse Duchesse de Bassano; but her reception-day being on the same day as the ball I was able, fortunately, to go there and to be presented to her. Mrs. M—— preferred to make the "preliminary steps" with me in her wake.

My wedding-dress, trimmed with the beautiful lace (which came in my *corbeille*), seemed the proper thing to wear. The gentlemen's costumes are "*culottes courtes blanches*, white silk stockings, and a dress-coat

25

with gold buttons." My mother-in-law had been under the coiffeur's tongs for hours, and when she reappeared, frizzled and curled, she looked so unnatural that we hardly recognized her. My father-in-law refused point-blank to go with us. When asked, "Don't you want to see Lillie's first appearance?" he answered, "I shall see her before she goes. It is not likely I shall see much of her when she is once there." Which would probably have been the case.

Mrs. Moulton, wishing to go in style, ordered the gala Cinderella coach which served at my wedding. It used to take my parents-in-law to and from the Tuileries in the time of Louis Philippe. One can see the like in Versailles, all glass in front, white satin inside, with steps to let down, and swung on eight undulating springs. Charles went in our coupé, and I must say I envied him.

It is a long drive from the Rue de Courcelles to the Tuileries, and it takes a long time, especially when the *queue* commences at the Place de la Concorde. I was almost dizzy as we advanced step by step, pulling up at every moment, rocking and swaying like a row-boat in a gentle swell, and when we got a chance to go faster the carriage rocked from side to side, all the fringe on the coachman's box waving about. The coachman was a study in himself, with his white wig and silk stockings, ensconced like a hen on her nest. The valet, with powdered hair, white silk stockings, and plush breeches, stood on his little platform behind the carriage, holding on to the two cords on the side. I felt very fine, but not fine enough to prevent my feeling a little sea-sick, and I could not help thinking that it was a great pity to put on such style at night, when no one could see us. I would have liked better to have been seen in the daytime in this pomp and glory.

When at last we did arrive my mother-in-law's feathers were somewhat awry. We mounted the stately staircase, lined on both sides by the superb Cent Gardes, standing like statues on each step.

Many chamberlains were waiting, and we were conducted to the Grand Maître de Cérémonie, who passed us on to a less grand Maître de Cérémonie, who showed us to the place where we were to stand in the ballroom. It was a magnificent sight, and as long as I live I shall never forget it.

The beautifully dressed ladies were covered with jewels, and the gentlemen in their showy uniforms were covered with decorations. Each lady showed to great advantage, as, on account of the width of their crinolines, they had to stand very far apart.

The entire ballroom was lighted with wax candles, and was really a fairy scene. At the end of the ballroom was the platform on which stood the throne of their Majesties, a row of red-velvet gilded fauteuils placed behind them for the Imperial family. The hangings over the throne, which were of heavy red velvet with the Napoleonic eagle in gold, fell in great folds down to the floor.

It was not long before the doors were thrown open, and every one who had been limp and lax while waiting, chatting with his neighbor, straightened himself up and bowed to the ground, as the Emperor and the Empress walked in. Their Majesties stood for a moment at the door, and then went immediately to the throne.

A few moments later the *quadrille d'honneur* was danced by the eight most princely of the guests. The Emperor danced with the Princess of Wales, who has the prettiest and sweetest face one can imagine. The Empress danced with the King of Saxony; the Prince of Wales with the Princess Mathilde, cousin of the Emperor; the Grand Duke of Russia with the Princess Clothilde.

Every one stood during the whole quadrille. After that was finished their Majesties circulated among us, talking to different people. Later on the Empress, when she had returned to the throne, sent a message to me by Prince Murat, that she wished me to come to her.

I was frightened to death to have to cross the ballroom, feeling as if all eyes were on me, and tripped along so quickly that Prince Murat, at my side, said, "Don't hurry so; I can't keep up with you."

While I stood before the steps of the throne the Empress came toward me, and with her exquisite smile, and with the peculiar charm she has when speaking, said, "I am so glad to see you here, Madame Moulton." "And I am so glad to be here, your Majesty; but I went through all the preliminary steps all the same," I said, "because *ma belle-mère* insisted upon it."

This seemed to amuse her, and after a few gracious words she left me.

As this was the first time I had seen her in evening dress, I was completely dazed by her loveliness and beauty. I can't imagine a more beautiful apparition than she was. Her delicate coloring, the pose of her head, her hair, her expressive mouth, her beautiful

EMPRESS EUGÉNIE

shoulders, and wonderful grace make a perfect ensemble.

She wore a white tulle dress trimmed with red velvet
bows and gold fringes; her crown of diamonds and
pearls and her necklace were magnificent.

On her breast shone the great diamond (the Regent)
which belongs to the Crown.

When I gazed on her in all her glory and prestige I
could hardly believe that we had been such chums a
few days before, when skating, and that I had held her
hands clasped in mine, and had kept her from falling.

Countess Castellane gave a beautiful costume ball the
other evening, which I must tell you about, because it
was so original. The stables were connected with the
salons by a long, carpeted gallery, at the end of which
was a huge fresco on the walls, representing a horse-race
in a very lifelike manner. Through a large plate-glass
window one could see the whole stable, which was, as
you may imagine, in spick-and-span order; and Count
Castellane's favorite horse was saddled and bridled, a
groom in full livery standing by its side. It was amusing to see ladies in their ball dresses walking about in
the stables, where the astonished horses were blinking
in the gas-light.

In one of the quadrilles the ladies and gentlemen were
dressed as children, in short socks and frocks with enormous sashes.

Princess Metternich was costumed as a milkmaid;
she had real silver pails hung over her shoulders.
Duchesse de Persigny was a *chiffonnière* with a *hotte* on
her back and a gray dress very much looped up, showing
far above her wooden shoes.

PARIS, *1863*.

DEAR M.,—The ice in the Bois continues very good; I am skating every day. I have commenced to teach the little Prince Imperial. He is very sweet, and talks very intelligently for his age. The other day, when I was skating with the Empress, a gentleman (I think he was an American), skating backward, knocked against us with such force that the Empress and I both fell. I tried with all my might to keep her from falling, but it was impossible. Her first words, when we were helped on our feet again, were, "Don't tell the Emperor; I think he did not see us."

That same evening there was a ball at the Tuileries, and when the Empress came to speak to me she said: "How are you? I can hardly stand up." I answered, "I am worse off, your Majesty; I can stand up, but I cannot sit down."

Yesterday, when I came home from my singing lesson with Delle Sedie, I found the family quite excited. The Empress's chamberlain had just been here to say that the Empress desired that we would come to the Tuileries next Monday, and expressed the wish that I should bring some music. I wrote to Delle Sedie and begged him to advise me what I should sing; he answered that he would come himself and talk it over with me, and Monsieur Planté, a young, budding pianist, who was ordered from the Tuileries to accompany my songs, was sent for, and Delle Sedie came at the same time.

Delle Sedie thought that I should begin with "Tre Giorni son che Nina," of Pergolesi, and then the air from "Lucia," and if I were asked to sing again the "Valse de Venzano."

On these occasions gentlemen wear the *pantalon collant*, which is a most unbecoming and trying costume, being of black cloth fitting very tight and tapering down to the ankle, where it finishes abruptly with a button. Any one with a protruding ankle and thin legs cannot escape criticism.

Le petit lundi of the Empress was not so *petit* as I expected; there were at least four or five hundred people present.

I was presented to the Princess Mathilde (the cousin of the Emperor), a very handsome and distinguished-looking lady, who is married to and separated from Prince Demidoff. Her palace is directly opposite our hotel. I was also presented to the Princess Clothilde, and many others. I was very nervous before singing, but after my first song I did very well.

There was dancing, and everything was very unceremonious and easy. I think (I will just say it to you, dear mama) that I had a success. Their Majesties were very kind, and thanked me many times, and the Duke de Morny said that he was very proud of his protégée, for it was he who had suggested to the Empress that I should sing for them. It was a delightful evening, and I enjoyed myself and my little triumph immensely. I made the acquaintance of the Austrian ambassador and the Princess Metternich. She seemed very pleasant, and put me directly at my ease. She is far from being handsome, but dresses better than any woman in Paris, and has more *chic*. In fact, she sets the fashion as much as the Empress does.

The Emperor, at the instigation of the Duke de Morny, has given orders for the construction of a bridge over the Marne near Petit Val—a thing we needed greatly. When you were here, if you remember, one had to walk from the station to the river, about a little quarter of a mile. Once there you had to wave and shout for the ferryman, who, before allowing you to get on the boat, would attend to what cattle or merchandise were waiting there for transport. I do not think the bridge would have been built had not the Duke de Morny come out by train to Petit Val to avoid the long drive of twelve miles from Paris, and had been bored by this primitive means of transporting his august person. He said he was astonished and mortified that such a state of things should exist so near Paris. So was every one else. Otherwise the "bac" would have gone on forever.

The Carnival has never been so whirlwindy as it has been this year; and I don't know how the purses of our lords and masters are going to hold out; and while the poor, "whom we have always with us," are getting rich, the rich, whom we don't always have, alas! are getting poor. For the private fancy-dress ball at the Tuileries last Monday, to which the guests were invited by the Empress, Worth alone made costumes to the tune of two hundred thousand dollars, and yet there were not four hundred ladies invited.

To begin at the top, the Empress was dressed as the wife of a doge of Venice of the sixteenth century. She wore all the crown jewels and many others. She was literally *cuirassée* in diamonds, and glittered like a sun-goddess. Her skirt of black velvet over a robe of scarlet satin was caught up by clusters of diamond brooches. The Prince Imperial was allowed to be present; he was dressed in a black-velvet costume and knee breeches; his little, thin legs black-stockinged, and a *manteau Vénitien* over his shoulders. He danced twice, once with Mademoiselle de Châteaubourg, and then with his cousin, Princess Anna Murat, who, being made on Junoesque lines, and dressed as a Dutch peasant with enormous gold ornaments over her ears, and a flowing white lace cap, towered above her youthful partner. He is only seven years old, and rather small for his age, which made the contrast between him and his colossal partner very striking. Princess Mathilde looked superb as Holbein's Anne of Clèves. She wore her famous collection of emeralds, which are world-known.

Princess Clothilde had also copied a picture from the Louvre; but her robe of silver brocade, standing out in great folds about her waist, was anything but becoming to her style of figure. Princess Augustine Bonaparte (Gabrielli) was in a gorgeous costume of something or other; one had not time to find out exactly what she was intended to represent; she was covered with jewelry (some people pretended it was false, but it did not look less brilliant, for that). A fancy ball is an occasion which allows and excuses any extravagance in jewelry; whereas, at an ordinary ball it is considered not in good taste to wear too much. I just mention this casually, in case you should want to make a display when you lunch at Miss Bryant's some Sunday.

Countess Walewski had powdered her hair and wore a Louis XV. amazon costume, a most unbecoming yellow satin gown with masses of gold buttons sewed on in every direction. This was not very successful.

Marquise de Gallifet, as the Angel Gabriel, with enormous real swan's wings suspended from her shoulders, looked the part to perfection, and most angelic with her lovely smile, blond hair, and graceful figure.

Princess Metternich was dressed as Night, in dark-blue tulle covered with diamond stars. Her husband said to me, "Don't you think that Pauline looks well in her nightgown?"

Countess Castiglione, the famous beauty, was dressed as Salammbô in a costume remarkable for its lack of stuff, the idea taken from the new Carthaginian novel of Gustave Flaubert. The whole dress was of black satin, the waist without any sleeves, showing more than an usual amount of bare arms and shoulders; the train was open to the waist, disclosing the countess's noble leg as far up as it went incased in black-silk tights.

The young Count de Choiseul, who had blackened his face to represent an Egyptian page, not only carried her train, but held over the head of the daughter of Hamilcar an umbrella of Robinson Crusoe dimensions. Her gold crown fell off once while walking about, and Choiseul made every one laugh when he picked it up and put it on his own black locks. She walked on all unconscious, and wondered why people laughed.

My costume was that of a Spanish dancer. Worth told me that he had put his whole mind upon it; it did not feel much heavier for that: a banal yellow satin skirt, with black lace over it, the traditional red rose in my hair, red boots and a bolero embroidered in steel beads, and small steel balls dangling all over me. Some com-

DANIEL FRANÇOIS ESPRIT AUBER

pliments were paid to me, but unfortunately not enough to pay the bill; if compliments would only do that sometimes, how gladly we would receive them! But they are, as it is, a drug in the market.

The Emperor was in domino—his favorite disguise— which is no disguise at all, for every one recognizes him.

I met the famous Auber at the Tuileries ball. The Duke de Persigny brought him and introduced him to me, not because Auber asked to be presented, but because I was most anxious to make his acquaintance, and begged the duke to bring him. He is a short, dapper little man, with such a refined and clever face. Wit and repartee sparkle in his keen eyes. His music is being very much played now—"Fra Diavolo" and "Dieu et la Bayadère," and others of his operas. His music is like himself—fine and dainty, and full of *esprit;* his name is Daniel François Esprit. M. de Persigny said, "Madame Moulton desires to know you, Monsieur Auber." I said, "I hope you will not think me indiscreet, but I did want to see you and know the most-talked-about person in Paris." In reply he said: "You have the advantage over me, Madame. I have never heard myself talked about." Then the Duke de Persigny said something about my voice. Auber turned to me, and said, "May I not also have the privilege of hearing you?" Of course I was tremendously pleased, and we fixed a day and hour then and there for his visit.

Prince Jérome, who is a cousin of the Emperor (people call him Plon-Plon), is not popular; in fact, he is just the contrary. But his wife, the Princess Clothilde, would be exceedingly popular if she gave the Parisians a chance to see her oftener. She is so shy, so young, and the least pretentious of princesses, hates society, and never goes out if she can avoid it. Prince Jérome is, of all the Napoleonic family, the one who most resembles Napoleon I. in appearance, but not in character. There is nothing of the hero about him. Since he had the misfortune to be suddenly indisposed the night before the battle of Solferino, and did not appear, they call him "craint-plomb." *Sé non è vero è ben trovato.*

The stories people tell of the Prince are awful; but one is not obliged to believe them if one does not want to.

There was such an amusing *soirée* at the Duke de Morny's in honor of the Duchess's birthday. They gave a play called "Monsieur Choufleuri restera chez lui le ......," which the Duke wrote himself, and for which Offenbach composed the music inspired by the Duke, who vowed that he "really did make the most of it." But, his conscience pricking him, he added, "At least some!" which I think was nearer the truth.

It was a great success, whether by the Duke de Morny or by Offenbach, and was the funniest thing I ever saw. Every one was roaring with laughter, and when the delighted audience called for "l'auteur," the Duke came out leading Offenbach, each waving his hand toward the other, as if success belonged to him alone, and went off bowing their thanks together. Apropos of the Duke de Morny, he said of himself: "I am a very complicated person. Je suis le fils d'une reine, frère d'un Empereur et gendre d'un Empereur, et tous sont illégitimes." It does sound queer! But he really is the son of Queen Hortense (his father being Count Flahaut); he is in this way an illegitimate brother of Napoleon III., and his wife is the daughter of the Emperor Nicholas of Russia. There you have a complicated case. My young sister-in-law has just married Count Hatzfeldt, of the German Embassy (second secretary). He is very good-looking without being handsome, and belongs to one of the most distinguished families in Germany. Countess Mercy-Argenteau appeared, comet-like, in Paris, and although she is a very beautiful woman, full of musical talent, and calls herself *une femme politique*, she is not a success. The gentlemen say she lacks charm. At any rate, none of the *élégantes* are jealous of her, which speaks for itself. She is not as beautiful as Madame de Gallifet, nor as *élégante* as Countess Pourtales, nor as clever as Princess Metternich.

Madame Musard, a beautiful American, has a friendship (*en tout deshonneur*) with a foreign royalty who made her a present of some—what he thought value-less—shares of a petroleum company in America. These shares turned into gold in her hands.

The royal gentleman gnashes his false teeth in vain, and has scene after scene with the royal son, who, green with rage, reproaches him for having parted with these treasures. But the shares are safely in the clutches of papa in New York, far away, and furnishing the where-withal to provide his daughter with the most wonderful horses and equipages in Paris. She pays as much for one horse as her husband gains by his music in a year, and as for the poor prodigal prince, who is overrun with debts, he would be thankful to have even a widowed papa's mite of her vast wealth. Another lady, whose virtue is some one else's reward, has a magnificent and much-talked-of hotel in the Champs Élysées, where there is a staircase worth a million francs, made of real alabaster. Prosper Mérimée said: "C'est par là qu'on monte à la vertu."

Her salons are filled every evening with cultured men of the world, and they say that the most refined tone reigns supreme—that is more than one can say of every salon in Paris.

I am taking lessons of Delle Sedie. He is a delightful teacher; he is so intelligent and has such beautiful theories, and so many of them, that he takes up about half the time of my lesson talking them over.

This is one of the things he says: "Take your breath from your boots." It sounds better said in French: *Prenez votre respiration dans vos bottines.* I don't think he realizes what he says or what he wants me to do. When I told him that I had sung somewhere unwillingly, having been much teased, he said: "You must not be too amiable. You must not sing when and what one asks. There is nothing like being begged. You are not a hand-organ, *pardieu*, that any one can play when they like." And this sort of talk alternates with my songs until time is up, when off I run or go, feeling that I have learned little but talked much. However, sometimes I do feel compensated; for when, to demonstrate a point, he will sing a whole song, I console myself by thinking that I have been to one of his concerts and paid for my ticket.

Yesterday I received the inclosed letter from the Duke de Morny, inviting us to go with him in his *loge* to see a new play called "Le déluge." It was not much

16 - 7bre

FACSIMILE OF LETTER FROM THE DUKE DE MORNY

voulez vous être assez bonne
pour en envoyer votre
photographie, je fais une
collection des jeunes et élégantes
femmes de Paris et vous donne,
j'espère, a un deux titres
je les fais colorier. quoique
ce ne soit pas un échange
égal, je vous recommande
donc demandant la votre
vous prie d'accepter la
mienne, reconnaissant
que je vous dois du retour,
je m'acquitterai à la
première occasion,

Je vous remercie encore de toutes vos bontés pour eux, je vous prie d'être mon interprète auprès de toute votre famille, veuillez demander à Mr Moulton ce qui est relatif à la poste aux lettres de Lucy. Je serai enchanté d'contribuer à améliorer ce sera ce... veuillez agréer chère ... l'assurance de mes sentiments dévoués et respectueux

Morny

of a play; but it was awfully amusing to see. Noah and his three sons and his three daughters-in-law marched into the ark dragging after them some wiry, emaciated débris of the Jardin des Plantes, which looked as if they had not eaten for a week. The amount of whipping and poking with sticks which was necessary to get them up the plank was amazing; I think they had had either too few or too many rehearsals. But they were all finally pushed in. Then commenced the rain— a real pouring cats-and-dogs kind of rain, with thunder and lightning and the stage pitch-dark. The whole populace climbed up on the rocks and crawled about, drenched to the skin, and little by little disappeared. Then, when one saw nothing but "water, water everywhere," the ark suddenly loomed out on top of the rocks (how could they get it up there?), and the whole Noah family stepped out in a pink-and-yellow sunset, and a dear little dove flew up to Noah's hand and delivered the olive branch to him. The dove was better trained than the animals, and had learned his rôle very well.

On coming out of the theater, we found, instead of the fine weather we had left outside, a pouring rain which was a very good imitation of the deluge inside. And none of us had an umbrella!

You see what the Duke de Morny writes: "I am making a collection of photographs of the young and elegant ladies of Paris. I think that you ought to figure among them, and though it is not an equal exchange, I am going to ask you to accept mine and give me yours." And he brought it to me last night.

An invitation for the ball at St. Cloud for the King

of Spain, who is now in Paris to inaugurate the new rail-road to Madrid, and another ball at the Tuileries will keep us busy this week.

PETIT VAL, *June 17th.* We have been here a week, rejoicing in the lilacs and roses and all the spring delights. The nightingales are more delightful than ever. There is one charmer in particular, who warbles most enchantingly in the cedar-tree in front of my window. He has a lady-love somewhere, and he must be desperately in love, for he sings his little heart out on his sky-larking tours to attract her attention. I try hard (naïve that I am) to imitate his song, especially the trill and the long, sad note. I wonder if either of them is deceived: whether she thinks that she has two lovers (one worse than the other), or, if *he* thinks he has a poor rival who can't hold a candle to him.

Auber wrote a cadenza for the "Rossignol" of Alabieff, which he thought might be in nightingale style. But how can any one imitate a nightingale? Auber, in one of his letters, asked me: "Chantez-vous toujours des duos avec votre maître de . . . champs?"

À MADAME LILLIE MOULTON

IN THE COURTS OF MEMORY

Paris, *January, 1864.*

The Princess Beauvau is a born actress, and nothing she loves better than arranging theatricals and acting herself. She rooted up some charity as an excuse for giving a theatrical performance, and obtained the theater of the Conservatoire and the promise of the Empress's presence. She chose two plays, one of Musset and the other, "l'Esclave," of Molière—and asked me to take part in this last one.

"Oh," I said, "I cannot appear in a French play; I would not dare to." But the Princess argued that, as there were only four words to say, she thought I could do it, and in order to entice me to accept, she proposed introducing a song; and, moreover, said that she would beg Auber to furnish a few members of the Conservatoire orchestra to accompany me. This was very tempting, and I fell readily into the trap she laid for me.

I consulted Auber about my song, and we decided on Alabieff's "Rossignol," for which he had written the cadenza. He composed a chorus for a few amateurs and all the orchestral parts.

I was to be a Greek slave; my dress was of white, flimsy, spangled gauze, with a white-satin embroidered bolero, a turban of tulle, with all sorts of dangly things hanging over my ears. I wore baggy trousers and *babouches*. You may notice that I did not copy Power's Greek slave in the way of dress.

I was completely covered with a white tulle veil, and led in by my fellow-slaves, who were also in baggy trousers and *babouches*. There could be no doubt that we were slaves, for we were overloaded with chains on

41

arms, ankles, and waist. I found circulation a very difficult matter shuffling about in *babouches*, which are the most awkward things to walk in. One risks falling forward at every step.

When they got me in front of the orchestra the slaves drew off my veil and there I stood. The chorus retired, and I began my song. I had had only one rehearsal with the orchestra, the day before; but the humming accompaniment to my solo, that the unmusical slaves had to learn, had taken a week to teach.

Every one said the scene was very pretty. My song was quite a success; I had to sing it over again. Then I sang the waltz of Chopin, to which I had put words and transposed two tones lower. I saw Delle Sedie in the audience, with his mouth wide open, trying to breathe for me. It has sixteen bars which must be sung in one breath, and has a compass from D on the upper line to A on the lower line. Applause and flowers were showered on me, and I was rather proud of myself. I felt like Patti when I picked up my bouquets!

Later on in the play I had to say my "four words," which turned out to be six words: *On ne peut être plus joli.* Though I was frightened out of my wits, I managed not to disgrace myself; but I doubt if any one heard one of the six words I said. The Empress sent me a little bunch of violets, which I thought was very gracious of her, and I was immensely flattered, for I think she took it from her corsage. I had noticed it there at the beginning of the evening.

One of the bouquets bore the card of Dr. Evans, the American dentist. It was very nice of him to remember me and send me such beautiful flowers. Dr. Evans

is so clever and entertaining. Every one likes him, and
every door as well as every jaw is open to him. At the
Tuileries they look on him not only as a good dentist,
but as a good friend; and, as some clever person said,
"Though reticent to others, their Majesties had to open
their mouths to him."

The other day we had a children's party. Auber
came, pretending that he had been invited as one of
the children. When he heard them all chattering in
French, English, and German, he said, "Cela me fait
honte, moi qui ne parle que le français." He was most
delighted to see the children, and seated himself at the
piano and played some sweet little old-fashioned polkas
and waltzes, to which the children danced.

I said to them: "Children, remember that to-day
you have danced to the playing of Monsieur Auber, the
most celebrated composer in France. Such a thing is
an event, and you must remember it and tell it to your
children."

Miss Adelaide Philips is here singing, but, alas! without the success she deserves. She appeared at Les
Italiens twice; once as Azucena in "Trovatore," and
then as the page in "Lucrezia Borgia." If it had not
been for her clothes, I think that her efforts would have
been more appreciated. The moment she appeared as
the page in "Lucrezia" there was a general titter in
the audience. Her make-up was so extraordinary, Parisian taste rose up in arms. And as for the Borgias,
they would have poisoned her on the spot had they
seen her! Her extraordinarily fat legs (whether padded
or not, I don't know) were covered with black-velvet
trousers, ending at the knee and trimmed with lace.

She wore a short-waisted jacket with a short skirt attached and a voluminous lace ruffle, a curly wig too long for a man and too short for a woman, upon which sat jauntily a Faust-like hat with a long, sweeping plume. This was her idea of a medieval Maffeo Orsini. As Azucena, the mother of a forty-year-old troubadour, she got herself up as a damsel of sixteen, with a much too short dress and a red bandana around her head, from which dangled a mass of sequins which she shook coquettishly at the prompter. The audience did not make any demonstration; they remained indifferent and tolerant, and there was not a breath of applause. The only criticism that appeared in the papers was: "Madame Philips, une Américaine, a fait son apparence dans 'Trovatore.' Elle joue assez bien, et si sa voix avait l'importance de ses jambes elle aurait eu sans doute du succès, car elle peut presque chanter." Poor Miss Philips! I felt so sorry for her. I thought of when I had seen her in America, where she had such success in the same rôles. But why did she get herself up so? There is nothing like ridicule for killing an artist in France, and any one who knew the French could have foreseen what her success would be the moment she came on the stage. She became ill after these two performances and left Paris.

PARIS, *May 7, 1863.*

DEAR M.,—Auber procured us tickets for Meyerbeer's funeral, which took place to-day; it was a most splendid affair. Auber, who was one of the pall-bearers, looked very small and much agitated. The music of the church was magnificent. Auber himself had written an organ voluntary and Jules Cohen played it. Auber said, on going to the cemetery: "La prochaine fois sera pour mon propre compte."

We went to a dinner at Mr. William Gudin's (he is the celebrated painter) last night. There were the Prince and Princess Metternich, old Monsieur Dupin, Duke de Bassano, Monsieur Rouher, Baron Rothschild, and many other people. The gallery was lit up after dinner, and they smoked there (as a great exception). Smoking is against Madame Gudin's principles, but not against his, as the huge table covered with every kind of cigars and cigarettes could bear witness. Collecting cigarettes is a sort of hobby of Gudin's; he gets them from every one. The Emperor of Russia, the Chinese, the Turkish, and Japanese sovereigns, all send him cigarettes, even the Emperor. These last are steeped in a sort of liquid which is good for asthma. Every one who could boast of asthma got one to try. I must say they smelled rather uninvitingly. The Emperor loves Gudin dearly, and orders picture after picture from him, mostly commemorative of some fine event of which the Emperor is, of course, the principal figure, and destined for Versailles later. Gudin has a beautiful hotel and garden near us in the Rue Beaujon. The garden used to be square; but now it is a triangle, as a new boulevard has taken a part of it. Gudin talked much about his debts, as if they were feathers in his cap, and as for his law-suits, they are jewels in his crown!

His famous picture of the Emperor's visit to Venice, now in the Luxembourg, is an enormous canvas, rather *à la Turner*, with intense blue sky deepening into a green sunset, pink and purple waves lashing the sides of the fantastic vessel in which the Emperor stands in an opalescent coloring. Some black slaves are swimming about, their bodies half-way out of the water, holding up their enormous black arms loaded with chains, each link of which would sink an ordinary giant.

Baroness Alphonse Rothschild has one desire, which, in spite of a fathomless purse, seemed difficult at first to fulfil. What she wants is to play a sonata with the orchestra of the Conservatoire, *rien de moins!* She begged me to ask Auber how much it would cost. After due reflection he answered, twelve hundred francs. She was quite surprised at this modest sum; she had thought it would be so many thousands. Therefore she decided to convoke the orchestra, and has been studying her sonata with all zeal and with a Danish coach. I don't mean a carriage, but a man who can coach, after the English school system.

She asked me to keep her in countenance, and wished me to sing something with the orchestra; but what should I sing? Auber could think of nothing better than "Voi che sapete," as the orchestra would have the music for it, and for frivolity he proposed "La Mando-linata," of Paladilhe. He said, "Il faut avoir de tout dans sa poche;" and the dear old master transcribed it all himself, writing it out for the different instruments. I shall always keep these ten pages of his fine writing as one of my most precious autographs.

On account of his *concours* Auber was asked to be present, as well as the Danish coach, whose occupation was to turn the leaves, and if necessary to help in critical moments. No one else was to be in the audience, not even our husbands. Well! the concert came off. We were four hours about it! It was a funny experience, when one thinks of it, and only Baroness Rothschild could have ever imagined such a thing or carried it through. In her enormous ballroom we two amateurs were performing with the most celebrated orchestra in the world—eighty picked musicians, all perfect artists —with no one to hear us. Auber professed politely to be delighted with all he heard, and clamored for more. The orchestra looked resignedly bored.

The Minister of Foreign Affairs, the Marquis Drouyn de l'Huys, gave a costume ball which was even finer than the last. Worth, Laferrières, and Félix outdid themselves. The Empress had a magnificent dress— *une ancienne dame Bavaroise*. She looked superb, actually covered and blazing with jewels.

The Comtesse de Castiglione had imagined a costume as "La Vérité." She was dressed entirely in white, looking severe and classically beautiful, cold as a winter day. She held in her hand a fan made of white feathers which had a mirror in the center. It must be amusing to be a professional beauty. When she goes to a ball, which she never does before midnight, she does not take the trouble to speak to any one; she walks into the ballroom and just stands in the middle of it to be looked at; people all make a circle around her and glare. A gentleman will go and speak with her, and they stand like two trees on an island, he doing the talking, and she gazing around her to see what effect she is producing.

The Emperor made a bet that he would make her speak three words, and he won it, because she answered a question of his by saying, "Pas beaucoup, Sire." She lives at Passy, and calls herself *la recluse de Passy;*

47

others call her *la recluse du Passé*. I do not admire her beauty half as much as I do the Empress's.

Countess Walewski was dressed like a fiery Vénitienne, all yellow and gold. She looked dazzling and like a thorough Italian, which was not difficult for her, as she is one.

The Duchesse de Mouchy's costume was a Louis XV. marquise, which did not suit her at all; neither did the powdered wig nor the black patches on her face become her.

I must tell you about my dress. It was really one of the prettiest there. Worth said that he had put his whole soul on it. I thought that he had put a pretty good round price on his soul. A skirt of gold tissue, round the bottom of which was a band of silver, with all sorts of fantastic figures, such as dragons, owls, and so forth, embroidered in different colors under a skirt of white tulle with silver and gold spangles. The waist was a mass of spangles and false stones on a gold stuff; gold-embroidered bands came from the waist and fell in points over the skirt. I had wings of spangled silvery material, with great glass-colored beads sewed all over them. But the *chef-d'œuvre* was the head-dress, which was a sort of helmet with gauze wings and the jewels of the family (Mrs. M.'s and mine) fastened on it. From the helmet flowed a mane of gold tinsel, which I curled in with my hair. The effect was very original, for it looked as though my head was on fire; in fact, I looked as if I was all on fire. Before I left home all the servants came to see me, and their *magnifique*, and *superbe*, and *étonnant* quite turned my head, even with the helmet on.

The Emperor and the Duke de Persigny went about in dominos, and flattered themselves that no one recognized them; but every one did. Who could have mistaken the broad back and the slow, undulating gait of the Emperor? And though he changed his domino every little while from blue to pink, and from white to black, there never was any doubt as to where he was in the room, and every eye followed him. I was quite agitated when I saw his unmistakable figure approaching me, and when he began, in a high, squeaky voice (such as is adopted by masked people) to compliment me on my toilette, it was all I could do not to make a courtesy. I answered him, feeling very shy about tutoying him, as is the custom when addressing a mask.

"Cela te plaît, beau masque (Do I please thee, handsome mask)?" I said.

"Beaucoup, belle dame, mais dis-moi ce que tu es (Very much, beautiful lady, but what are you supposed to be?)."

"Je suis une salamandre; je peux traverser le feu et les flammes sans le moindre danger (I am a salamander; I can go through fire and flame without the slightest danger)."

"Oses-tu traverser le feu de mes yeux (Dost thou dare to brave the fire of my eyes)?"

"Je ne vois pas tes yeux à travers ton masque, mon gentilhomme (I cannot see thy eyes through thy mask, my gallant gentleman)."

"Oserais-tu traverser la flamme de mon cœur (Wouldst thou dare to go through the flame of my heart)?"

"Je suis sure que j'oserais. Si la flamme est si dangereuse, prends garde que ton beau domino ne brûle pas (I am sure that I would dare. If the flame is so dangerous take care your beautiful domino does not burn)." Such silly talk! But he seemed amused, as he probably thought that I had no idea to whom I was talking.

Taking a red counter out of his pocket and handing it to me he said, "Will you take supper with me?"

"Not alone," I answered. "You are too dangerous."

He laughed and said, "I shall not be alone, my pretty lady." Then, giving me another counter, he said: "This is for your husband. If you will be at two o'clock at that door"—pointing to it—"it will be opened for you."

At two o'clock we presented ourselves at the door of the said salon, which was immediately opened on our showing the *jetons*, and we found ourselves, as I thought we should, in the salon where their Majesties were to sup. There were already many people assembled: the Metternichs, the Persignys, the Gallifets, the Count and Countess Pourtales, etc.—I should say, twenty-five in all. There was a magnificent display of flowers and fruit on the table. The Emperor came in with the Empress, not looking in the least Cæsar-like, with his hair matted down on his forehead and his mustaches all unwaxed and drooping; but he soon twisted them up into their usual stiffness. I noticed that people looked at me persistently, and I fancied all sorts of awful things, and felt dreadfully embarrassed.

After supper the Empress came up to me and said, "Where can one buy such lovely curls as you have, *chère Madame?*" I understood the reason now for the notice I was attracting. They had thought that the curls were false. I answered, hoping it would sound amusing, "Au Magasin du Bon-Dieu."

The Empress smiled and replied; "Nous voudrions toutes acheter dans ce magasin-là; but tell me, are your curls real or false? You won't mind telling me (and she hesitated a little). Some people have made bets about it. How can we know," she said, "unless you tell us?" "My hair is all my own, your Majesty, and, if you wish to make sure, I am perfectly willing that you should see for yourself." And, removing my helmet, I took out the comb and let my hair down. Every one crowded around me, and felt and pulled my hair about until I had to beg for mercy. The Emperor, looking on, cried out, "Bravo, Madame!" and, gathering some flowers off the table, handed them to me, saying: "Votre succès tenait à un cheveu, n'est-ce pas?"

Supposing the curls had been false, how I should have felt!

I put on my head-dress again with the flowing tinsel threads, and, some one sending for a brush, I completed this exhibition by showing them how I curled my hair around my fingers and made this coiffure. I inclose the article about this supper which came out in the *Figaro* (copied into a New York paper).

The Emperor and Empress not unfrequently take a great liking to persons accidentally presented to them, invite them to their most select parties, make much of them, and sometimes rousing a little jealousy by so doing among the persons belonging to the Court. Of the ladies officially foremost, the reigning favorites are Princess Metternich, extremely clever and piquante, who invents the oddest toilettes, dances the oddest dances, and says the oddest things; the Marquise de Gallifet, whose past life is a romance, not altogether according to the French proverb (fitting school-girl reading), but who is very handsome, brilliant, merry, and audacious; and two others, the handsome and dashing wives of men high in the employment of the Emperor. These ladies spend enormous sums on their toilette, and are perpetually inventing some merry and brilliant nonsense for the amusement of the Empress. Among the persons from the "outside" most in favor just now, in the inner circle of the court, is a very handsome and accomplished American lady, the youthful wife of a millionaire, possessing a magnificent voice, a very amiable temper, and wonderfully splendid hair. After a very small and very merry party in the Empress's private apartments a few nights ago, the Imperial hosts and their guests sat down to an exquisite "little supper," this lady being one of the party. During the supper one of the Empress's ladies began playfully to tease Mrs. —— about her hair, declaring that no human head could grow such a luxuriant mass of lustrous hair, and inviting her to confess to sporting certain skilfully contrived additions to the locks of nature's bestowing. Mrs. —— modestly protested that her hair, such as it was, was really and truly her own; in right of growth, and not of purchase. All present speedily took part in the laughing dispute; some declaring for the opinion of the Lady of Honor, the others for that of Mrs. ——. The Emperor and Empress, greatly amused at the dispute, professed a strong desire to know the facts of the case; and the Emperor, declaring that it was clearly impossible to get at the truth in any other way, invited Mrs. M—— to settle the controversy by letting down her hair, and giving ocular demonstration of its being her own. The lady, whereupon, drew out the comb and the hairpins that held up her hair, and shook its heavy and shining masses all over her shoulders, thus giving conclusive proof of the tenure by which she held it. As Frenchwomen seldom have good heads of hair, it is probable that some little disappointment may have been caused to some of the ladies by this magnificent torrent of hair, displayed by Mrs. M——, but the gentlemen were all in raptures at the really beautiful spectacle, the lady's husband, who worships her, being as proud of her triumph as though his wife's luxuriant locks were his own creation.

March, 1864.

Dear M.,—Auber, on hearing that the Empress had asked me to sing in the chapel of the Tuileries, offered to compose a *Benedictus* for me. The orchestra of the

Conservatoire was to accompany me, and Jules Cohen was to play the organ. I had several rehearsals with Auber and one on the preceding Saturday with the orchestra. The flute and I have a little ramble together which is very pretty. The loft where the organ is, and where I stood, was so high up that I could only see the people by straining my neck over the edge of it, and even then only saw the black veils of the ladies and the frequent bald heads of the gentlemen. The Empress remained on her knees during the whole mass. The Emperor seemed attentive; but stroked and pulled his mustaches all the time.

My *Benedictus* went off very well. The chapel was very sonorous and I was in good voice. I was a little nervous at first, but after the first phrase I recovered confidence and did all that was expected of me. The Duke de Bassano came up to the loft and begged me to come down into the gallery, as their Majesties wished me and Charles to stay for breakfast. I was sorry Auber was not invited. We found every one assembled in the gallery outside the chapel. The Empress came straight toward me, thanked me, and said many gracious things, as did the Emperor. There were very, very few people at breakfast—only the household. I sat between the Emperor and the little Prince, who said, "I told mama I knew when you sang, for you said '*Benedictus*'; we say *benedicteus*."

The Princess Metternich receives after midnight every evening. If one is in the theater or at a *soirée* it is all right, but to sit up till twelve o'clock to go to her is very tiresome, though when you are once there you do not regret having gone. It is something to see her smoking her enormous cigars. The other night Richard Wagner, who had been to the theater with the Metternichs, was there. I was glad to see him, though he is so dreadfully severe, solemn, and satirical. He found fault with everything; he thought the theaters in Paris horribly dirty, *mal soignés*, bad style, bad actors, orchestra second-rate, singers worse, public ignorant, etc. He smiled once with such a conscious look and scanned people's faces, as if to say, "I, Richard Wagner, have smiled!" But he can very well put on airs, for he is a genius. At Les Italiens, Patti, Mario, Alboni, and Delle Sedie are singing "Rigoletto." They are all splendid. Alboni is immensely fat and round as a barrel—but what a voice! It simply rolls out in billows of melody. The "quartette" was magnificent, and was encored. Patti and Mario are at daggers drawn, and hate each other like poison, so their love-making is reduced to a minimum, and they make as little as possible. In their fondest embraces they hold each other at arm's length and glare into each other's eyes. Mario is such a splendid actor one would think he could conquer his dislike for her and play the lover better. The *Barbier de Séville* is, I think, his best rôle; he acts with so much humor and sings so exquisitely and with such refinement. Even in the tipsy scene he is the fine gentleman. Patti sings in the singing lesson Venzano's waltz and "Il Bacio." Her execution is wonderful, faultless, and brilliant.

We went to a *soirée* given by the Marquise de Boissy, better known as Byron's Countess Guiccioli, who inspired so many of his beautiful poems; but when you see her dyed and painted you wonder how the *blasé* Byron could have been all fire and flame for her. Fagnani, the painter, who did that awful simpering portrait of me, painted her, it being stipulated that he should make her look ten years younger than she is. He had a hard time of it! But now, being old and married to the senator, Marquis de Boissy, she has lost all claim to celebrity, and is reduced to giving forlorn *soirées* with a meager buffet.

Beaumont is a charming painter, and a friend of Henry's. When he comes here, as he does very often, he puts us all in a good-humor; even my father-in-law forgets to grumble at the reduced price of stocks and the increased rate of exchange. His picture of Circé charming the pigs is very pretty. Helen and I are both in it; he wanted her ear and hair and my eyes and hair. I am not Circé; I only stand in the background admiring a pig. To reward us he painted a fan for each: mine has arrows, doves, my initials, "Beware," and cherubim all mixed up, making a lovely fan.

Baroness Alphonse Rothschild sent me her box for the opera, and I asked the Metternichs and Herr Wagner, the composer, who was dining at the Embassy, to go with me, and they accepted. The Rothschilds' box is one of the largest in the opera-house. The Princess Metternich created a sensation when we entered—she always does—but Herr Wagner passed unnoticed. He sat behind and pretended to go to sleep. He thought everything most mediocre. The opera was "Faust," which I thought was beautifully put on the stage, with Madame Miolan Carvalho as Marguerite and Faure as Mephistopheles. They both sang and acted to perfection; but Wagner pooh-poohed at them and everything else. *Abscheulich* and *gräss-*

lich alternated in his condemning sentences. Nothing pleased him.

He fidgeted about and was very cross during the fifth act, where the ballet is danced.

"Why did Gounod insert that idiotic ballet? It is *banal* and *de trop*." (France is the only place where this fifth act is performed.)

"You must blame Goethe for that," retorted the Princess Metternich. "Why did he make Faust go to the Champs Élysées if he did not want him to see any dancing?"

"Why, indeed?" grumbled Wagner. "Goethe had much better have let Marguerite die on her straw and not send her up in clouds of glory like the Madonna to heaven, and with ballet music."

"Well," said the Princess, "I don't see any difference between a ballet in heaven and a ballet in Venusberg."

The Emperor has made a fine *coup de popularité*. He refused to have the new boulevard named after his mother, and cleverly proposed it to be called Richard Lenoir, the man who led his fellow-workmen in the Revolution.

We were invited to one of Rossini's Saturday evenings. There was a queer mixture of people: some diplomats, and some well-known members of society, but I fancy that the guests were mostly artists; at least they looked so. The most celebrated ones were pointed out to me. There were Saint-Saëns, Prince Poniatowski, Gounod, and others. I wondered that Richard Wagner was not there; but I suppose that there is little sympathy between these two geniuses.

Prince Metternich told me that Rossini had once said

to him that he wished people would not always feel obliged to sing his music when they sang at his house. "J'acclamerais avec délice 'Au clair de la lune,' même avec variations," he said, in his comical way. Rossini's wife's name is Olga. Some one called her Vulgar, she is so ordinary and pretentious, and would make Rossini's home and salon very commonplace if it were not that the master glorified all by his presence. I saw Rossini's writing-table, which is a thing never to be forgotten: brushes, combs, toothpicks, nails, and all sorts of rubbish lying about pell-mell; and promiscuous among them was the tube that Rossini uses for his famous *macaroni à la Rossini*. Prince Metternich said that no power on earth would induce him to touch any food *à la Rossini*, especially the macaroni, which he said was stuffed with hash and all sorts of remnants of last week's food and piled up on a dish like a log cabin. "J'ai des frissons chaque fois que j'y pense."

Not long ago Baron James Rothschild sent Rossini some splendid grapes from his hothouse. Rossini, in thanking him, wrote, "Bien que vos raisins soient superbes, je n'aime pas mon vin en pillules." This Baron Rothschild read as an invitation to send him some of his celebrated Château-Lafitte, which he proceeded to do, for "the joke of it," he remarked. "It is so amusing to tell the story afterward." Rossini does not dye his hair, but wears the most wiggy of wigs. When he goes to mass he puts one wig on top of the other, and if it is very cold he puts still a third one on, curlier than the others, for the sake of warmth. No coquetry about him!

Rossini asked me to sing.

"I will, with pleasure," I said. "I only wish that I knew what to sing. I know that you do not like people to sing your music when they come to your house."

"Not every one," he said, beaming with a broad smile; "but I have heard that you have an unusually beautiful voice, and I am curious to hear you."

"But," I mischievously answered, "I do not know 'Au clair de la lune,' even with variations."

"Oh! the naughty Prince," said he, shaking his finger across to where Prince Metternich was standing. "He told you that. But tell me, what do you sing of mine?"

Auber had told me to take "Sombre Forêt," of "William Tell," in case I should be asked. Therefore I said that I had brought "Sombre Forêt," and if he liked I would sing that.

"Bene! bene!" he replied. "I will accompany you."

I was dreadfully nervous to sing before him, but when I had finished he stretched out both hands to me and said:

"Merci! C'est comme cela que ça doit être chanté. Votre voix est délicieuse, le timbre que j'aime—mezzo-soprano, avec ces notes hautes et claires."

Auber came up flushed with delight at my success, and said to Rossini, "Did I say too much about Madame Moulton's voice?"

"Not enough," replied Rossini. "She has more than voice; she has intelligence and *le feu sacré—un rossignol doublé de velours;* and more than all, she sings my music as I have written it. Every one likes to add a little of their own. I said to Patti the other day: '*Ma chère* Adelina, when you sing the "Barbiere" do not make it too *strakoschonée'* [Strakosch is Patti's brother-in-law, and makes all her cadenzas for her]. If I had wanted to make all those little things, don't you think that I could have made them myself?"

Auber asked me, "Do you know what Rossini said about me?"

"No," I answered, "I know what he ought to have said. What did he say?"

"He said," Auber replied, with a merry twinkle in his eye, 'Auber est un grand musicien qui fait de la petite musique.'"

"That was pure envy," I said. "I should like to know what you said about Rossini."

"Well, I said," and he hesitated before continuing, "I said that Rossini *est un très grand musicien et fait de la belle musique, mais une exécrable cuisine.*"

Rossini adores Alboni, but deplores her want of confidence in herself. She has such stage frights that she swears that she will have to leave the stage. He has written "La Messe solennelle" for her voice. The "Agnus Dei" is perfectly wonderful. She sang it after I had sung. If she had been first, I never should have had the courage to open my mouth.

Auber asked him how he had liked the representation of "Tannhäuser"? Rossini answered, with a satirical smile, "It is a music one must hear several times. I am not going again."

Rossini said that neither Weber nor Wagner understood the voice. Wagner's interminable dissonances were insupportable. That these two composers imagine that to sing is simply to *dégoiser* the note; but the art of singing, or technic was considered by them to be secondary and insignificant. Phrasing or any sort of *finesse* was superflous. The orchestra must be all-powerful. "If Wagner gets the upper hand," Rossini continued, "as he is sure to do, for people will run after the New, then what will become of the art of singing? No more *bel canto*, no more phrasing, no more enunciation! What is the use, when all that is required of you is to *beugler* (bellow)? Any *cornet à piston* is just as good as the best tenor, and better, for it can be heard over the orchestra. But the instrumentation is magnificent. There Wagner excels. The overture of Tannhäuser is a *chef-d'œuvre;* there is a swing, a sway, and a rush that carries you off your feet. . . . I wish I had composed it myself."

Auber is a true Parisian, adores his Paris, and never leaves it even during the summer, when Paris is insufferable. He comes very often to see me, and we play duets. He loves Bach, and we play Mendelssohn overtures and Haydn symphonies when we are through with Bach. Auber always takes the second piano, or, if a four-handed piece, he takes the base. Sometimes he says: "Je vous donne rendez-vous en bas de la page. Si vous y arrivez la première, attendez-moi, et je ferai de même." He is so clever and full of repartees.

I do not think I ever talked with a wittier person than he is. I always wish I could remember what he says; but, alas! when he goes my memory goes with him.

Though so old (he must be over eighty) he is always beautifully dressed in the latest fashion, trim and neat. He says that he has never heard his operas seated in the audience; it makes him too nervous. He has his seat every night in the parquet of all the theaters in Paris. He only has to choose where to go. He once said: "Je suis trop vieux; on ne devrait pas viellir, mais que faire? c'est le seul moyen de devenir vieux. Un vieillard m'a toujours paru un personnage terrible et inutile, mais me voici un vieillard sans le savoir et je n'en suis pas triste." He is not deaf, nor does he wear glasses except to "déchiffrer ma propre musique"—as he says. Another time he said: "I am glad that I never was married. My wife would now have been an old, wrinkled woman. I never would have had the courage to come home of an evening. Aussi j'aurais voulu avoir une fille (une fille comme vous), et elle m'aurait certainement donné un garçon."

I quote the following from a Paris newspaper:

Parmi les dames qu'on admire le plus, il convient de citer Mme Moulton.—C'est la première fois que nous revoyons Mme Moulton au théâtre depuis son retour d'Amérique. —Serait-elle revenue exprès pour la pièce d'Auber.—On dit, en effet, que dans tous ses opéras, Auber offre le principal rôle à Mme Moulton, qui possède une voix ravissante.

The Emperor once said to Auber: "Dites-moi, quel âge avez-vous? On dit que vous avez quatre-vingt ans." "Sire," answered Auber, "je n'ai pas quatre-vingt ans, mais quatre fois vingt ans." Is he not clever? Some one was talking about the Marquise B—— and her friendship (*sic*) for Monsieur de M——, and said, "On dit que ce n'est que l'amitié." "Oh," said Auber, "je connais ces amitiés-là; on dit que l'amour et l'amitié sont frère et sœur. Cela se peut, mais ils ne sont pas du même lit."

And another time (I am remembering all his witty sayings while I can), Prince Metternich, who smokes one cigarette after the other, said to Auber, "Vous me permettez?" wanting to put his ashes in Auber's tea-saucer. Auber said, "Certainement, mais j'aime mieux monter que descendre." In other words, *J'aime mieux mon thé que des cendres.* How can people be so quick-witted?

Auber has given me all his operas, and I have gone through them all with him for his music. I sing the laughing song in "Manon Lescaut" and the bolero in "Diamants de la Couronne." These two are my favorite songs and are very difficult. In the laughing song I either laugh too much or too little. To start laughing in cold blood is as difficult as to stop laughing when once started. The bolero is only a continuous display of musical fireworks.

NEW YORK, *May, 1864.*

When we arrived in New York (we went to visit my sister and my mother) we were overwhelmed with invitations of all kinds.

I made a most (to me) interesting acquaintance at this *soirée,* a Mrs. Henry Fields, who I found out was the famous and much-talked-about "Lucie," the governess in the trial of the Duc de Praslin. Every one was convinced of her innocence (she pleaded her own case, refusing the aid of a lawyer). Nevertheless, she was the cause of the death of the Duchess, as the Duke killed his wife because she refused to give "Lucie" a letter of recommendation, and he became so enraged at her refusal that he first tried to strangle her, and then shot her. I had heard so much about this murder (it was along ago), and knew all the details, and, what was more, I knew all the children of the unhappy woman whose only crime was to love her husband too much, and to resent "Lucie's" taking away the love of her children from her! Warning to young women: Don't love your husbands too much, or don't engage a too attractive governess.

PHILADELPHIA, *July, 1864.*

DEAR AUNTY,—We came from New York a few days ago, and are staying with mama's friend, Mrs. M——, who is a very (what shall I say?) fascinating but a very peculiar person. She is a curious mixture of a poetess and a society woman, very susceptible, and of such a sensitive nature that she seems always to be in the hottest of hot water, and at war with all her neighbors; but she routs all her enemies and manages everything with a high hand.

Her daughter is just engaged to a Swedish naval officer. To celebrate the engagement they gave a big dinner, and, as the Sanitary Fair is going on just now, President Lincoln is here, and Mrs. M—— had the courage to invite him, and he had the courage to accept. It is the first time that I have ever seen an American President, and I was most anxious to see him, particularly as he has, for the last years, been such a hero in my eyes. He might take the prize for ugliness anywhere; his face looked as if it was cut out of wood, and roughly cut at that, with deep furrows in his cheeks and a huge mouth; but he seemed so good and kind, and his eyes sparkled with so much humor and fun, that he became quite fascinating, especially when he smiled. I confess I lost my heart to him. . . . The dinner, I mean the food part of it, was a failure. It came from Baltimore, and everything was cold; the *pâté de foie gras* never appeared at all! When Mrs. M—— mentioned the fact to Mr. Lincoln, pointing to the menu, he said "the *pâté*" (he pronounced it *patty*) has probably walked off by itself. Every one laughed, because he said it in such a comical, slow way.

After the gentlemen had smoked (I thought they were a long time at it) we were requested to go into the gallery, where all the gas-lights were turned up to the fullest and chairs placed in rows, and Professor Winter began to read a lecture on the brain—of all subjects! Who but Mrs. M—— would ever have arranged such an entertainment?

Professor Winter told us where our 50,000 ideas were laid up in our brains (I am sure that I have not 50,000 in mine). One might have deducted 49,999, and still, with that little one left, I was not able to understand the half of what he said.

Another wonderful thing he told us was, that there are five thousand million cells in our brain, and that it takes about ten thousand cells to furnish a well-lodged perception. How in the world can he know that? I think he must have examined his own ten thousand cells to have discovered all this exuberance of material. The President looked bored, and I am sure everybody else wished Professor Winter and his theories (because they can't be facts) in the Red Sea. . . . After this *séance manquée* I was asked to sing. Poor Mr. Lincoln! who I understood could not endure music. I pitied him.

"None of your foreign fireworks," said Mr. Trott,

in his graceful manner, as I passed him on my way to the piano. I answered, "Shall I sing 'Three Little Kittens'? I think that is the least fireworky of my *répertoire*." But I concluded that a simple little rocket like "Robin Adair" would kill nobody; therefor I sang that, and it had a success.

When the gaunt President shook my hand to thank me, he held it in a grip of iron, and when, to accentuate the compliment, meaning to give a little extra pressure, he put his left hand over his right, I felt as if my hand was shut in a waffle-iron and I should never straighten it out again.

"Music is not much in my line," said the President; "but when you sing you warble yourself into a man's heart. I'd like to hear you sing some more."

What other mild cracker could I fire off? Then I thought of that lovely song, "Mary Was a Lassie," which you like so much, so I sang that.

Mr. Lincoln said, "I think I might become a musician if I heard you often; but so far I only know two tunes."

"'Hail, Columbia'?" I asked. "You know that, I am sure!"

"Oh yes, I know that, for I have to stand up and take off my hat."

"And the other one?"

"The other one! Oh, the other one is the other when I don't stand up!"

I am sorry not to have seen Mr. Lincoln again. There was something about him that was perfectly fascinating, but I think I have said this before.

IN THE COURTS OF MEMORY

DEAR AUNTY,—My last letter, written from Philadelphia, told you of my having made Mr. Lincoln's acquaintance. A few days after we left for Niagara,
taking Rochester on our way. I had not seen Rochester
since I was eleven years old, and mama and I both
wanted to go there again.

We slept in Rochester that night. The next morning a deputation headed by the director of the penitentiary, flanked by a committee of benevolent ladies,
called upon us to beg me to sing for the penitents at
the penitentiary the next day, it being Sunday. They
all said, in chorus, that it would be a great and noble act.

I did not (and I do not now) see why pickpockets and
burglars should be entertained, and I could not grasp
the greatness of the act, unless it was in the asking.
However, mama urged me (she can never bear me to
say no), and I accepted.

At the appointed time the director called for us in a
landau, and we drove out to the penitentiary. As we
entered the double courtyard, and drove through the
much belocked gates, I felt very depressed, and not at
all like bursting forth in song. Mama and I were led
up, like lambs to the slaughter, on to a platform, passing
the guilty ones seated in the pews, the men on one side,
the women on the other, of the aisles, all dressed in
stripes of some sort; they looked sleepy and stupid.
They had just sat through the usual Sunday exhortation.

The ladies of the committee ranged themselves so as
to make a background of solemn benevolence on the
platform, in the middle of which stood a primeval

66

melodion with two octaves and four stops. One stop would have been enough for me, and I needed it later, as you will see.

Here I was! What should I sing? I was utterly at a loss. Why had I not thought this out before coming? French love-songs; out of the question.

Italian prayers and German lullabies were plentiful in the *répertoire*, but seemed sadly out of place for this occasion.

I thought of Lucrezia Borgia's "Brindisi"; but that instantly went out of my mind. A drinking song urging people to drink seemed absurdly inappropriate, as probably most of my audience had done their misdeeds under the influence of drink.

I knew the words of "Home, Sweet Home," and decided on that. Nothing could have been worse. I attacked the squeaky melodion, pushed down a pedal, pulled out the "vox humana" stop—the most harmless one of the melodion, but which gave out a supernaturally hoarse sound—I struck the chord, and standing up I began. These poor, homeless creatures must have thought my one purpose was to harass them to the last limit, and I only realized what I was singing about when I saw them with bowed heads and faces hidden in their hands; some even sobbing.

The director, perceiving the doleful effect I had produced, suggested, "Perhaps something in a lighter vein." I tried to think of "something in a lighter vein," and inquired, "How would 'Swanee River' be?"

"First-rate," said the kind director; "just the thing —*good*," emphasizing the word *good* by slapping his hands together. Thus encouraged, I started off again in the melancholy wake of the melodion. Alas! this fared no better than "Home, Sweet Home." When I sang "Oh; darkies! how my heart grows weary!" the word *weary* had a disastrous effect, and there was a regular breakdown (I don't mean in the darky sense of the word, the penitents did *not* get up and perform a breakdown—I wish they had!); but there was a regular collapse of penitents. I thought that they would have to be carried out on stretchers.

The poor warden, now at his wits' end, but wishing to finish this lugubrious performance with a flourish, proposed (unhappy thought) that I should address a few words to the now miserable, broken-hearted crowd. I will give you a thousand guesses, dear aunty, and still you will never guess the idiotic words that issued from your niece's lips. I said, looking at them with a triumphant smile (I have no doubt that, at that moment, I thought I was in my own drawing-room, bidding guests good night)—I said (I really hate to write it): "I hope the next time I come to Rochester I shall meet you all here again."

This was the first speech I ever made in public—I confess that it was not a success.

PARIS, *1865.*

The Princess Mathilde receives every Sunday evening. Her salons are always crowded, and are what one might call cosmopolitan. In fact, it is the only salon in Paris where one can meet all nationalities. There are diplomats, royalists, imperialists, strangers of importance passing through Paris, and especially all the celebrated artists.

She has great taste, and has arranged her palace most charmingly. She has converted a small portion of the park behind it into a winter garden, which is filled with beautiful palms and flowering plants. In this attractive place she holds her receptions, and I sang there the other evening.

Rossini was, as a great exception, present. I fancy that he and his wife had dined with the Princess; therefore, when the Princess asked him to accompany me, saying that she desired so much to hear me sing, he could not well refuse to be amiable, and sat down to the piano with a good enough grace. I sang "Bel Raggio," from "Semiramide," as I knew it by heart (I had sung it often enough with Garcia). Rossini was kind enough not to condemn the cadenzas with which Garcia had interlarded it. I was afraid he would not like them, remembering what he had said to Patti about hers.

I was amused at his gala dress for royalty: a much-too-big redingote, a white tie tied a good deal to one side, and only one wig.

He says that he is seventy-three years old. I must say that this is difficult to believe, for he does not look it by ten years. He never accepts any invitations. I know I have never seen him anywhere outside his own house, and it was a great surprise to see him now. We once ventured to invite him and his wife to dinner one evening, when the Prince and Princess Metternich were dining with us; and we got this answer: "Merci, de votre invitation pour ma femme et moi. Nous regrettons de ne pouvoir l'accepter. Ma femme ne sort que pour aller à la messe, et moi je ne sors jamais de mes habitudes." We felt snubbed, as no doubt we deserved to be.

Gounod played most enchantingly some selections from "Roméo et Juliette," the opera he has just composed. I hear that he wants Christine Nilsson to sing it. The music seems to me even more beautiful than "Faust." Rossini talked a long time with Gounod, and Auber told me that Rossini said, patting Gounod on the back, "Vous êtes le chevalier Bayard de la musique."

Gounod answered, "Sans peur, non!"

Rossini said, "Dans tous les cas, sans reproche et sans égal."

Gounod is, I think, the gentlest, the most modest, and the kindest-hearted man in the world. His music is like him, gentle and graceful. Princess Mathilde asked me to sing again; but, as I had not brought any music, Auber offered to accompany me in the "Song of the Djins," from his new opera, which I had so often sung with him. It was not the song I should have selected; but, as Auber desired it, I was glad to gratify him, and was delighted when I saw Rossini compliment Auber, who (like the tenor before the drop-curtain, who waves his hand toward the soprano as if all the merit of the performance was due to her) waved his hand toward me, which suggested to Rossini to make me a reflected compliment.

This was a great occasion, seeing and hearing Rossini, Gounod, and Auber at the same time. I shall never forget that evening. I wonder that I had the courage to sing before them. Among the guests was an Indian Nabob dressed in all his orientals, who in himself would have been sufficient attraction for a whole evening, had he not been totally eclipsed by the three great artists. The Nabob probably expected more homage than he received; but people hardly looked at him.

I was presented to him, and he seemed glad to speak English, which was not of the best, but far better than his French. He told me a great deal about his journey, the attractions of Paris, and about his country and family.

I asked him, by way of saying something (I was not particularly interested in him or his family), how many children he had. He answered, "Quite a few, milady."

"What does your Highness call a few?" I asked.

"Well, I think about forty," he replied, nonchalantly.

"That would be considered quite a large family here," I said.

The Nabob, of course, did not appreciate the profundity of this remark.

A few days after, the Princess Mathilde sent me a lovely fan which she had painted herself, and Mr. Moulton is going to have it mounted. I am very happy to have it as a souvenir of a memorable evening, besides being an exquisite specimen of the Princess's talent as an artist. The Princess is what one might call miscellaneous. She has a Corsican father, a German mother, and a Russian husband, and as "cavaliere servente" (as they say in Italy), a Dutchman. She was born in Austria, brought up in Italy, and lives in France. She said once to Baron Haussmann, "If you go on making boulevards like that, you will shut me up like a vestal."

"I will never make another, your Highness," he answered.

Every one is very much excited about a young Swedish girl called Christine Nilsson, who has walked right into the star-light, for she really is a star of the first magnitude. She has studied with Wachtel only one year, and behold her now singing at the Théâtre Lyrique to crowded audiences in the "Flûte Enchantée." Her voice has a wonderful charm; she sings without the slightest effort, and naturally as a bird. She has some phenomenal high notes, which are clear as bells. She makes that usually tedious *grand aria*, which every singer makes a mess of, quite lovely and musical, hovering as she does in the regions above the upper line like a butterfly and trilling like a canary-bird. A Chinese juggler does not play with his glass balls more dexterously than she plays with all the effects and tricks of the voice. What luck for her to have blossomed like that into a full-fledged prima-donna with so little effort. I have got to know her quite well, as Miss Haggerty, who was at some school with her in Paris, invites her often to lunch and asks me to meet her.

Nilsson is tall, graceful, slight, and very attractive, without being actually handsome. She acts well and naturally, and with intelligence, without exerting herself; she has the happy faculty of understanding and seizing things *au vol*, instead of studying them. She has a regal future before her. A second Jenny Lind! Their careers are rather similar. Jenny Lind was a singer in cafés, and Nilsson played the violin in cafés in Stockholm. She is clever, too! She has surrounded herself by a wall of propriety, in the shape of an English *dame de compagnie*, and never moves unless followed by her. This lady (Miss Richardson) is correctness and primness personified, and so *comme il faut* that it is actually oppressive to be in the same room with her. Nilsson herself is full of fun and jokes, but at the same time dignified and serious.

Christine Nilsson gave Mrs. Haggerty a box at the Théâtre Lyrique, where she is now playing "Traviata" (I think it was the director's box), and I was invited to go with her and Clem. The box was behind the curtain and very small and very dark. But it was intensely amusing to see how things were done, and how prosaic and matter-of-fact everything was. If ever I thanked my stars that I was not a star myself it was then.

Everything looked so tawdry and claptrap: the dirty boards, the grossly painted scenery, the dingy workmen shuffling about grumbling and gruff, ordered and scolded by a vulgar superior. Of course the stars do not see all these things, because they only appear when the heavens are ready for them to shine in.

The overture, so it sounded to us, was a clash of drums, trumpets, and trombones all jumbled together. After the three knocks of the director, which started up the dust of ages into our faces until we were almost suffocated, the curtain rose slowly with great noise and rumbling.

The audience looked formidable as we saw it through the mist of cloudy gas-light, a sea of faces, of color and vagueness. The incongruity of costumes was a thing to weep over. If they had tried they could not have made it worse. The lady guests, walking and chatting, in a *soi-disant* elegant salon, were dressed, some in Louis XV. splendor, some in dogesses' brocades, some in modern finery, with bows and ribbons and things looped up any way. Nilsson was dressed in quite modern style— flounces, laces, and fringes, and so forth, while Alfredo had donned a black velvet coat *à la* something, with a huge jabot which fell over a frilled shirt-front. He wore short velvet trousers, and black-silk stockings covered his thin legs without the least attempt at padding.

The "padre" was in a shooting-jacket, evidently just in from a riding-tour. He held a riding-stick, and wore riding-gantlets which he flourished about with such wide gesticulations that I thought he was going to hit Nilsson in the face.

We could not hear the singing so well from where we sat; but the orchestra was overpowering, and the applause deafening, like peals of thunder.

I laughed when the gang of workmen rushed on to the stage as soon as the curtain came down, and began sweeping and taking down one set of furniture and putting on another; especially in the last act, when Violetta's bed came on and the men threw the pillows from one to the other, as if they were playing ball. They hung up a crucifix, which I thought was unnecessary, and brought in a candlestick. I wondered if they were going to put a warming-pan in the bed. A mat was laid down with great precision. Then Nilsson came in, dressed in a flounced petticoat trimmed with lace, a "matinée," and black slippers, and got into the bed.

After the performance was over the curtain was raised and the artists came forward to bow; the stage was covered with flowers and wreaths. And Nilsson, in picking up her floral tributes, was wreathed in smiles; but they faded like mist before the sun the minute the curtain was lowered, and she looked tired and worn out. Her maid was there, waiting with a shawl to wrap around the shoulders of the hot prima-donna, and the prim Miss Richardson ready to escort her to her room, while the army of shirt-sleeved men invaded the stage like bees, with brooms which, though anything but new, I hope swept clean. Then everything was dark and dismal, lit only by one or two candles and a solitary lantern. All that was so brilliant a moment before was now only a confused mass of disillusions.

Nilsson and her duenna drove to Mrs. H——'s and had supper with us. One would never have dreamt that she had been dying of consumption an hour before, to see her stow away ham, salad, and pudding in great quantities. Then she embraced us all and drove off in her coupé. The star was going to set. I went home, glad that my life lay in other paths.

PARIS, *March, 1865.*

DEAR M.,—Do not be anxious about me. When Mrs. M—— wrote, I was really in danger of a *fluxion de poitrine*. I am sorry she worried you unnecessarily. I am much better; in fact, I am far on the road to recovery. If every one had such a nice time when they are ill as I had they would not be in a hurry to get well. When I was convalescent enough to come down-stairs, and the doctor had said his last word (the traditional "you must be careful"), I had my *chaise-longue* moved down into Henry's studio, and Monsieur Gudin, who is the kindest man in the world, offered to come there and paint a picture in order to amuse and divert me.

75

Bierstadt, the American painter, who is in Paris, also proposed to come. Then those two artists ordered canvases of the same size, and Beaumont, not to be outdone, ordered a larger canvas, and Henry announced his intention of finishing an already commenced landscape.

Behold, then, your invalid, surrounded by these celebrated artists, reclining on a *chaise-longue*, a table with *tisanes* and remedies near by, and the four painters painting. Gudin is painting a seascape; Bierstadt, a picture of California; Beaumont, of course, his graceful ladies and cherubs. It amused me to see how differently they painted. Gudin spread his paints on a very large table covered with glass, and used a great many brushes; Bierstadt used a huge palette, and painted rather finically, whereas Beaumont had quite a small palette and used few brushes. I was very sorry when my convalescence came to an end and the pictures were finished; but I had the delight of receiving the four pictures, which the four artists begged me to accept as a souvenir of the "pleasant days in the studio."

Another pleasant thing happened during "the pleasant days in the studio," which was the gift of a beautiful gold medal which the Emperor sent me as a souvenir of the day I sang the *Benedictus* in the chapel of the Tuileries. It is a little larger than a five-franc piece, and has on one side the head of the Emperor encircled by "Chapelle des Tuileries," and on the other side "Madame Moulton" and the date.

We are all dreadfully sad about the Duke de Morny's death. He was very much appreciated, and a favorite with every one. They say that the Duchess cut off all her hair and put it into his coffin. I never heard before that she was such a loving wife. I only hope that she will not need her braids to keep on her next wedding-wreath.

We have just heard of the assassination of that good, kind President Lincoln. How dreadful!

I have a new teacher called Delsarte, the most unique specimen I have ever met. My first impression was that I was in the presence of a *concierge* in a second-class establishment; but I soon saw that he was the great master I had heard described so often. He is not a real singing teacher, for he does not think the voice worth speaking of; he has a theory that one can express more by the features and all the tricks he teaches, and especially by the manner of enunciation, than by the voice. We were (Aunty and I) first led into the salon, and then into the music-room, so called because the piano is there and the stand for music, but no other incumbrances as furniture.

On the walls were hung some awful diagrams to illustrate the master's method of teaching. These diagrams are crayon-drawings of life-sized faces depicting every emotion that the human face is capable of expressing, such as love, sorrow, murder, terror, joy, surprise, etc.

It is Delsarte's way, when he wants you to express one of these emotions in your voice, to point with a soiled forefinger to the picture in question which he expects you to imitate. The result lends expression to your voice.

The piano is of a pre-Raphaelite construction, and stands in the middle of the room like an island in a lake, with a footstool placed over the pedals (he considers the pedal as useless). The lid of the piano was absent, and, to judge from the inside, I should say that the piano was the receptacle for everything that belonged to the Delsarte homestead. There were inkstands, pens, pencils, knives, wire, matches, toothpicks, half-smoked cigars, even remnants of his luncheon, which seemed to have been black bread and cheese, and dust galore. Delsarte had on a pair of much-worn embroidered slippers, a velvet *calotte*, the tassels of which swayed with each of his emotions, and a dilapidated *robe de chambre* which opened at every movement, disclosing his soiled plaid foulard doing duty for a collar.

On my telling him that I desired to take some lessons of him, he asked me to sing something for him. Seeing the music of Duprato's "Il était nuit déjà," I proposed singing that, and he sat down at the pedal-less piano to accompany me. When I arrived at the phrase, "Un souffle d'air léger apportait jusqu'à nous l'odeur d'un oranger," he interrupted me. "Repeat that!" he cried. "Il faut qu'on sente le souffle d'air et l'odeur de l'oranger." I said to myself, ". . . no one could 'sentir un oranger' in this room; one could only smell Delsarte's bad tobacco."

He begged me to sing something else.

"Will you accompany Gounod's 'Medje' for me?" I asked him.

"No," he replied. "I will listen; you must accompany yourself. There are certain songs that cannot be accompanied by any one but the singer. This is one of them! You feel yourself, don't you, that it is absolutely necessary for you to clutch something when singing this? A weak chord or a too powerful one struck in a wrong place would spoil entirely the effect, and even the best accompanist cannot foresee when that effect is going to be produced." I think this is so clever! "'Voi che sapete' can be accompanied by any school-girl," he continued. "It is plain sailing; but in 'Medje' the piano must be part of the singer and breathe with him." I sat down at the piano and sang. When I came to "Prends cette lame et plonges la dans mon cœur," he stopped me short, and pointing to a horrible picture on the wall indicating bloody murder and ter-ror (No. 6), he cried, "Voilà l'expression qu'il faut avoir." I sang the phrase over again, trying to imagine what Medje's lover must have felt; but I could not satisfy Delsarte. He said my voice ought to tremble; and, in fact, I ought to sing false when I say, "Ton image encore vivante dans mon cœur qui ne bat plus." "No one," he said, "in such a moment of emotion could keep on the right note." I tried again, in vain! If I had had a dagger in my hand and a brigand before me, I might perhaps have been more successful. However, he let it pass; but to show that it could be done he sang it for me, and actually did sing it false. Curiously enough, it sounded quite right, tremolo and all. There is no doubt that he is a *great artist*. One can see that Faure and Coquelin (the actor) have both profited by his unique teaching. He assured me that there is no art like that of making people believe what you want them to. For instance, he pretends that he can sing "Il pleut, il pleut, bergère," and make you hear the patter of the *bergère's* heels on the wet sod, or wherever she was trying to *rentrer ses blancs moutons*. He sang it with the fullest conviction, and asked me what I thought of it. I shut my eyes and tried to conjure up the *bergère* and her heels. My head began to whirl with all this talk, and, in taking leave of my new master, I promised him that I would try to sing false until the next lesson. Another thing he said was: "Never try to accompany yourself when the accompaniment is difficult. There is nothing so painful as to see a singer struggling with tremolos, and arpeggios." How right he is!

He has one theory about the trembling of the chin. It certainly is very effective. When in "Medje" I say, "Tu n'as pas vu mes larmes, tout la nuit j'ai pleuré," Delsarte says, "Make your chin tremble; just try it once," pointing to a diagram, "and every one will be overcome." I have tried it and have seen the effect. But I am letting you into all Delsarte's most innermost secrets.

PARIS, *July, 1865.*

DEAR M.,—You must forgive me if I have not written lately; but we have been on a visit to the Duke and Duchess de Persigny for the past week. I did not have time to do more than dress for driving and drive, dress for afternoon tea, dress for dinner, and dine.

The estates of Chamarande are beautiful, the château itself is very magnificent and arranged with the Duchess's taste, which is perfect though ultra-English.

The château has a moat around it, over which is a stone bridge which leads to the entrance on the side opposite the broad terraces bordered by cut trees, as in Versailles. The park is very large, filled with beautiful old trees, and most artistically laid out.

The Duke de Persigny is perfectly delightful, genial, kind, and certainly the cleverest man of the day, with a temper which is temper-proof. I never saw him out of it, and, well as I know him, I have never seen him ruffled in any way, and sometimes there were occasions, goodness knows!

The Duchess is still handsome and attractive; her pronounced originality lends her a peculiar charm. She has many admiring friends who are true to her, and I must say that when she is a friend she is a true one, and never fails you. Her originality frequently leads her beyond conventionality; for instance, the other day she took it into her head to dine out of doors. If she wanted to picnic *al fresco*, why did she not choose some pretty place in the park or in the woods? But no, she had the usual elaborate dinner served directly outside the château, and on the gravel walk. The servants, powdered and in short breeches as usual, served us in their customary solemnity; but they must have wondered why we preferred to sit on the gravel, with a draught of cold air on our backs, when we might have been comfortably seated in a big and airy room with a carpet under our feet. However, such was the wish of the châtelaine, and no one dared say a word, not even the Duke, though he protested meekly.

Later on the Duke had his revenge, for in the midst of our breezy repast there came a downpour of rain, accompanied by lightning and peals of thunder, which necessitated a hasty retreat.

The Duchess, who is very timid in thunder-storms, was the first to rush into the house, the guests following pell-mell, and our dinner was finished indoors.

After our return to Petit Val we had the visit of Auber's protégé, a young man called Massenet. One day, in Paris, two months ago, Auber said to me:

"I am very much interested in a former pupil of the Conservatoire who took the Grand-Prix de Rome, and has just come back from his four years' musical studies in Rome. As he is more or less a stranger in Paris, I should be very thankful if you would interest yourself for him. He really is a genius; but, as so often happens, geniuses don't have pocket-money."

I answered: "Please tell him to come and see me. I have some music I wish to have transposed. Do you think that he would be willing to do it?"

"Certainly; he would be glad to do anything," was the answer.

The next day a pale young man presented himself. "You are Monsieur Massenet?" I inquired.

"Yes, Madame," came the gentle answer.

Thereupon I gave him the music, and I showed him to a quiet little room in the upper part of the house, which contained a piano, writing-table, pen and ink, etc., and left him to his fate. He came two or three times before I heard him play, and then it was only by chance that I passed through the corridor, and imagine my astonishment at hearing the most divine music issuing from the room where the young man was working. I rushed in, saying:

"What is that?"

"Nothing," he answered.

"Nothing!" I exclaimed. "I never heard anything so exquisite. Do play it again."

"It was simply something that passed through my head," he answered.

"Then let something else pass through your head. I must hear more," I said. Then he played, and I sat and listened to the most bewildering and beautiful music that I ever heard. From that moment there was no more copying. What a genius he is! I wish you could hear him improvise!

We have invited him frequently, and when we are at Petit Val he comes often out to see us, and luxuriates in the repose and comfort of our life here. He has already written some lovely songs under its influence. He composed one called "l'Esclave," and dedicated it to me for my birthday. He accompanies me as no one has ever done before.

Auber, who drives out occasionally, is delighted to see that "Our Massenet," as he generally calls him, is getting color in his pale cheeks and his bright and eager eyes are brighter than ever, and he is actually getting fat.

PARIS, *January, 1866.*

We have just returned from Nice and Cannes, also from a very disappointing yachting cruise in the Mediterranean, which proved to be a complete fiasco. I must tell you about it. Lord Albert Gower had invited us to go to Spezia on his beautiful yacht. From there we were to go to Florence, and later make a little trip in Italy. We had all been asked to a dinner at the Duke de Vallombrosa's villa at Cannes, and some of us to spend the night there.

The evening before we started there was a large dinner at the prefect's given in honor of the Austrian Ambassador, Prince Metternich, who had come on an official visit concerning an archduke, at which Lord Albert proposed that we should take Cannes *en route*, spend the night there, and start the next day for Spezia.

I thought that I was going to have a beautiful time when we left Nice. The sun was shining brightly, and there was every prospect of a good breeze, and I settled down on deck with books and work, thinking how delightful it was all going to be, and how pleasant it was to get away from the fatiguing gaieties of Nice, where there had been a perfect avalanche of dinners, balls, and theater-parties which even surpassed Paris.

Well! A dead calm set in about an hour after we had started, and only a vestige of a breeze wafted us along on our way, and we never arrived at Cannes till seven o'clock, just in time to disembark, jump into a carriage, and reach the Duke de Vallombrosa's villa. I thought that I was very expeditious over my toilette, notwithstanding which I found myself half an hour late for dinner. Fortunately, however, our hosts were lenient and accepted my excuses.

Lord and Lady Brougham, Duke de Croy, and many others were there. And who else do you think? No less a personage than Jenny Lind! You may imagine my delight at seeing her—"the Goddess of Song," the idol of my youth—about whom still hung a halo.

She is neither handsome nor distinguished-looking; in fact, quite the contrary: plain features, a pert nose, sallow skin, and very yellow hair. However, when she smiled, which was not often, her face became almost handsome.

After dinner the Duchess de Vallombrosa begged her to sing; but she flatly refused, and there was no other music, thank heaven! I was presented to her, in spite of her too evident dislike for new acquaintances; but when she heard that I sang she seemed more amiable and interested. She even asked me to come to see her the next day. "That is," she said, "if you can climb my hill." I told her that I was sure I could climb her hill, and would, even if I had to climb on all fours.

After having been on the glaring Mediterranean all day I could hardly keep my eyes open, and retired before the last carriage had driven away. The next morning I looked out of my window and saw our yacht dancing on the sparkling waves. We expected to leave for Spezia that afternoon.

At eleven o'clock, the hour appointed, I commenced my pilgrimage to the hill of the "Swedish nightingale," with what emotion, I can hardly tell you! I left the carriage at the foot of the hill, and climbed and climbed, until I reached the heaven where the angel lived. It was the reverse of Jacob's dream. His angel climbed down to him, whereas I had to climb up to mine. She always used a donkey for her climbings.

She received me very cordially, saying, "I welcome you to my *bicoque*," and led me through a few badly furnished rooms with hay-stuffed sofas and hard, uncompromising chairs and queer-looking tables painted in red and green out on to the veranda, which commanded a magnificent view over the sea and the Esterel Mountains.

I wish you could have seen her! She was dressed in a white brocade trimmed with a piece of red silk around the bottom, a red, blousy waist covered with gold beads sewed fantastically over it, perhaps odds and ends of old finery, and gold shoes!

Just fancy, at eleven o'clock in the morning! We talked music. She hated Verdi and all he had made; she hated Rossini and all he had made; she hated the French; she hated the Americans; she abhorred the very name of Barnum, who, she said, "exhibited me just as he did the big giant or any other of his monstrosities."

"But," said I, "you must not forget how you were idolized and appreciated in America. Even as a child I can remember how they worshiped Jenny Lind."

"Worshiped or not," she answered, sharply, "I was nothing more than a show in a showman's hands; I can never forget that."

We sat on her veranda, and she told me all about her early life and her musical career. She said she was born in 1820, and when only ten years old she used to sing in cafés in Stockholm. At seventeen she sang "Alice" in "Robert-le-Diable"! Then we talked of our mutual teacher, dear Garcia, of whom she took lessons in 1841 and whom, for a wonder, she liked.

At the *Rhein-fest* given for Queen Victoria in 1844 she said that she had had a great success, and that Queen Victoria had always been a friend to her since that time.

I asked her when she first sang in London.

"I think it was in 1847, or thereabouts," she replied. "Then I went to Paris; but I do not wish to speak of that horrid place."

"Is Paris such a horrid place?" I asked. "I wish you would come while I am there."

JENNY LIND

"Never, never!" she cried. "They treated me so abominably I vowed that I would never set foot in Paris again, and although they have offered me every possible inducement I have always refused."

"What a pity!" I exclaimed. "Would you not like to see the Exposition in Paris next year? I think it might interest you."

"Yes, that might interest me; but Paris! Paris!"

"Do you know Auber?" I asked.

"Auber. No, I have always wanted to know him, but have never had an opportunity."

"If you will come to Paris, I will arrange that you meet him."

"I will! I will! And then I will sing for him!" she said, with almost girlish glee.

How delighted I was to think that I might be the medium to bring them together.

She asked me a great many questions about my singing. Suddenly she said, "Make a trill for me."

I looked about for a piano to give me a note to start on. But a piano was evidently the thing where the Goldschmidts had drawn the line. I made as good a trill as I could without one.

"Very good!" said she, nodding her head approvingly. "I learned my trill this way." And she made a trill for me, accentuating the upper note.

Pointing her finger at me, she said, "You try it."

I tried it. Unless one has learned to trill so it is very difficult to do; but I managed it somehow.

Then she said, in her abrupt way, "What vocalizes do you sing?"

I replied that I had arranged Chopin's waltz in five flats as a vocalize.

"In the original key?" she asked. "I know it well. It is one of Goldschmidt's favorite concert pieces."

"Not in the original key. I have transposed it two notes lower, and put some sort of words to it. I also sing as a vocalize the first sixteen bars of the overture of Mendelssohn's 'Midsummer Night's Dream.'"

"I don't think that I could do that," she said.

"I am sure you could," I answered, upon which she tried it. She sang it slowly but perfectly, shutting her eyes as if feeling her way cautiously, for the intonations are very difficult.

Twelve o'clock sounded from a cuckoo-clock in the next room, and I felt that my visit, fascinating as my angel was, must come to an end. I left her still standing on the veranda in her white brocade, and as I walked off she made the trill as an adieu.

I reached the villa in time for breakfast, after which our hosts drove us down to the pier, where the little rowboat was waiting to take us out to the yacht.

I said that our trip was a failure! It was more than a failure. It meant a gale, thunder, lightning, and sudden death, and everything in the Litany, and we finished ignominiously by taking refuge in the first port we could reach, and going on to our destination by train.

PARIS, *February 12, 1866.*

DEAR AUNTY,—There has been a regular deluge of balls in Paris this winter. The Minister of Marine gave a gorgeous one, the *clou* of which was the entrance at midnight precisely of *Les Quatres Continents*, being four long *cortèges* representing Europe, America, Africa, and Asia.

I was quite provoked that they did not ask me to be in the American *cortège*. I should have loved to have been an Indian squaw, except that a blanket is a rather warm *toilette de bal*. They wanted me to take a costume of a Spanish lady in the *cortège* of Europe, but I refused; if I could not be in the American I did not want to be in any of the others.

Taking part in the *cortège* meant waiting till midnight before appearing, and then, being in it, you did not see it. I had a banal and not a correct costume of an Amazone Louis XIII., and stayed in the ballroom all the evening, and saw the procession when it came in. It was very interesting and really beautifully arranged.

Africa (Mademoiselle de Sèvres) was brought in on a camel fresh from the jungle of the Jardin des Plantes, and followed by quantities of natives of every variety of shade, from sepia to chocolate, as near to nature as they dared go without spoiling their beauty. Some of the costumes were very fantastic. Ladies dressed in skirts made of feathers, and beads hanging everywhere, copied after well-known pictures, and especially after the costumes of "l'Africaine," of the Opera. The men wore enormous wigs made of black wool, and black *tricots*, blacker than the most African of negroes.

Asia (Baronne Erlanger) was standing on a platform carried by menials hidden from view and smothered under tiger and other skins. She was poised with one foot on the head of a tiger, one hand was clutching a date-tree, and the other hand clinging to the back of a stuffed leopard. It must have been difficult for her to keep her balance; her platform seemed very shaky, and the date-tree waved as if it had been in a tornado. The natives who followed her were more beaded and feathery and multicolored than the Africans, otherwise they looked much alike.

America was represented by a pretty girl (a Miss Carter, of Boston). She was brought in reclining in a hammock of gay colors. The American natives were not of the kind one meets in New York and Boston; they were mostly the type taken from the most popular books. There was the sedate Puritan from Long-fellow's "Evangeline"; the red Indians from Cooper's books; Hiawatha and Pocahontas, of course; and the type most beloved in the European market, that of the plantation tyrant who drags his victim to the whipping-post with pointed stakes and cudgels, *à la Oncle Tom*, and lastly the Mexican types with slouched hats and picturesque shirts and leather leggings, pistols bulging from their belts.

Europe (Madame d'Arjuson) was seated in a Roman chair, and looked very comfortable, in comparison with the other Continents; the platform on which she sat was loaded with flowers and dragged in on wheels. All the national costumes of Europe were extremely pretty and varied. The German peasants in great variety, the Italian *ciociara*, the Spanish toreador, and the Dutch fisherwoman with her wooden shoes—all were complete.

Worth and Bobergh had not slept for nights, thinking out the different costumes and worrying over the de-tails. Worth had the most-brain work, and Bobergh was the sleepy partner.

The cotillon was superb; it commenced at two o'clock and finished at the break of day. The favors were of every nationality, imported from all over the world, and tied up with every imaginable national color. I danced with the Count Vogüé, who is by far the best dancer in Paris. He got masses of favors and gave them all to me, and I also received a great quantity; so that when I went to the carriage I almost needed a dray to carry them.

PARIS, *March, 1866.*

DEAR M.,—I think of your sitting in your Cambridge home and reading this account of the frivolities of your daughter. While the scene of last night is just in my mind, I will tell you about it.

Yesterday was Count Pourtales's birthday, and Prince Metternich thought out a wonderful scheme for a surprise for Count Pourtales and the rest of us. Princess Metternich and Countess Pourtales were the only ones taken into his confidence.

There was a dinner at the Pourtales' in honor of the occasion, and the guests were Baron Alphonse Rothschild, Count and Countess Moltke, Prince Sagan, the Duke de Croy, and ourselves.

On arriving at seven o'clock we were ushered into the salon, and later went in to dinner. All the lights were placed on the table, leaving the rest of the room in darkness. The servants seemed to me principally butlers with the traditional side-whiskers, or chasseurs with beards or mustaches. I thought that they might be extra servants brought in for the occasion.

The first course was served. A little awkward spilling of soup on the table-cloth was not remarked upon. The fish came on with its sauce. A startled cry came from a lady on receiving some drops of it on her bare neck, to which no one paid any particular attention. Then, a few moments later, some wine was carelessly spilled on one of the gentlemen's heads. These things can so easily happen, no one said anything.

The filet was handed to me, and at the same time the sauce-dish was uncomfortably near my neck, and directly under my nose. This was too nonchalant, and my surprise was still greater when the servant, in an unnatural and gruff voice, said, "Do you want any of this stuff?" I looked up at the man, and recognized a twinkle in a familiar eye, and as the twinkle was accentuated by a powerful wink I began to understand and held my tongue.

Things might have gone on longer if one of the waiters had not been too bold, and on serving Countess Moltke, a very pretty American lady married to a Dane, pushed her arm a little roughly, and in an obviously disguised voice said, "Better take some of this, you won't get another chance."

She called out in an indignant voice, "Did you ever hear the like?" Count Pourtales seemed dazed, while his wife looked as unconcerned as if there was nothing unusual. Then the insolent waiters began talking across the table to each other. One said, "Don't you see that lady with the rose has not got any salad?" The other answered, "Attend to your own affairs." Count Pourtales, crimson with mortification, was about to get up and apologize, when he was suddenly pulled back into his seat, and the absurd waiters began throwing pellets of bread at him.

Imagine his feelings! To be treated in this way in one's own house, by one's own servants! Every one of them must have suddenly gone crazy, or else they were drunk. For a moment consternation was depicted on all the countenances; we thought the end of the world had come.

When things had gone so far, Prince Metternich stood up and made a pretty little speech for the host, and we all drank his health, and the waiters all took off their wigs and false beards and waved them in the air.

Six of the most fashionable young gentlemen of Paris had been serving us! The Pourtales' own servants, who had kept aloof, now came in, and the *ci-devant* waiters drew up chairs between those at the table, and the dinner finished amidst great hilarity.

PARIS, *August, 1866.*

DEAR M.,—We were invited to go out to Fontainebleau yesterday for dinner. We found it a very hot ride from Paris, and really suffered in the crowded train. When we arrived at the station we found a coupé from the Imperial stables waiting for us, and an extra carriage for the maid, the valet, and the trunk, which contained our change of dress for dinner. I wished that the coupé had been an open carriage. I love to drive through those lovely avenues in the park. Princess Metternich suggested that we should take some green corn with us, as the Empress had expressed the wish to taste this American delicacy, and I took some from Petit Val.

On reaching the palace we were met by the Vicomte Walsh, who led the way to the apartment of the Baroness

93

de Pierres, one of the *dames d'honneur* of the Empress
(an American lady, formerly Miss Thorne, of New York),
who was expecting us.

You may imagine my astonishment at seeing her
smoking—what do you think? Nothing less than a
real common clay pipe, and you may imagine her
surprise at seeing me, followed by my servant, who
carried a large basket containing the corn. I told her
about it, and that I had brought some at the instigation
of the Princess Metternich, in order that the Empress
could try it. She seemed to be delighted at the idea,
and exclaimed, "We must get hold of the chef at once
and tell him how to cook it." She rang her bell and
gave the order. Promptly Monsieur Jean appeared in
his fresh white apron and immaculate jacket and
white *couvre-chef.* Baroness de Pierres and I surpassed
ourselves in giving contradictory directions as to the
cooking of it. She thought it ought to be boiled a long
time, while I maintained that it required very little
time.

"You must leave the silk on," said she.

"Has it got silk?" asked the bewildered chef.

I was of the opinion that the husks should be taken
off. "By no means!" she declared, and explained that
in America the corn was always served in the husk.

The chef, trying to analyze this unusual article of
food, lifted one of the ears from the basket and examined it.

"En robe de chambre, alors, Madame!" said he, and
looked dismayed at these complications.

"Yes," she replied, "just like a potato—*en robe de
chambre.*"

We could hear him as he left the room, followed by
the basket, muttering to himself, "Soie! robe de chambre! Soie! robe de chambre!" in his most satirical tone.
I began to feel a little nervous about it myself, and
wondered if for this broth there had not been too many
cooks.

We went out before dinner to see the famous carp;
I looked in vain for the one with the ring in its nose.

At dinner, besides the Household, were the Princess
Mathilde, Monsieur Ollivier, Monsieur Perrière, the
Duke de Persigny, Baron Haussmann, and several
statesmen.

The corn came in due time served as *légume*.

I was mortified when I saw it appear, brought in on
eight enormous silver platters, four ears on each. It
looked pitiful! Silk, *robe de chambre* and all, steaming
like a steam-engine. Every one looked aghast, and no
one dared to touch it; and when I wanted to show them
how it was eaten in its native land they screamed with
laughter. Baron Haussmann asked me if the piece I
was playing (he meant on the flute) was in *la-bémol?*

I looked to the Baroness de Pierres for support; but,
alas! her eyes refused to meet mine and were fixed on
her plate.

I tried to make the corn less objectionable by un-
wrapping the cobs and cutting off the corn. Then I
added butter and salt, and it was passed about; first,
of course, to the Emperor, who liked it very much;
but the Empress pushed her plate aside with a grimace,
saying, "I don't like it; it smells like a baby's flannels."

The Emperor, seeing the crushed look on my face,
raised his glass and said, with a kind glance at me,

"Here's to the American corn!" I reproached the Princess Metternich for having suggested my taking it there.

COMPIÈGNE, *November 22, 1866.*

DEAR A.,—You know it has always been my wish to see the life at Compiègne, and behold, here I am!

We received the invitation twelve days ago. It reads thus:

MAISON   *Palais des Tuileries, le 10 Novembre 1866.*
DE L'EMPEREUR
Premier Chambellan

    Monsieur,
    Par ordre de l'Empereur, j'ai l'honneur de vous prévenir que vous êtes invité, ainsi que Madame Charles Moulton, à passer huit jours au Palais de Compiègne, du 22 au 29 Novembre.
    Des voitures de la Cour vous attendront le 22, à l'arrivée à Compiègne du train partant de Paris à 2 heures ½, pour vous conduire au Palais.
    Agréez, Monsieur, l'assurance de ma considération très distinguée.
          Le Premier Chambellan,
Monsieur,   Vte de Laferrière.
Madame Charles Moulton.

This gave me plenty of time to order all my dresses, wraps, and everything else that I needed for this visit of a week to royalty.

I was obliged to have about twenty dresses, eight day costumes (counting my traveling suit), the green cloth dress for the hunt, which I was told was absolutely necessary, seven ball dresses, five gowns for tea. Such a quantity of boxes and bundles arrived at the house in Paris that Mademoiselle Wissembourg was in a blue fidget, fussing about, boring me with silly, un-

THE MAIN FAÇADE—CHÂTEAU DE COMPIÈGNE

necessary suggestions, and asking so many useless questions that I wished her at the bottom of the Red Sea.

A professional packer came to pack our trunks, of which I had seven and C—— had two; the maid and the valet each had one, making, altogether, quite a formidable pile of luggage. As we saw it on the wagon driven from the house, it seemed an absurdly large amount for only a week's visit.

We arrived at the St. Lazare Station at 2.30, as indicated on the invitation.

We found the Vicomte Walsh (the Chamberlain of the Emperor) waiting to show the guests where the train was. It would have been rather difficult not to have seen it, as it was the only one in the station, and was marked "Extra and Imperial."

There were several large salon carriages with large, comfortable *fauteuils*, and some tables covered with newspapers and *journaux illustrés* to beguile the time. It would take too much time to tell you the names of all the people I recognized at the station; but in the carriage with us were the Duke and Duchess Fernan Nuñez, Madame de Bourgogne (whose husband is Equerry of the Emperor), the two Princes Murat, Joachim and Achille, Monsieur Davilliers, Count Golz (the German Ambassador), Baron Haussmann and his daughter, and Mr. de Radowitz of the German embassy, who immediately stretched himself out contentedly in a comfortable arm-chair and fell fast asleep.

I should say there were about fifty or sixty guests.

We actually flew over land and dale. I never traveled so fast in all my life; but then I had never been in an Imperial train before. We did not stop until we reached the station of Compiègne.

I think the whole twelve thousand inhabitants of Compiègne were gathered there to stare at us, and they did stare persistently, until we had mounted the many equipages waiting for us and had driven away.

It certainly must have been very entertaining for them to see the long procession of carriages, the hundreds of trunks, the flurrying maids, and the self-important valets.

There were two landaus: one for the Metternichs and one for the German Ambassador.

The *chars-à-bancs*, of which there must have been at least ten, were dark green outlined with red, each with four prancing horses whose tails, jauntily braided with red cords, were tied to the saddles.

Each carriage had two postilions, who looked very trim in their short velvet jackets embroidered with gold and covered with endless buttons. They wore white breeches, long top-boots, black-velvet caps over their white wigs, and their little pigtails, tied with a black bow, hung down their backs, flapping up and down as they galloped.

The Princess Metternich had fourteen trunks and two maids; the Prince had his private secretary and valet, and a goodly number of trunks. This will give you a vague idea of the amount of baggage which had to be transported in the *fourgons*.

Don't you think we must have made a very imposing spectacle, as we rattled through the quiet town of Compiègne, over its old stone pavement, the postilions blowing their horns, cracking their whips, the horses galloping full speed, the *chars-à-bancs* filled with handsomely dressed ladies, and after this long procession came the maids and the valets and mountainous piles of baggage?

When we entered the *grande cour* (inclosure), the sentinels grasped their guns and saluted, as we passed by them, before we pulled up in front of the grand staircase of the château, where an army of lackeys were waiting to help us alight.

The Grand Chamberlain received us at the head of the stairs with pleasant cordiality and waved us toward a *huissier*, who, dressed in a black livery with heavy chains around his neck, looked very important. He, in his turn, passed us on to the particular valet allotted to us, who pompously and with great dignity showed us the way to our apartments.

Our names were on the doors, and we entered the brilliantly lighted rooms, which, after our journey, seemed most welcome with their bright fires and cheerful aspect.

Tea and chocolate were on the table waiting us, and I regaled myself while the soldiers (who seem to be the men-of-all-work here) brought in the trunks and the maid and valet were unpacking.

I must describe our rooms. We have a large salon, two bedrooms, two servants' rooms, and an antechamber. In the salon there are two long windows which reach to the floor and overlook the park. The walls are paneled with pink and mauve brocade. The covering of the furniture and the curtains are of the same stuff.

My bedroom is furnished in white and green with a

delightful *chaise-longue* and large *fauteuils*, which to me are more inviting than the stiff Empire style of the salon.

I made my toilette in a maze of excitement; my maid was confused and agitated, and I thought I should never be ready. I think you will be interested to hear what I wore to-night. It was light-green tulle, embroidered in silver, the waist trimmed with silver fringe. If one could see the waistband, one would read WORTH in big letters. I thought it was best to make a good impression at the start, so I put on my prettiest gown.

On leaving our apartment, a little before seven, we found the lackey waiting to show us the way to the *Grande Salle des Fêtes*, and we followed his plump white calves through the long corridors, arriving at last at the salon where the company was to assemble.

Here we found more white calves belonging to the gorgeous liveries and the powdered heads of the lackeys, who stood there to open the doors for all comers. We were not the last, but of the latest, to arrive.

The salon seemed immense to me. On one side the windows (or rather the doors) opened on to the terrace; on the opposite side of the walls, between the pillars, were mirrors resting on gilded consoles. At one end of the room was the statue of Lætitia Bonaparte (*Madame Mère*), and at the other end was one of Napoleon I. Banquettes and tabourets of Gobelins tapestry stood against the walls. The ceiling is a *chef-d'œuvre* of Girodet—*style Empire*.

The Vicomte de Laferrière and the Duchesse de Bassano, the *grande maîtresse*, came forward to receive the guests.

SALLE DES FÊTES—CHÂTEAU DE COMPIÈGNE

My first feeling, when I entered the room, was that I knew no one in this numerous assemblage. There must have been a hundred people at least; but gradually the faces of my acquaintances loomed one by one out of the mist, and among them I recognized the lovely Marquise de Gallifet, who kindly beckoned me to come and stand by her, for which I felt very grateful.

The chamberlains — there were many of them — bustled about, constantly referring to some papers which they had in their hands, in order to tell each gentleman which lady he was to take in to dinner.

The Grand Chamberlain glanced round the room with an all-comprehensive look, and seemed intuitively to know when we were all present. He then disappeared into his Majesty's private salon.

There was an ominous hush, a flutter of agitation, a stiff attitude of expectancy, the guests arranging themselves according to their own consciousness of their rank; and presently the doors of the salon were quietly opened and their Majesties entered. The gentlemen bowed reverentially; the ladies courtesied very low, and the sovereigns, responding with a gracious inclination of the head, advanced toward us.

The Empress turned to the ladies, the Emperor to the gentlemen, speaking a word of welcome to as many of the guests as the time allowed. Fifty or sixty *bon soirs* and *charmé de vous voir*'s occupy some time; but their Majesties kept their eyes on the Grand Maréchal, and he kept his eye on the clock.

The Empress looked lovely. She wore a beautiful gown, a white-spangled tulle, with a superb tiara of diamonds, and on her neck a *collier* of huge pearls.

The Emperor was in white *culottes courtes*, white-silk stockings and low shoes, as were the rest of the gentlemen. He wore the ribbon of the *Légion d'honneur*, and on his left breast the star of the same.

The Grand Maréchal, waiting his opportunity, approached his Majesty, who went up to the Empress and gave her his arm. The Grand Maréchal then led the way slowly and with due stateliness to the banqueting hall.

The gentlemen offered their arms to their respective ladies, and we marched in procession through the long gallery, trying to prevent ourselves from slipping on the waxed floor, and passed between the splendid *Cent Gardes*, who lined both sides of the entire length of this enormous hall. Their uniforms are magnificent and dazzling; they wear light-blue coats under their silver cuirasses, white breeches, and high, shiny top-boots; and on their heads silver helmets, from which flow long manes of white horsehair that hang down their backs.

There the men stood, motionless as statues, staring stolidly before them, without so much as a stolen side-glance at the beauty and elegance passing before their eyes.

This procession of ladies glittering with jewels, the officers and diplomats in their splendid uniforms covered with decorations and gay-colored *cordons*, made a sight never to be forgotten; at least, *I* shall never forget it.

When their Majesties entered the dining-room they separated, and took their places on opposite sides of the table, half-way down its length and exactly facing each other. The Emperor had Princess Metternich on his right hand, and the Duchess of Fernan Nuñez on his left. The Empress had the Austrian Ambassador, Prince Metternich, on her right, and the German Ambassador, Count Golz, on her left.

The other *invités* were placed according to their rank and position: all the *gros bonnets* were in their right places, you may be quite sure. I was such a little *bonnet* among all those great people that I was practically nowhere, and at the tail end of everything except the members of the Household and the ladyless gentlemen, who, of course, were below me.

There must have been about one hundred persons seated at the table. I never saw such a tremendous long stretch of white linen.

The flowers, stiffly arranged at intervals, alternated with white *épergnes* filled with bonbons, and larger fruit-dishes filled with the most delicious-looking fruit. All along the whole length of the table were placed, at regular intervals, the groups of *pâte tendre* representing the Hunt. These, as my cavalier (Count de Bourgogne, told me, are made only at the Sèvres manufactory, expressly for the French sovereigns. They were designed in the time of Louis XV. by an artist called Urbain, and have been reproduced ever since. It would seem as if nothing had been found worthy to replace them.

The *service de table* was of white Sèvres porcelain with only the letter "N" in gold surmounted by the Imperial crown; many of the courses were served on silver plates, in the center of which were engraved the arms of France.

A strip of red velvet carpet laid over the polished floor surrounded the table. On the outer side of this carpet were the chairs, to be pushed forward as soon as people were ready to sit down. The lackeys stood in a line all the way down the room, making a very imposing sight in their red-and-white liveries; there must have been forty or fifty of them at least. The Emperor's *chasseur* always stands behind his chair and serves him, and him alone, taking a dish of each course, as it is brought in, from the *maître d'hôtel*. No one but this privileged *chasseur* can hand anything in the way of food to his Majesty. When the Emperor has served himself, the *chasseur* hands the dish back to the *maître d'hôtel*, who passes it on to the other servants, who then serve the guests. The Empress is served in the same way.

I suppose this custom dates back to the time of the Borgias, when, in order to save their own lives, they were willing to risk those of their trusty menials by making them taste the food before it was put on the table.

A military band played during the dinner. It was placed in a large circular loggia having windows opening on to a courtyard, thus serving two purposes: to let in the air and let out the music, which, fortunately, it did, otherwise we could not have heard ourselves speak.

The dinner lasted about an hour. (The Emperor dislikes sitting long at table.) It seemed almost impossible that so much eating and drinking and changing of plates—in fact, such an elaborate repast—could be got through within such a short time. But it was!

When their Majesties had finished they rose, and every one followed their example. All the chairs were drawn from under you, *tant pis* if you were in the act of eating a pear and had not yet washed your fingers; but, no matter, you had to skip across the red carpet in order to let their Majesties pass.

A rather amusing incident occurred at dinner. One of the foreign ministers, who is very vain of the smallness of his feet, had donned a pair of patent-leather shoes evidently much too tight for him. During the dinner he relieved his sufferings by slipping his aching toes out of them. All went well until his chair was suddenly drawn from underneath him, as their Majesties were about to pass. In utter despair he made the most frantic efforts to recover the wandering shoes from under the table; but, alas! the naughty things had made their escape far beyond reach (a little way shoes have of doing when left to themselves); consequently, he was obliged to trip across the red carpet as best he could without them. The Empress, who keenly appreciates a comical situation, had noticed with great amusement his manœuvers and embarrassment, and (was it just for a little fun?) stopped in passing and spoke to him, much to his confusion, for it was impossible to prevent her from seeing his little, white shoeless feet.

On our returning to the salon the magnificent *Cent Gardes* stood just as we had left them, and I wondered if they had unbent for a moment all the time we had been at dinner.

The *cercle* began, and their Majesties circulated about among their guests. When the Empress was in front of me, she gave me her hand and said some very kind words to me. She noticed I wore the bracelet she had given me and seemed pleased. I do not know if you ever saw this handsome bracelet—it is composed of large rubies and diamonds set in three heavy gold coils. The date when the Empress gave it to me and her name are inscribed inside. The Prince Imperial spoke to every one he knew. He has a very sweet voice, such gentle manners and winning ways. He speaks excellent English and, of course, several other languages.

Waldteufel, *le fabricant de valses*, put himself at the piano (an upright one, standing at the extreme end of the immense ballroom), and played some of his charming *entrainante* music. But, though he played as loudly as possible, it was difficult to distinguish what sort of music it was, the ballroom being so enormous. However, it did not make much difference, as there were only a few who wanted to dance, and one could see that they were urged to do so by the chamberlains. Waldteufel has an apartment in the town of Compiègne, where he fabricates his waltzes by day and comes here to play them by night.

At ten o'clock their Majesties went into the Emperor's private salon with a selected few; then the dancing became general and livelier. Tea and cakes were served at eleven o'clock, and their Majesties reëntered, conversed a few moments, bowed to every one, and withdrew, turned round on reaching the door, and, with a sweeping inclination of the head, disappeared.

We bade good night to our friends about us and withdrew, as did every one else, and I, for one, was glad to go to my Royal couch. Good night!

IN THE COURTS OF MEMORY

DEAR M.,—When we came down this morning into
the salon we found it almost deserted, and only realized
the reason why when we saw the Empress and other
ladies holding their prayer-books devoutly in their
hands returning from mass, which is celebrated in
the chapel of the château. They wore black-lace veils
in place of hats, the Empress wearing hers draped in
true Spanish fashion, which was infinitely becoming to
her, being, as she is, "to the *manner* born."

We remembered *then* that it was Sunday, and felt
subdued, seeing so many who were more pious than we
were. In fact, I felt so much so that I think it would
have been impossible for me to have laughed during
the *déjeuner.* Perhaps it was fortunate I sat next to
the Duke de Fernan Nuñez, whose sedate and polished
manners suited the occasion perfectly. He did not
encourage any attempt at gaiety. Oh dear, no! Far
from it! I felt myself gradually freezing, and our conversation was of the most uninteresting character and
dry almost to parching.

I began talking to him about Spain. I said I thought
it must be such a lovely country, so full of romance,
sentiment, and so forth. But he nipped my enthusiasm
in the bud by informing me that he was not Spanish.

"I thought you were," I murmured.

"No; I am Italian." This staggered me a little.
He was certainly the husband of the Duchess de Fernan
Nuñez, who was Spanish; why had he not the same
name?

He told me that he was "Dei Principi Pio-Trivulzio,"

one of the oldest families in Milan, and that when he married his wife (who is a *Grande d'Espagne*) he was obliged, according to the traditions of Spain, to take her name and give up his own.

The *déjeuner* finished, we returned to the salon, and after their Majesties had talked a little with their guests the programme for the afternoon, which was to be an excursion to Pierrefonds, was offered to those who wished to go. We hurried to our rooms to put on our hats, coats, and furs, reappearing equipped for the fray.

The *chars-à-bancs* and the carriages of their Majesties were drawn up on the garden side of the terrace. The Emperor took Prince Metternich in his dog-cart; the Empress drove herself in her English phaëton, accompanied by the Duchess de Fernan Nuñez. The rest of us were provided with big *chars-à-bancs*, each holding six or eight people, and had four horses ridden by two postilions. In the same carriage with me was the Duchess de Persigny, Count Golz, and others; and although it was very cold, we did not mind, as we were well wrapped in furs and had plenty of rugs. We enjoyed intensely the beautiful drive through the forest of Compiègne. Monsieur Davilliers told me that the forest contains about fifteen thousand hectares. I should think so, judging from the endless roads and cross-roads, the interminable avenues and wonderful vistas. There were sign-posts at every turn; those painted red pointed toward Compiègne.

It took us a long time to reach the forest at Pierrefonds, which joins that of Compiègne. By an abrupt turn of the road we came suddenly in view of the enormous castle of Pierrefonds and the little town, which is

CHÂTEAU DE PIERREFONDS

known for its sulphur baths, and only frequented in summer. No one need inform you what kind of baths they are, as their fumes pervade space and inform you themselves.

The imposing castle looks entirely out of place in its surroundings; the little hill on which it stands seems as if it had been put there in order to accommodate the castle.

We passed over two bridges and over a *pont-levis* at the foot of the castle; then through a second gateway into a court, and finally over a drawbridge to reach the entrance.

There we got out of the carriages, passed through a dark, vaulted chapel and mounted to the platform, where we had a splendid view of the town and the forest.

Viollet-le-Duc, who was with us, is the pet architect of the Emperor; he is working hard to restore these magnificent ruins, and has now been ten years about it, but says that they will never be finished in his lifetime. The Emperor is very proud of showing them as the work of his favorite architect, and Viollet-le-Duc is just as proud of having been chosen for this stupendous undertaking.

We were spared no details, you may be sure, from the smallest of gargoyles to the biggest of chimneys. There is a huge fireplace which reaches to the ceiling in the *salle des gardes*, with funny little squirrels peering at you with cunning eyes. I wish it had occurred to the great architect to have utilized this fireplace, for he could very well have put a few logs in it and prevented us poor visitors from freezing to death.

We walked (it must have been miles), examining every-thing in detail. We mounted two hundred steps to see the view, and then descended three hundred steps to see the arched cellars. The castle was first bought one hundred years ago as a ruin by some one, who only paid eight thousand francs for it; then Napoleon I. bought it, and now Napoleon III. is restoring it. It is seven thousand meters square. It has eight big towers, etc. I could go on forever, I am so brimful of statistics, but I spare you.

While the hampers brought from Compiègne were being unpacked we tried to rest our weary limbs in some prehistoric chairs, whose carvings pierced our bones to the marrow. I suppose this is what they call *payer de sa personne*. I consoled myself, while drinking my tea and eating my cake, with the thought that my *personne* was paying its little private tax to art.

After this interesting but fatiguing visit, and after the long drive through the cold, misty forest, the dead and dry leaves rustling under the horses' feet as they galloped along, I was glad to rest a moment by my cozy fire before dressing for dinner.

I was a little dismayed when I was told that the famous poet, Théophile Gautier, was to be my dinner companion. I was awed at the idea of such a neighbor, and feared I should not be able to rise to the occasion. Would he talk poetry to me? And should I have to talk poetry to him?

I tried to remember, during our promenade down the hall, Longfellow's "Psalm of Life," in case he should expect anything in this line, and I tried to remember something he himself had written; but for the life of me I could think of nothing but a very improper book called *Mademoiselle de Maupéon*, which I had never been allowed to read, so that would be of no use as conversation.

I might have spared myself this worry, for, from the time he sat down at the table, he talked of little else than cats and dogs. He loves all animals. I liked him for that, and one could see that he preferred them to any other topic.

I can't remember all the nonsense he talked. In appearance I think he must resemble Charles Dickens. I have only seen the latter's photographs; but had he not rather a skimpy hair brushed any which way and a stringy beard? I fancied him so to myself. At any rate, Gautier looks like the Dickens of the photographs.

He said he had eight or ten cats who ate with him at the table; each had its own place and plate, and never by any chance made a mistake and sat in another cat's place or ate off another cat's plate. He was sure that they had a heaven and a hell of their own, where they went after their death, according to their deserts, and that they had souls and consciences. All his cats had classical names, and he talked to them as if they were human beings. He said they understood every word he said. He also quoted some of his conversation with them, which must have sounded very funny:

"Cleopatra, have you been in the kitchen drinking milk on the sly?

"Cleopatra puts her tail between her legs and her ears back and looks most guilty, and I know then what the cook told me was true."

Then again: "Julius Cæsar, you were out extremely

late last night. What were you doing?" He said that
when he made these reproaches Julius Cæsar would get
down from his chair and, with his tail high in the air,
would rub himself against his legs, as much as to say
he would never do it again.

"Depend upon it," he added, "they know everything
we do, and more."

I asked, "When Julius Cæsar comes from his noc-
turnal walks is he *gris* (tipsy)?"

"Gris! Que voulez-vous dire?"

"You once wrote a poem (how proud I was that I
had recollected it), 'A minuit tous les chats sont gris.'"

"C'est vrai, mais je parlais des Schahs de Perse."

"Est-ce que tous les Schahs de Perse sont gris a minuit?"

"Madame, tous les Schahs de Perse que j'ai eu l'honneur de voir à minuit ont été gris comme des Polonais."

"But the 'chats' you wrote about go mewing on roofs
at midnight. Do the Schahs de Perse do that?"

"Did I write that?" said he. "Then I must have
meant cats. You are very inquisitive, Madame."

"I confess I am," I answered. "You see, that poem
of yours has been set to music, and I sing it; and you
may imagine that I want to know what I am singing
about. One must sing with an entirely different expression if one sings of gray cats or of tipsy Persian
sovereigns."

He laughed and asked, with an innocent look, "Do
you think I could have meant that at midnight nothing
has any particular color—that everything is gray?"

"I don't know what you meant; but please tell me
what you want me to believe, because I believe everything I am told. I am so naïve."

"You naïve! You are the most *blasée* person I ever met."

"I *blasée!* I! What an idea!"

Such an idea could only emanate from a poet's brain with an extra-poetical poet's license. I was very indignant, and told him so, and said, "Est-ce que tous les poètes sont fous à cette heure de la soirée?"

"Vous voyez," he retorted, "you are not only *blasée;* you are sarcastic."

I enjoyed my dinner immensely in spite of being *blasée*, and Gautier's fun and amusing talk lasted until we were back in the salon. The Emperor approached us while we were still laughing, and began to talk to us. I told him that Monsieur Gautier had said that I was *blasée*. The Emperor exclaimed: "Vous blasée! Il faut y mettre beaucoup de bonne volonté pour être blasée à votre âge!"

I said I did not know whether to be angry or not with him.

"Be angry with him," answered the Emperor. "He deserves it."

Waldteufel began playing his delightful waltzes, and every one was soon whirling about. I never heard him play with so much dash; he really seemed inspired. Prince Metternich asked him to order a piano to be sent to his salon in the château. "I cannot exist without a piano," said he. "It helps me to write my tiresome *rapports*."

There were only two pianos, I believe, in the château; the one (upright) in the ballroom and the Erard in the *salle de musique*.

At eleven o'clock we went into the Emperor's salon, where tea was served.

MONDAY, *November 24, 1866.*

DEAR M.,—At breakfast this morning I sat next to Prince Metternich. He told me that there was to be *conseil de ministres* to-day, and therefore there was no question of their Majesties' presence at excursions, and no particular plans projected for this afternoon.

Thus we were left to our own devices. Prince Metternich's fertile brain was already at work to imagine something amusing to divert their Majesties for the evening. He suggested charades. He is excellent at getting them up.

When we met in the salon he spoke to the different people who he thought would be helping elements.

The Marquise de Gallifet thought that tableaux would be better; Count de Vogüé suggested games (he knew several new ones, which he proposed). All in vain! Prince Metternich insisted on charades; therefore charades carried the day, of course.

The Prince had already thought of the word "Exposition," and arranged in his mind what part each one of us was to have. The Vicomte de Laferrière, whom he was obliged to take into his confidence, told him that he would show us the room in which there was a stage for amateur performances.

As soon as their Majesties had departed we proceeded to the said room, where there was a little stage, a very little one, with red-velvet curtains. Next to this room was a long gallery, in which there was a quantity of chests containing every variety of costumes, wigs, postiches, tinsel ornaments, and all sorts of appurtenances—enough to satisfy the most dramatic imagination.

Each garment, as it was held up to view, suggested endless possibilities; but the Prince stuck firmly to his first inspiration, and we were despatched to our different apartments to think out our rôles and to imagine how funny we were going to be.

The Empress is always present at the *conseils de ministres*, which to-day must have lasted an unusually long time, as no one was invited to her tea. So we took ours with the Metternichs. The Prince had just returned from town, and was childishly eager to display the various and extraordinary purchases he had made, which he considered absolutely necessary for the finishing touches to our toilettes. His requisites consisted of an oil-can, a feather duster, a watchman's rattle, and wax enough to have made features for the whole Comédie Française, and paint and powder for us all. He would not tell us what he had procured for his *own* costume, as he said he wanted to surprise us, adding, what he could not buy he had borrowed.

Count Vogüé gave me his arm for dinner. Of course, we talked of little else but the charade.

Their Majesties were informed of the surprise which was awaiting them in the little theater. The Empress said to Prince Metternich, after dinner, "I hear you have prepared something to amuse us this evening. Do you not wish to go and make your arrangements? We will be ready to join you in half an hour."

All of us who were to take part disappeared to dress, and returned to the gallery connecting with the stage in due time. Peeping through the hole in the curtain, we could see the imposing and elegant audience come in and take their seats with much ceremony and calmness. They little thought how impatient we were to begin and yet trembling with nervousness. Their Majesties, the guests, and all the ministers who had stayed for dinner more than filled the theater. It looked, indeed, uncomfortably crowded.

At last every one was seated, and the first syllable, "Ex," was played with great success. It represented a scene at Aix-les-Bains.

Invalids met (glasses in hand) and discussed and compared their various and seemingly very complicated diseases. They made very funny remarks on the subject of getting their systems in order in view of the possible incidents which might come up during the Exposition of the next year.

The Marquis de Gallifet was one of the invalids, and seeing the Minister of the Interior in the audience, looked straight at him and said, "C'est à vous, Monsieur le Ministre, de remédier à tout cela (It is your business, Monsieur le Ministre, to cure all that)," which made every one roar with laughter, though Prince Metternich (our impresario) was very provoked, as he had particularly forbidden any one to address the audience.

The Princess Metternich looked very comical dressed as a Parisian coachman, with a coachman's long coat of many capes; she wore top-boots, and had a whip in her hand and a pipe in her mouth, which she actually smoked, taking it out of her mouth every time she spoke and puffing the smoke right into the faces of the audience. She sang a very lively song, the words of which her husband had found time to write for her during the afternoon. It began, "C'est à Paris, qu' ça s'est passé." She cracked her whip and stamped her feet, and must have been very droll, to judge from the screams of delight in the audience. The song was full of quips and puns, and pleased so much that she had to repeat it.

The next word was "Position," and acted only by gentlemen. An amateur, or rather a novice, was taking lessons in fencing, in order to defend himself against probable attacks upon him by the barbaric foreigners who next year would invade Paris, and he wished to be prepared sufficiently to resent all their insults.

When the curtain came down all the sky came with it, which put the public in great glee.

The whole word "Exposition" was what we call "Mrs. Jarley's Wax Works."

Count de Vogüé was the showman, and the servant assisting him was no less a person than the Austrian Ambassador himself, Prince Metternich. As the stage was small, it could not contain more than two couples at a time, so they were brought on in pairs.

First came Antony, and Cleopatra (the latter Marquise de Gallifet, beautiful as a dream) drank mechanically (having been wound up by the servant) an enormous pearl, and Antony (Prince Murat) looked on wonderingly and admiringly.

Madame de Bourgogne and Count Grammont were a Chinese chop-sticking couple. When wound up, their chop-sticks went everywhere except into their mouths. The Marquise de Chasselouplobat and the Marquis de Caux were shepherd and shepherdess, with the usual rakes, baskets, ribbons, etc.

I was a mechanical doll sent from America (the latest invention) for the Exposition. I was dressed as a Tyro-

9   117

lienne with a red skirt, a black bodice, and a hat with a ridiculous feather sticking out from the back of it, which Prince Metternich said I *must* have.

While the others were on the stage Princess Metternich wrapped a lot of silk paper around me and tied it with bows of wide ribbon, thus covering me completely, head and all. I was carried in and placed on a turning pedestal.

The showman explained the wonderful mechanism of this doll, unique of its kind, and capable of imitating the human voice to such a degree that no one could hear any difference.

When he had finished talking (I thought, as I stood there, motionless and stifling under my paper covering, he never would stop) he tore off the paper and called his assistant to wind me up.

I had so far been very successful in keeping my countenance; but I assure you, when I saw Prince Metternich's get-up, my efforts to keep myself from bursting out laughing almost amounted to genius. He had said he wished his costume to be a surprise. Well! The surprise almost made the mechanical doll a failure, and had not Count de Vogüé quickly turned the pedestal around I don't know how I should have saved myself from disaster.

Prince Metternich was dressed as a servant. He had a velvetine coat, red vest, knickerbockers, white stockings, and servant's low shoes, and he wore a huge black beard and a black wig. He had made his eyebrows so bushy that they looked like mustaches; but his nose had preoccupied him more than anything else—I don't know how much time he had spent in making it. First, he made it hooked and then changed it to *retroussé*, then again back to hooked, which he thought suited his style best. He commenced it when the first scene was being acted, and had just got it at the right angle when it was time for him to go on the stage. The result of his afternoon's labors must have been most gratifying, for he was a stupendous success.

He wound me up and I began singing; but everything went wrong. I sang snatches of well-known songs, cadences, trills, arpeggios, all *pêle-mêle*, until my exhibitors were in despair.

"Mais, c'est terrible," cried Vogüé. "Ne pouvez-vous pas l'arrêter? Est-ce qu'il n'y a pas de vis?"

"Il n'y a pas le moindre vice, Monsieur," shaking his head in despair.

Then I stopped short. How could I sing when I was convulsed with laughter?

"Il faut la remonter," the showman said, with a resigned air, and, turning to the audience, he announced that such a thing had never happened before. "La poupée a été probablement dérangée pendant le voyage." This caused much merriment. "Elle a besoin de l'huile," said the Prince in a loud stage whisper, and took the oil-can and flourished it about my shoulders.

They made so many jokes and puns that they were continually interrupted by the peals of laughter which followed each joke.

"Faites-la donc chanter," implored Vogüé. "N'y a-t-il pas un clou?"

"S'il y en avait eu un, je l'aurais trouvé, puisque c'est le clou de la soirée."

"Mon Dieu! Que faire? Et tout le monde qui

attend. Cherchez bien. Vous trouverez peut-être un bouton."

The Prince answered, sadly, "Not a sign of a button, Monsieur." And he added, in a loud voice, "We ought to have a button in *gold*, so that one can see it."

He said this with intention, thinking it might suggest to the Emperor to give me the gold button which he only gives to those he wishes to make life-members of his Hunts. Ladies do not often get them. At last, the mortified assistant applied the rattle and wound me up again. I gave a little nod with my head; they both struck attitudes of satisfaction, and one said, "Now she is going to sing 'Beware!'" which called forth a burst of applause from the audience. I sang "Beware!" and the Prince, thinking I made the trill too long, tried to stop me by using the rattle again, which was almost the death of me. I wore some long ribbons around my neck, and the more the Prince turned it, the tighter the ribbons choked me. Happily I had breath enough to go on singing; but I turned my head and fixed a glassy eye on my tormentor, and, instead of singing "Trust her not, she's fooling thee," I sang, "Trust him not, he's choking me, he's choking me."

Luckily he understood, and the people who knew English understood and appreciated the situation.

When it was all finished the Empress came hurriedly toward me, exclaiming: "Thank Heaven! I thought the Prince was going to strangle you. I was so frightened." She then kissed me on both cheeks, and the Emperor gallantly kissed my hand.

They both said they had never laughed so much in their lives, and were most profuse in their thanks, com-

IN THE COURTS OF MEMORY

plimenting all those who had taken part in the charade; certainly Robert de Vogüé and the Prince Metternich both outdid themselves.

It was one o'clock when tea was served in the Emperor's salon. You may imagine if I was tired.

November 25th.

DEAR M.,—As the programme announced this morning that there was to be a *chasse à tir* this afternoon, I put on my green costume brought for this purpose.

The Empress appeared also in a green dress, with a coquettish three-cornered hat trimmed with gold braid, and looked bewitchingly beautiful; the Emperor wore a shooting suit with leather gaiters, as did all the gentlemen. Every one looked very sportsmanlike.

M. Davilliers gave me his arm for *déjeuner*. He told me a great deal which I did not *want* to know about hunting-dogs.

For instance, "Les chiens anglais," he said, "étaient très raillants, très perçants, mais hésitants dans les fourrés." So much Greek to me; but I pretended to understand. He continued to say that the Emperor had an excellent trainer, who obtained the best results because he treated the dogs with kindness. I inwardly applauded the trainer.

He said it was better to let them have the entire use of their faculties; whereas, if the unhappy animals are stupefied by bad treatment they lose their *initiative*, being pursued by the thought of a beating, and they don't know what to do, instead of following their natural instincts.

I agreed with him entirely, and thought that our conversation was an excellent preface to the afternoon's sport.

As the Emperor passed me, before we started off, he said, handing me a little package he held in his hand, "Here is the gold button which you did *not* have last night; it makes you a life member of all Imperial hunts." (So Prince Metternich's ruse had succeeded.)

I bowed very low and thanked him, and asked if it would necessitate my hunting. "Certainly not, if you don't want to," his Majesty answered; "but have you ever seen a *chasse à tir?*"

At my answer that I had never seen one, nor anything nearer to one than people going out with a gun and coming back with nothing else, he laughed and said, "I must tell that to the Empress."

It is the Emperor's habit to say, when he hears anything which amuses him, "I must tell that to her Majesty." She is always in his thoughts.

I said, looking at the button, "Last year your Majesty gave me a gold medal for singing a *Benedictus*; now I shall sing a hallelujah for this."

"It is not worth so much," the Emperor said, with a kind smile.

"Would you like to accompany me this afternoon," he asked, "and see for yourself what a *chasse à tir* is?"

I answered that I should be delighted, and said, "Shall I come with a gun?"

"Oh dear, no! Please don't!" the Emperor exclaimed, hurriedly. "But come with stout boots and a warm coat."

The carriages were waiting, and we were soon packed in our rugs and started for the shooting.

The Emperor drove Baron Beyens in his dog-cart; the Empress drove with the Princess Metternich in a victoria to the field, where she left her and returned to the château. I fancy she was afraid of the dampness of this bleak November day.

We arrived at a great open place and found all the company assembled, and I should say the whole populace of Compiègne had turned into beaters and spectators. The gentlemen took their places in a long line, the Emperor being in the middle; on his right the person highest in rank (Prince Metternich), on his left Count Golz, and so forth.

Madame de Gallifet and I were a little behind the Emperor, between him and Prince Metternich. Behind us were the gamekeepers, loading and handing the guns to their masters as fast as they could. The three first gentlemen had their own *chasseurs* and two guns each. After the gamekeepers came the men whose duties were to pick up the dead and wounded victims and put them in the bags.

It was a dreadful sight! How I hate it! I am sure I shall not sleep for a week, for I shall always see the forms and faces of those quivering, dying creatures in my dreams. I never will go to a *chasse* again.

And the worst was, they had frightened the birds and animals into a sort of circle, where they could not escape; the butchery was awful. The victims numbered close on four thousand. Prince Metternich alone shot twelve hundred.

How happy I was when it all was over and I could get away from these horrors and this miserable sport! We were invited to the tea in the Empress's salon. I had time to change my dress and put on the high silk gown prescribed for this function.

Such beautiful rooms! First an antechamber, with cabinets of Italian carving and vitrines and inlaid tables; then the Empress's salon, a very large room filled with low arm-chairs, tables covered with knickknacks, books with paper-cutters still in them, as if they were just being read, screens with engravings *à la Louis Seize*, and beautiful fans on the walls, also splendid tapestries. It had a lovely ceiling, painted by some celebrated artist, mostly angels and smiling cherubs, who seemed to possess more than their share of legs and arms, floating about in the clouds.

The Empress generally has a distinguished person, or some kind of celebrity, either a traveler or an inventor, even a prestidigitateur (ugh, what a word!), always some one who is *en vue* for the moment. To-day it was a man who had invented a machine to count the pulse. He strapped a little band on your wrist and told you to concentrate your thought on one subject, then a little pencil attached to the leather handcuff began muffing up and down slowly or quickly, as your pulse indicated.

The Empress seemed much interested, and called those in the room whose pulse she wished to have tested. She said, "Now let us have an American pulse." My pulse seemed to be very normal, and the exhibitor did not make any comments, neither did any one else.

"Shall we now have a Germanic pulse?" the Empress asked, and called Comte Solms. "Think of something pleasant," said the inventor. "A ballet is a nice thing to think of," said the Princess Metternich, in her shrill voice.

IN THE COURTS OF MEMORY

"Regarde, comme il va vite," the inventor cried, and he showed the paper with the most extraordinary wavy lines. Every one laughed, and no one more than Comte Solms himself.

Six o'clock came very quickly, and the Empress, rising, gave the signal for our departure.

The Marquis de Caux took me in to dinner. He is the most popular and sought-after gentleman in all Paris. No ball is complete without him, and his presence at any dinner is sufficient to assure its success. He leads all the cotillons worth speaking of, and is a universal favorite. He allowed his secret to leak out (*un secret de Polichinelle*), which all Paris is talking about.

I swore secrecy; but I can tell *you* that it can be contained in one word, and that word is SIMPATICO, which is Italian for his rendezvous with HER at the American Doctor Sim's house, for it is there he meets her. *Devine qui peut!* (Guess who can!) I have not said anything.

At nine o'clock we all adjourned to the theater in the Palace, to reach which we passed through many rooms we had never seen before, and through a long gallery. The theater is very handsome, and as large as most of the theaters in Paris. There is always one theatrical performance during each week while their Majesties are in Compiègne. The company of the Théâtre Français had been commanded to play this evening. The piece chosen was the latest one of Émile Augier, which has had a great success in Paris, called "Le fils Giboyer." Émile Augier, who was invited specially, was present.

Madeleine Brohan, Coquelin, Breton, and Madame Favard had the principal rôles. Such distinguished artistes as those could not but give the greatest enjoy-

ment. The theater is very handsome; there are only
boxes and the parquet; the Imperial Loge reaches from
the first tier of boxes to the last seats of the parquet in
the shape of a shell. Any one standing up there could
touch, on raising the arm, the velvet draperies of the
Imperial box.

The theater is entirely lighted by wax candles, of
which there must have been thousands, and all the
scenery belonging to the play was sent especially from
Paris.

Their Majesties sat in the center of the Imperial
Loge, and the lady guests and the most important gentlemen, according to their rank, were placed beside and
behind them.

The other gentlemen sat in the parquet, and circulated
about between the acts.

In the boxes were places for the Court ladies, also
the ladies invited from the neighboring château and
from Compiègne.

The whole assemblage certainly presented the most
dazzling and magnificent sight. The ladies in their
beautiful toilettes and superb jewels showed to the
greatest advantage in this brilliantly lighted theater.
The Empress was gorgeous in yellow tulle covered with
lace and jewels. She wore the famous Regent diamond,
which belongs to the French Crown, in her corsage, and
a superb diamond tiara and necklace. Princess Metternich, who is known to be the best dressed lady in
Paris, had a black tulle dress embroidered in gold; she
wore a tiara of diamonds and emeralds and a necklace
of the same.

When their Majesties entered every one rose and

courtesied deeply; their Majesties bowed graciously in response. The Master of Ceremonies gave the signal, and the curtain rose immediately.

The actors seemed inspired to do their best, as well they might, with such a brilliant audience before them.

I wondered if they did not miss the *claque*, to which actors are so accustomed in France. You know the *claque* is a set of men who are hired to clap at certain points in the play indicated beforehand to them, in order that the audience may appreciate the most salient points and join the applause, if they wish to.

Every one enjoyed the play immensely. There were portions of it which were very pathetic. I noticed the Emperor was visibly affected, and the Empress wiped from her eyes *una furtiva lagrima*, as Donizetti's song has it.

I know *I* cried my lace handkerchief wet.

The representation lasted till about half-past ten, and after our return to the salon the Emperor sent for the artists, who had by this time changed their toilettes. Their Majesties talked long, and, I should say, familiarly with them, and, judging from the way they laughed and chatted, they seemed to feel quite at their ease, especially Coquelin, who apparently put the Emperor in a very good humor. At eleven o'clock refreshments were passed round, the carriages were announced, and making a deferential "reverence" the artists took their leave, carrying with them an ornament with the monograms of their Majesties as a souvenir of their visit.

I never saw the Empress look so beautiful as she did to-night. She certainly is the most exquisite creature,

and what is so charming about her is her utter lack of
self - consciousness. Her smile is bewitching beyond
description; her complexion perfect; her hair of the
Venetian type, and her profile classical. Her head is
so beautifully put on her shoulders; her neck and shoulders are absolutely faultless. None of the many portraits painted of her, not even Winterhalter's, do her
the least justice; no brush can paint and no words
can describe her charm. I think the famous beauty,
Countess Castiglione, cannot begin to compare with
her.

Their Majesties withdrew. The guests from the
château and those from Compiègne took their departure, and we all dispersed to our several apartments.

I am beginning to learn the ways of the life of Compiègne.

At nine o'clock our tea, coffee, or chocolate (as we
choose) is brought to our rooms by a white-stockinged
and powdered valet.

If you are very energetic, you can go for a walk in the
park, or (as I did to my sorrow) a visit to the town.
But you are not energetic more than once, because you
do not find it worth your while, as you must hurry back,
and change your dress and shoes before appearing in the
salon a little before eleven o'clock, the hour for breakfast.
You remain in the same dress until you change for
dinner or the Empress's tea. You find every morning in
your room a programme for the day.

Déjeuner à onze heures.

Chasse à tir à deux heures.

Comédie Française à neuf heures.

So you know what to wear and what to expect; but

the invitation to tea is always made by the Empress's private *huissier*, who knocks at your door toward five o'clock and announces, "Her Majesty the Empress desires your presence at five o'clock."

The *toilette de rigueur* for this occasion is a high-necked long silk dress, and you generally remain until six o'clock.

If you are not summoned to her Majesty's tea, tea is served in your own salon, where you can invite people to take tea with you, or you are invited to take tea with other people.

If there is a hunt, the ladies wear their green-cloth costumes and the gentlemen wear their hunting gear (a red coat, velvet cap, and top-boots). The gentlemen wear *culottes courtes* the first evening they arrive, and on such fine occasions as the *curée*, and at the Gala Theater, where outsiders are invited; otherwise they always wear *pantalon collant*, which is the most unbecoming thing one can imagine in the way of manly attire.

At six o'clock you dress for dinner, always in ball dress, and a little before seven you meet in the Grande Salle des Fêtes. At dinner the guests are placed according to their rank; but at *déjeuner* there is no ceremony, and you engage your partner after your heart's desire. Those who are high up at dinner try to get as far down at the end of the table as possible.

With me it is all ups and downs; at breakfast I am 'way up to the very top, and at dinner 'way down.

After *déjeuner* the Master of Ceremonies inquires what you wish to do; that is to say, if there is nothing special mentioned on the programme, such as a review, or manœuvers, or a *chasse à courre*, when all are expected to join.

Do you wish to walk? You can tramp up and down the one-thousand-metre-long trellis walk, sheltered from wind and rain.

Do you wish to drive? There are carriages of all descriptions, *chars-à-bancs*, landaus, pony-carriages, and even a donkey-cart, at your service.

Do you care to ride? There are one hundred and fifty horses eating their heads off in the Imperial stables waiting for you.

Do the gentlemen wish to go shooting? There are countless gamekeepers booted and spurred, with guns and game-bags on their shoulders, impatient to accompany you.

Whatever you do, you are expected to be in your rooms before four o'clock, which is the time the Empress will send for you, if she invites you for tea.

The *cercle* always follows each repast, and dancing or music always follows the *cercle*. Tea is served at the Emperor's salon at eleven o'clock, after which their Majesties retire, and you do the same.

November 26th.

DEAR M.,—A very embarrassing thing happened to me this morning.

We thought we could manage an excursion to the town. I wanted to see the Cathedral, and it did not seem far away.

Therefore, bright and early, at nine o'clock we started on our trip.

We saw the Cathedral; but I had not counted on the time necessary for the change of toilette, which I had to make before *déjeuner*.

IN THE COURTS OF MEMORY

I found on my table an envelope containing this poetry, which I inclose, from Théophile Gautier. I suppose he considered it as a sort of *amende honorable*.

À MADAME CHARLES MOULTON

Vos prunelles ont bu la lumière et la vie;
telle une mer sans fond boît l'infini des cieux,
car rien ne peut remplir l'abîme de vos yeux,
où, comme en un lotus, dort votre âme assouvie.

Pour vous plus de chimère ardemment poursuivie,
quel que soit l'idéal, votre rêve vaut mieux,
et vous avez surtout le blasement des Dieux,
Psyché, qu'Éros lui-même à grand'peine eût ravi.

Votre satiété n'attend pas le banquet,
et connaissant la coupe où le monde s'enivre,
dédaigneuse à vos pieds vous le regardez vivre.

Et vous apparaissez par un geste coquet,
rappelant Mnémosyné à son socle appuyée
comme le souvenir d'une sphère oubliée.

THÉOPHILE GAUTIER.

Charles had gone long before, and I became absorbed in reading it, and forgot to look at the clock, when suddenly, seeing how late it was, I rushed down into the gallery, and what was my horror at finding myself alone with the *Cent Gardes*, who were standing at ease! It was the first time I had ever seen them look like mortal beings, and not like statues, and it signified, naturally, that every one was in the *salle à manger*, and that I was too late. However, I thought I could slip into the room unnoticed, and a place at the table would be offered to me; but, alas! it happened that just this morning the Emperor had desired me to sit next to him at

131

the table, and the Marquis de Caux had been (and was still) waiting for me at the door to conduct me to my place on the sovereign's left hand.

I cannot tell you how I felt as I was being marshaled up the whole length of the room, stared at by every one, and criticized, probably, for this horrible breach of etiquette. I never was so mortified in all my life. I took my place, speechless and confused, and Prince Murat, who sat on the other side of me, kept saying, "The Emperor is piping mad." The Prince Murat is half American (his mother was a Miss Frazier, from New Jersey), therefore I will forgive him for wanting to tease me.

I suppose I must have looked very red, and I certainly was very out of breath, for the Emperor, probably noticing my embarrassment, kindly said, "Don't worry; you are not late."

I told him I had been sight-seeing in Compiègne, and I hoped he would forgive me.

The Empress smiled and nodded to me in the most gracious manner across the table, as if to put me at my ease.

The Emperor told me that he had sent up to Paris for a game of croquet, having heard from Prince Metternich that we all loved so much to play it, adding that he would like to see the game himself. "We are going to have a mock battle this afternoon," said he. "All these generals and officers who are here have come from everywhere to take part. I think it will amuse you to see it, if you have never seen anything of the kind."

I assured him I had never seen a battle, mock or otherwise, and had no idea what it could be like.

"Well, you shall see," he said.

"Is there," I inquired, "as much firing as yesterday?"

"Much more; but this time with cannons," he replied.

"I hope the cannon-balls are also mock," I ventured to say.

I told the Emperor of the poetry which Gautier had sent to me, and, having it in my hand, showed it to him, saying, "Ought I to forgive him?"

"You ought to forgive him," he said. "This is the most exquisite thing I ever have read."

"If your Majesty says so, I will."

The manœuvers were to commence at two o'clock. All the ladies wore their hunting-dresses, and I was proud to don my gold button.

The various equipages were waiting to take us to the field.

The Duchess de Persigny, Princess Murat, Baron Beyens, the Marquis de Caux, and I got in the same carriage; many of the ladies appeared on horseback. Princess Ghika rode one of the three horses she had brought with her to Compiègne. Madame de Vatry rode one of the Emperor's.

All the carriages, on reaching the field where the manœuvers were to take place, were drawn up in line, in order that every one should have a good view. Then the Emperor and Empress, on their beautiful horses, and the Prince Imperial, full of youthful dignity, on his cream-colored pony, arrived, accompanied by the staff of splendidly uniformed generals and officers, who took up their positions behind their Majesties before the manœuvers commenced.

10

The Empress looked radiantly beautiful, her well-fitting riding-habit showing her fine figure to the greatest advantage.

It was, as the Emperor had said, a mock battle; but it seemed to me, not having had much experience in battles, to be very real.

Officers careered over the field for dear life; orderlies with enormous flat, four-cornered things flapping across their backs, scurried to and fro; trumpeters sounded bugles, waved flags, and made signals. . . . What could look more real and less mock than this?

It was France *versus* an imaginary enemy.

It seemed as if the one thing France craved and coveted was a poor, lonely farm-house in the distance, apparently unprotected. All the stratagems of war, all the trumpeting and capering about, were brought to bear on conquering that little house. The artillery collided up against it; the infantry, with drums beating, marched boldly to the very door-steps; the cavalry pranced around it. . . . But for the life of me, though I was staring as hard as I could through my opera-glasses, I could not tell whether France had got it or not. However, there was so much smoke, it might have capitulated without my noticing. I suppose the generals knew.

It made me think of Tennyson's "Charge of the Light Brigade."

> Cannon to right of them,
> Cannon to left of them,
> Cannon in front of them,
> Volley'd and thunder'd.

The guns and cannons kept up such a continual firing that the ground actually shook under our feet.

I wondered why so much powder and energy should be wasted on a helpless farm-house, and dreaded to think what the real thing must be, if this was only sham.

When it was apparently finished, and every one in the neighborhood had surrendered, they sounded a grand fanfare, and blew a mighty blast of trumpets, the officers dashed up full tilt to the Emperor, and announced, "Victory all along the line!"

I can't tell you how sweet the little Prince looked when he distributed the *médaille de mérite* to the brave warriors, who received it with due modesty, saluting gravely.

The Emperor rode about among the carriages and asked us ladies how we had liked it, and if there had been too much noise.

The company at dinner to-night looked particularly brilliant; there must have been a hundred and fifty people present, as the generals and the officers were asked to remain to dinner. I had one general next to me at table, the famous General Changarnier, who my other neighbor said had one foot in the grave and the other *dans le plat*. He was so old and thin and bony that if his uniform had not kept him up he would have crumbled together before my eyes, and have become a zero instead of a hero. However, he kept together while dinner lasted, for which I was thankful, and I returned him safely to posterity and to the salon.

Their Majesties devoted themselves exclusively to the Army after dinner; but they sent word by a chamberlain that we were to commence dancing, though they had not finished the *cercle*.

Waldteufel was already seated at the piano, waiting.

The officers danced vigorously. The elder ones ventured on quadrilles, and danced them with great gusto.

Prince Murat, noticing the old generals skipping about so youthfully, proposed a Virginia reel, with a view to giving them a little more exercise.

Every one entered into the spirit of it; but there were only a few who knew how to dance it.

Both Prince and Princess Metternich had learned it at Petit Val. Madame Gallifet knew it as "Sir Roger de Coverley" from her English days, and Prince Murat must have learned it from his American mother.

The Emperor danced with me, as he said he would only dance with an *expert!*

The Empress had Count Golz for her partner, and stood next to me; Princess Metternich (full of fun) chose one of the most ancient warriors. Madame de Persigny and Prince Murat were at the end of the line; the other guests filled the intermediate places.

Prince Metternich, knowing the music, thought he was absolutely necessary at the piano, consequently he took Waldteufel's place there.

I, as "the expert," led off. The Emperor tried to imitate me, but became confused by the constant shouting from his cousin (Prince Murat) at the other end. However, he and I managed to finish our part; but the Emperor refused to be *swung*, and we marched down the middle of the line, hand in hand, disregarding the rules in a truly royal manner. Then, having watched the Empress go through her part (she also marched down in a royal manner), the Emperor seemed bored at looking at the others, and called the Marquis de Caux to take his place. Next, Prince Metternich began improvising reels of his own invention, which turned into all sorts of fantastic measures, which were impossible to dance by. Madame de Persigny, in turning, fell flat on her back; every one rushed to her rescue, which caused great confusion, as people lost their places and could not find them again.

This brought our famous reel, which proved to be a dead failure, to an abrupt close; and the old generals, for whose sake we danced it, never got a chance to show what they could do; and we were thankful when Waldteufel returned to the piano and played a waltz, to which we could dance until it was time for the Emperor's tea, and then,

Bonsoir!

November 27th.

DEAR M.,—Baron Haussmann took me in to *déjeuner* this morning. The Baron is the Préfet de Paris. He is very tall, bulky, and has an authoritative way of walking ahead and dragging his partner after him, which makes one feel as if one was a small tug being swept on by a man-of-war! I wondered if the *Cent Gardes* noticed how I tripped along, taking two steps to his one, until he reached his seat at the table, into which he dropped with a sigh of relief.

His body in profile defies any one's looking around the corner, so to speak. I could only see at intervals Marquise Chasselouplobat's shapely elbows and hands. Our conversation turned on the new improvements he intends to make in Paris. He asked me how I liked the boulevard of his name, just completed.

"I like it," I answered, "though it has deprived us of a good part of our garden." (It had cut off just half of it.)

"It brings you nearer the Bois," he added. "I hope the Government paid you well for it."

"I suppose the Government thinks it did; but our croquet-ground is gone forever."

"Forever!" he repeated. "Where do you play now?"

"Sometimes at the Austrian embassy."

"Is its garden large enough for that?"

I answered, "It is not large enough for a real croquet-ground; but the ambassador is such an ardent player that he has arranged a place under the trees where we play—sometimes at night with lamps on the ground."

"I should think that would be very difficult; quite impossible, in fact."

"What else can we do? We have no other place."

After a moment's hesitation he asked, "How would you like it if I put a piece of ground in the Bois at your disposal?"

I could have screamed with joy! What a piece of news to tell my friends after breakfast. I chanted a little *Gloria* under my breath, and asked him if he really meant it. He said, "Of course I mean it, and as soon as I return to Paris I will have the formal papers made out and sent to you, and you can claim the ground when you like." He added, gallantly, "I will have the document made out in your name, Madame, in souvenir of our breakfast to-day."

Is he not a very generous man? But if every time he sits next to a lady he gives her a slice of the Bois de Boulogne he will soon be out of the government books.

You can readily imagine the delight of my fellow-players when I told them all this after our return to the salon.

The weather looked unsettled; no one felt like driving or walking. However, later, the wind veered about, the sun came out of the heavy clouds, our spirits rose with the barometer, the elements seemed to point to out-door amusements. What better than a game of croquet?

The Emperor, as I said before, had sent to Paris for the game, and Prince Metternich felt it would be rude not to use it. We have been playing it so much this year that we have quite got it on the brain, and we were very excited and most eager to play, and orders were given to have the box brought out on the terrace.

Both their Majesties were highly interested; they examined everything with the greatest curiosity, un-wrapped the balls themselves, and were quite anxious to begin.

The question was, where should the game be put up, and where should the wickets be put down? The lawn was wet, the gravel walks were too narrow. The only place that could be found was under the *charmille* on the terrace, where stood a grove of old platane trees.

Prince Metternich was, of course, the moving spirit, and undertook to manage everything. He and d'Es-peuilles got a meter measure and measured off the dis-tances with great care and precision before placing the wickets. This took a long time. Then he distributed the mallets and the corresponding balls to each person, and we stood in front of our weapons ready to commence. Prince Metternich was so long and particular about telling the rules that he succeeded only in confusing all the beginners.

The Empress was to play with the Prince Metternich, the Marquis de Gallifet with the Princess Metternich. The Emperor was to play with the Marquise de Gallifet, Monsieur d'Espeuilles was to play with me— eight people in all! Nothing is so dreadful as a game of croquet with people four of whom are beginners.

The Empress was the first to play; her ball was placed so near the wicket that nothing short of genius could have prevented her from going through, which she did with great triumph; her next stroke went far beyond, and she worried it back by a succession of several pushing knocks into its position. No one made any remarks. Then the Emperor made a timid stroke, which gently turned the ball over. Prince Metternich remarked that he (the Emperor) should hit harder, at which his Majesty gave such a whack to his ball that it flew into the next county.

"Never mind," said Prince Metternich, and put another ball in front of the Emperor's mallet, and somehow it got through the wicket.

Princess Metternich played next, and she was an adept, so all went well with her. I came after her, and managed to get his Majesty's ball on its way a bit. Tiresome pauses and long explanations followed.

Prince Metternich shouted, trying to rally the players.

"Marquis, where are you?" disturbing the Marquis from a flirtation. "It is your turn to play."

"Really; what shall I do?"

"Try to hit this ball."

"*Par exemple!* Which ball? Where is it? I do not even see it."

"Here it is behind this tree; if you *caramboler* against the tree you might hit it." And in this way it went on until the Emperor, bored to death, slowly disappeared and the Empress suddenly discovered that her feet were cold and went away, and couples flirtatiously inclined began wandering off, and it was nearly dark and tea-time before Prince Metternich (who was worn out trying to make people understand or take any interest in the game) realized that there were only a few devotees left on the battle-field amid damaged trees and chipped balls.

So ended our game of croquet; we felt crushed and crestfallen.

At the Empress's tea, to which we were bidden, we were not spared satirical gibes on the subject of our luckless game.

The Marquis de Gallifet, *Officier d'Ordonnance de l'Empereur*, whom I sat next to at dinner, is what one might call sarcastic—he actually tears people to pieces; he does not leave them with a shred of reputation, and what he does not say he implies. He thinks nothing of saying, "He! He's an abominable scoundrel. She! She is a shameless coquette!" and so forth. He spares no one; nevertheless, he is most amusing, very intelligent, and an excellent talker. He told me of his awful experience in the war of Mexico. He had been shot in the intestines and left for dead on the field of battle. He managed, by creeping and crawling, "*toujours tenant mes entrailles dans mon képi*," to reach a peasant's house, where the good people took care of him until he was able to be transported to a hospital. There he stayed through a dismal year of suffering. In order to keep the above-mentioned *entrailles* in their proper place, the doctors covered them with a silver plate. "I had my name engraved on it," he said.

He asked me, "Did you ever hear anything like that?" I tried to fancy how any one would look placarded like that, but replied that I had never heard of anything quite so awful; but I *had* heard that every cloud had a silver lining. He laughed and said, "I shall call myself a cloud in future."

The dinner to-night was very good. I give you the menu:

> Potage tortue clair,
> Crême de volaille,
> Brisotins de foie gras,
> Saumon Napolitain,
> Filet de bœuf à la moderne,
> Suprême de perdreaux,
> Homards à la Parisienne,
> Gelinottes rôties,
> Salade,
> Petits pois à l'Anglaise,
> Ananas Montmorency,
> Glacés assorties,
> Café—Liqueur (both served at the table).

Dinner over, we filed before the *Cent Gardes* in their shining uniforms through the long gallery.

It was earlier than usual when we began to dance; but we were (at least I was) interrupted by receiving a message from their Majesties, asking me if I would kindly sing something for them. Of course I did not refuse, and we adjourned to the music-room, where the Erard piano was.

THE MUSIC HALL—CHÂTEAU DE COMPIÈGNE

I did not exactly know what to sing; but Prince Metternich soon relieved my mind on that score by saying, "Don't bother about singing anything serious, and especially *don't* sing anything classical." The Princess Metternich could accompany anything which was not too difficult; therefore we thought I had better sing "Ma mère était bohémienne," of Massé, which I did. I saw directly that this melodramatic music, beautiful as it is, did not suit the occasion, for though the gaily attuned audience was visibly affected by the phrase, *Et moi j'ai l'âme triste*, they did not show more signs of emotion than by making a little dab at their eyes with their pocket-handkerchiefs.

The Princess remained at the piano, ready to accompany the other songs I had brought, which were of the same character, and I stood by her, trying to decide what I should sing next, when the Emperor came up and asked me for "Beware!" Charles accompanied that, and I sang it. The Empress asked me if I would sing some Spanish songs for her. I sang "Chiquita," which I learned with Garcia, and the "Habañero." She seemed very pleased, and made me many compliments. Then the Emperor begged me for some negro songs, and asked me if I knew "Massa's in the Cold, Cold Ground," or "Suwanee River," or "Nelly Bly," all of which he remembered having heard in America.

I sat down at the piano and commenced with "Suwanee River." I fortunately knew the words of that.

(Oh, Delsarte! what would you have said had you seen your pupil singing this claptrap music before your sovereigns and their most distinguished guests?")

Delsarte says that one can force the tears into one's

eyes, one can make one's lips tremble, one can express the most harrowing emotions in one's voice, and not sing more than "do, re, mi, fa." I tried to profit by his teachings, and brought them to bear upon the pathetic words of "Oh, darkies, how my heart grows weary," and I could see that both their Majesties were deeply moved. I sang the word "weary" with such pathos that every one was more or less affected, and the phrase, "All the world is dark and dreary," I rendered in the most heart-broken tones.

I was sorry that I could not remember the words of "Massa's in the Cold, Cold Ground," as the Emperor wanted it; but I could not. I knew the music of "Nelly Bly," but had never known the words, so I tried to improvise some; but it was impossible for me to think of more than two words which rhymed with "Bly," and those were "sly" and "eye."

With shameful *aplomb* I sang these senseless words:

> Nelly Bly wipes her eye,
> On her little frock,
> Nelly Bly, Nelly Bly,
> Dick a dick a dock.

Happily the Emperor did not notice anything wrong, and was delighted to hear those old songs again, and thanked me repeatedly.

Once seated at the piano, I was not allowed to leave it until my *répertoire* of music of this character had been exhausted.

This brought the evening to a close.

Tea was served; their Majesties withdrew, and I fled to my apartment feeling that metaphorically I was covered with laurels.

November 28th.

DEAR A.,—To-day I was very high up, *'way up in the clouds*, for I sat next to the Emperor.

Davilliers, one of the chamberlains, gave me his arm and conducted me to my place. The Emperor's first words were:

"I can't thank you enough for the pleasure you gave us last evening."

I tried to express my pleasure at these kind words.

"Did you see how we were affected when you sang 'Suwanee River'? I thought to laugh, instead of which I cried; how could you make it so pathetic?"

"That is my teacher's art," I replied.

"Who is your teacher?"

"Monsieur Delsarte. Your Majesty has perhaps heard of him?"

"No," answered the Emperor. "I have never heard of him. Is he a great singer?"

"He cannot sing at all, your Majesty; but he has wonderful theories which go to prove that one does not need any voice at all to sing; one only needs features to express one's emotions."

"He must be wonderful," the Emperor remarked.

"He is, your Majesty, and quite unique in his way. He says, for instance, when he sings, 'J'ai du bon tabac dans ma tabatière,' and comes to 'Tu n'en auras pas,' he can make people shed bitter tears, as though it were too much to bear."

"His tobacco must be very good?" laughed the Emperor.

"It is the worst thing of its kind, your Majesty, one can imagine," I answered.

"Is it perhaps Caporal?" said he, with a merry twinkle in his eye.

"I don't know anything about military grades; but, if there were anything lower than a Caporal I should say it was the name of his tobacco."

"Well," he said, "if he taught you to sing as you sing, *il mérite de la patrie.*"

The Emperor was perfectly delightful, witty, amusing, and laughing continually, with such a keen appreciation he seemed really to enjoy himself.

As the programme in our room this morning read, *chasse à courre*, on went the green dress for the second time, and, of course, the button. The Duchess de Fernan Nuñez asked me to drive with her, which I was happy to do, as I like her very much. We sat on the front seat, so as to have the best view of the proceedings.

The Emperor and Empress were on horseback; all the gentlemen were in red coats, white breeches, top-boots, and velvet caps, which made them look very picturesque.

The rendezvous was at the Carrefour l'Étoile, and when we arrived the hunters and equipage, with the *piqueurs* and the *chasseurs* from the neighborhood, who belonged to the Imperial Hunt, were already there.

The Imperial *équipage de chasse* is composed of ten *piqueurs*, *valets de chien*, *valets à pieds*, *valets à cheval*, and *valets de limiers*, and one hundred English hounds. The hounds are trained by the use of drags, which are, as perhaps you know, bundles of something saturated in blood, which the horses drag and the scent of which the hounds follow. The carriages were drawn up on the side of the road to wait until their Majesties appeared.

The ladies dressed in rich furs and velvets, the riders in brilliant red coats on prancing horses, the attendant grooms, the *piqueurs* in their gay liveries, green and gold with green-velvet jockey caps, made a wonderful spectacle. The day was superb, the sun shone brilliantly through the autumn foliage, the hazy distances were of a tender hue, and everything had an exquisite tint. Never shall I forget it!

Unfortunately our coachman neglected to follow the other carriages, and we drove about a long time before we discovered that we were on the wrong road, and then he became quite bewildered and seemed to lose his head completely.

After driving from one cross-road to another, we at last chanced upon Monsieur de Bourgogne, who told us that he was just in advance of their Majesties, and that they would be there presently. He said that we had better wait where we were, as the stag would probably pass by that way.

It seemed as if, in fact, we must be near, as we could hear the dogs yelping and the horns sounding (they call it "hallali"). Count de Grammont rode up to us and said we had better follow him, as we would then soon come in sight of the hunters. Despite all these contradictory advices, our coachman managed to arrive on the scene of action just in time for us to see the poor stag, who had taken to the water for dear life (they call it *bat l'eau*), and the dogs in a frenzy of excitement barking furiously and plunging after him.

We could not see *all* that happened, thank heaven! as our carriage was behind the whole assembled crowd. With my tenderness toward all animals, my heart ached for the poor beast, and I hoped sincerely that he would escape his cruel pursuers. I could not see any pleasure or excitement in watching this painful spectacle, and was glad when the time came to turn our backs on the whole thing and return to the château.

At the Empress's tea no one talked of anything else but the events of the afternoon. I pretended that I had seen it all, even to the very end. Princess Ghika, beaming all over with joy, was given the foot, as she was in at the death.

Count de l'Aigle took me in to dinner. He is one of the neighbors, not one of the guests; but, as he belongs to the Imperial Hunt, he is always invited to this dinner.

The Empress looked superb in a brown tulle over satin, looped up with brooches of diamonds. She had had a diamond crescent in her hair like Diana. The Marquise de Gallifet was lovely in light-green tulle, with an aigret of diamonds in her blond hair.

The table was arranged most appropriately for the occasion, decorated by the whole *biscuit de Sèvres service de chasse*. Every one seemed gay and stimulated by the excitement of the day.

When the usual after-dinner ceremonies and the *cercle* in the salon were terminated, the Grand Chamberlain announced to his Majesty that all was ready for the *curée*, which was awaiting his permission to begin.

The Emperor and the Empress led the way into the long gallery, which overlooks the *cour d'honneur*. We ladies had provided ourselves with wraps and shawls, as we knew we should need them either on the balcony or at the windows of the gallery, of which there are about twenty.

The Empress braved the weather and stood out on the balcony with the Emperor, well wrapped in furs, for the night was cold; and the gentlemen, not finding sufficient room, went below and stood on the steps of the "Perron," which gives on to the courtyard.

All the lackeys, valets, grooms, in fact, all the household servants, formed a large circle in the enormous *cour d'honneur* opposite the Imperial balcony, all bearing flaming torches made of tar, which lighted up the whole place. Behind these stood the populace of Compiègne, who are allowed to be present on these occasions.

At the farther side of the courtyard, and directly opposite their Majesties, the chief huntsman held up the skin of the stag, which contained the entrails, waving it backward and forward, in order to excite the hounds. The *piqueurs* stood in front of the "Perron," holding the dogs back with great difficulty, for they were struggling to get loose, and yelping in their eagerness and greediness to rush forward.

As the *chasseur* waved the skin, the *piqueurs* let the hounds loose, and when they were half-way across the court, approaching the object of their desire, the *piqueurs* called them back, in order to show how well disciplined and under what complete control they were.

The tantalizing of the poor animals was repeated several times. At last the fanfare was sounded, and the hounds were allowed to rush forward midst the tooting of horns, the cracking of whips, and the cries and shouts of the crowd. The torches were waved high in the air, giving a weird light to the whole scene, and the entrails at last were thrown to the dogs, and before you could

11 149

say "Jack Robinson" everything was devoured. You can picture to yourself what a unique and fantastic sight this must have been!

It was eleven o'clock when we returned to the salon, where tea and refreshments were served. Those returning to Paris took leave of their Majesties and drove to the station, where the special Imperial train provided for them was waiting.

Later their Majesties took leave of us.

We lingered a little, as it was our last evening.

On returning to my apartment, I saw on my table a package, on which was written, *De la part de l'Empereur.* You can imagine how eager I was to open it. Those magic words brought untold visions before my eyes. What might it not be?

I opened the package feverishly, and what was my surprise and *disappointment* to find a rather ordinary-looking *tabatière* and a package of tobacco, written on it, *Du bon tabac pour le maître de chant de Madame Moulton.*

Was it not a cruel blow?

November 30th.

Here we are again in Paris, glad to be at home after our gay week in Compiègne, charming and delightful as it was; there is always great fatigue and tension attending such visits. To-day I luxuriate in one dress; no changing five times a day. I allowed my maid to go out for the day, and we are going to dine at a restaurant. . . . What a contrast! It seems as if I had been away a month!

Before we left Compiègne yesterday, when we were

taking our morning tea, we were interrupted by the coming in of the majordomo, who handed us a paper. We were not unprepared for this visit, as we had been told by one of the guests, who had been here before, that every one was expected to remain in their rooms until this important personage had made his rounds, in order to collect the *pourboire*. I say THE *pourboire*, because what one generally gives separately is lumped into one sum. This paper, which he handed to us almost at the point of his *hallebarde*, proved to be a *già scritto* receipt for six hundred francs—our *pourboire!*

During breakfast yesterday the Emperor took up his glass, and, looking at me across the table, drank my health. Among the guests there was a great deal of health-drinking.

Gustave Doré had made some very clever caricatures of some events which he had drawn beautifully and touched off with aquarelle, as he alone could do it. The little album was passed stealthily from hand to hand under the shelter of the table, with the strictest injunctions not to let any one see it except your *immediate* neighbor! With these injunctions it managed to travel about half-way down the table.

He had made a lovely sketch of her Majesty driving a chariot like the "Aurora" in the Rospigliosi Gallery, and had depicted the Emperor seated on an enormous white horse, leading a charge of cavalry, his arm uplifted.

The Princess Metternich was represented as the coachman in the charade, hat on one side, pipe in her mouth, and looking very *débonnaire*. Prince Metternich was shown standing in the middle of an arena, in full diplomatic uniform, with masses of decorations and *cordons*. He had a long whip, such as are used in circuses, and men and women (meaning us, I suppose) capering around doing their tricks.

The sketch of Madame de Persigny was very funny. A mass of tulle petticoats, in the midst of which two little feet in the air, and a crown rolling away in the distance.

The picture he made of me was the mechanical doll, ribbons floating all about, and on every turn of the ribbons was written "Beware!"

The diplomat's shoe was not forgotten. There was a table a mile long, and at the very end of it a little shoe seen underneath.

We were in our traveling costumes, and on our return to the salon their Majesties went about saying pleasant and gracious things to every one. They hoped we would remember our visit with as much pleasure as they would, etc.

There was a greater animation than usual, and less ceremony; people talked louder and with less restraint; every one bade good-by to the ladies and gentlemen of the Household who remained. The Empress gave her hand to be kissed by the gentlemen (some of them, not all), kissed some ladies, and shook hands with others.

When their Majesties were ready to dismiss us they bowed, and we all departed to get our hats and wraps,

I gave a lingering look at the lovely rooms I was leaving, which were now devoid of our trunks and little personal trinkets, nodded a farewell to our particular valet, who was probably thinking already of our successors, descended *l'Escalier d'honneur*, and passed through the beautiful *Galerie des Gardes* to the colonnades, where the *chars-à-bancs* were ready waiting to carry us to the station.

We were a rather subdued party in the train; the conversation mostly turned on the subject of *pourboires*. The *huissier* decides the exact amount that each ought to give. For instance, he knows an ambassador ought to give two thousand francs. For a minister of state one thousand francs suffices. Unofficial people like ourselves cannot be expected to be out of pocket more than six hundred francs. As for the poor nobility of France, they escape with five hundred!

Some were of opinion that it was pleasanter to give *en masse*, in one big sum, than to give in driblets; others thought it more satisfactory to hand one's offering personally to the different servants; but we all, with one voice, voted the officious beadle an imposition.

The daily expenses of Compiègne, so the *Gouverneur de la Maison* told us, and he ought to know, are not less than ten thousand francs a day, and there are more than nine hundred people living in the Palace at a time, to be fed and warmed.

To-day, at five o'clock, the fourth *série* will come; it is called *la série des oubliés*, as ours was called *la série élégante*. The first is called *la série obligatoire*, the second *les ennuyeux*.

We found our carriage at the station. Our simple coupé seemed a great come-down from the beautiful carriages we had been driving in, and good Louis and the footman, in their quiet liveries, seemed in fierce contrast to the gorgeous creatures we had been familiar with so lately.

The family is at Petit Val, and we remain there quietly until January.

We found among our belongings an enormous *bourriche*, containing a quantity of game, hares, pheasants, and so forth.

Good night! I am tired.

PARIS, *1867*.

DEAR M.,—You will have heard so much about the Exposition, that I cannot tell you anything new. It is now in full swing, and I think it is magnificent. Of course I cannot compare it to any other, as it is the only one that I have ever seen.

I have a season ticket (costing one hundred francs) containing my photograph and my autograph; therefore no one but myself can use it. The Exposition building is round, and the section of one thing goes through all the countries; for instance, art, which seems to be the smallest thing, is in the inner circle. If you only want to study one particular industry you go round the circle; but if you want to study a country you go down a section. The outer circle is for machinery, and outside in the grounds, in front of the different countries, are the cafés belonging to them. Here you can listen to the different national musics, and see the different national types and costumes, and eat the different national foods. We go almost every day, and it is always a delight. You can see the whole art of cutting diamonds, from the gravel in which they are found to their final polish. The villa of the Bey of Tunis, a Buddhist temple, a Viennese bakery, where people flock to taste the delicious rolls hot from the oven, and where

Hungarian bands of highly colored handsome zitherists play from morning till night, and a hundred other attractions, make the Exposition a complete success. You pass from one lovely thing to the other. The gardens are laid through avenues of trees and shrubs, where fountains play, and beds of flowers and bouquets of plants are arranged with the most artistic taste. All these wonders will in six months' time be reduced to the level and monotony of the Champ de Mars. One can't believe that these large horse-chestnut trees in full bloom are only temporary visitors, like the people.

The Prince Oscar of Sweden (he will one day be the King) came often to the Exposition, and went about with us. He was very much interested in everything he saw, especially in the American Steinway pianos. He sent me several times some of the famous punch they make in Sweden, also some silver brooches which the Swedish peasants wear. He has a *bâteau mouche*, in which he takes his friends up and down the Seine. The Princess Mathilde and Madame de Gallifet were of the party last Monday. We *mouched* as far as Boulogne, where Baron James Rothschild has a charming place called Bagatelle, which the Prince wanted very much to see.

We got out of the boat and walked up to the entrance of the park; but the porter refused, in spite of all pleadings, to let us in, and was almost rude until Monsieur Dué mentioned the name of the illustrious visitor; then the gates were thrown wide open, and we walked in and all over the place. The porter, becoming most humble and servile, offered to escort us over the house, and even asked us to take tea; but we did not succumb to either of these temptations.

There are so many kings and sovereigns here: the Emperor of Russia, who is very handsome and stately; the King of Prussia, who is accompanied by the colossal Count Bismarck, very noticeable in his dazzling white uniform, and wearing a shining helmet with an enormous spread eagle on top of it, which made him tower still more above ordinary mortals, and reminded me of all the mythological heroes I knew of. He clanked his sword on the pavement, quite indifferent to the stare of wondering Frenchmen, and was followed by several other tall Germans, who regarded everything *de haut en bas* with Teutonic phlegm. The Prince of Italy (Umberto) looks rather small by the side of these German giants. The Khedive of Egypt, the Shah of Persia, the ex-Queen of Spain, and other sovereigns are flitting about.

The Baron James Rothschild invited us to go to Ferrière's with Prince Oscar of Sweden. That was very amusing! We had a special train from Paris and Rothschild's special car; when we arrived at Ferrière's we first had refreshments, then we walked in the grounds till it was time to dress for dinner. We met before dining in the enormous salon in the center of the château. This salon is two stories high, with a gallery around it, and was so large that a billiard-table in one corner seemed too small to be noticed, and the concert-grand piano standing at the other end looked insignificant. The dining-table was beautifully decorated with garlands of roses and a whole collection of antique goblets, worth a fortune. There were huge bouquets of roses for the ladies, almost too big to carry.

Prince Oscar's brother had once written a very pretty song, called "I Rosens duft," which some one had arranged as a duet, and the Prince wanted me to sing it with him (he had thoughtfully brought the music). All through dinner he was teaching me the Swedish words, so that we could sing it afterward. He was so intent (and so was I) that every one, I am sure, thought we were having a tremendous flirtation, as they saw our heads almost touching when he was writing the words on the menu. He also wrote a poem to me (which I inclose), which he said he composed on the spot. How can he be so clever?

PRINCE OSCAR'S POEM
WRITTEN AT THE DINNER-TABLE AT LAFERRIÈRE'S
1867

Din sång, hur skön, hur underbar!
En balsamdoft på dina läppar hvila,
En välljudsström från ditt hjärta ila,
Vill mana fram ur verldens haf ett svar:
Din sång, hur skön, hur underbar!

Din ton, hur stärk, hur ljuf, hur ren!
En altareld som ingen flägt få störa,
Och dock en storm som själens djup kan röra,
En glöd som smälta kan "de visas sten":
Så är din ton—så stark, så ren.

Sjung mer, sjung mer, det här så godt
En stund få glämma verldens hvimmel
Och lyss till samklang ur en öppnad himmel,
Om ock för en minut i drömma blott:
Sjung mer, sjung mer, det gör mit hjärta godt.

(Translated literally)

Your voice, how beautiful, how wonderful!
A perfume of balsam rests on your lips,
A torrent of melody rushes from your heart,
That can only be echoed by the world's ocean:
Your voice, how beautiful, how wonderful!

Your voice, how full of power, how enchanting and pure!
A sacred fire which no breeze can trouble,
And yet a tempest that stirs the very soul,
A glowing flame which can melt the philosopher's stone:
Such is your voice—so powerful, so pure.

Sing more, sing more, it is so good
For one moment to forget the tumult of this world
And listen to the harmony of a heaven unveiled,
And if only for a moment to dream:
Sing more, sing more, it makes my heart rejoice.

We sang the duet after dinner with such success that we had to repeat it. Before our departure there was a grand display of fireworks: O's appeared in every dimension and design, and a blaze of fire and Bengal lights in rapid succession kept us in a continual state of admiration.

I received a little note from Jenny Lind. She is in Paris, and wished to know when she could come to see me. I wrote to her directly that I would let Monsieur Auber know, and he would probably come at four o'clock (his usual hour). Therefore, it all came about. Jenny Lind came, so did Auber. The meeting was a pleasure to them both. They talked music, art, told many anecdotes of celebrated acquaintances: Alboni, Nilsson, Patti, etc. He had brought some of his music with him, and Jenny Lind and I sang the duo of his latest opera "Le Premier Jour de Bonheur." He consulted me as to whether he might dare to ask her to dine with him, with a few congenial spirits. I said I was sure she would be enchanted to do so, which she was.

As to the congenial spirits, Auber suggested the Met-

Hotel de Louvre
Thursday.

Dear Mrs Moulton.
Certainly — I will
with the greatest
pleasure write
with Mr Auber
to the yes. Mr Aubra
tout ce que vous voulez.

FACSIMILE OF LETTER FROM JENNY LIND

I was going to drive
over to you tomorrow
morning — to take my
book! and to tell
you — that I am
very proud of my
Commissioners

for he got me 3
beautiful places
11ᵗ Scholars for

l'Opera Comique
tonight! he he!
I of course would
prefer to dine
at Mrs Arbats
own house: and
you probably too.
Tomorrow — if he
is alone — or at
least in no great
company — and

them — I would
screw my voice
up a little to
sing him a song if
he likes — [illegible] a [illegible]
Many thanks for
your kindness
&. Yours very
affectionately
Truly J. [signature]

ternichs, Gounod, Duke de Massa, and ourselves, making ten in all.

No one refused, and we had the most delightful dinner. The Princess proposed to Auber to give his arm to Jenny Lind, and to put her at his right hand, *la place d'honneur*, adding, with her most ironical smile, "le génie avant la beauté." Auber made a charming host, telling one funny anecdote after the other in his quiet and typical manner. Gounod, in his low and drawly voice, said: "Vous nous donnez, mon cher Auber, des choses par trop ennuyeuses aux concerts du Conservatoire. À la pensée des 'Quatre saisons' de Haydn je m'endors. Pourquoi ne s'est-il pas contenté d'une saison?" Princess Metternich replied, "Que probablement en les composant Haydn s'est mis en quatre." "La moitié m'aurait suffi," said Auber; "pour moi, elles sont toutes *mon automne*" (monotone).

When we returned to the salon we discreetly waited for the promised song.

Suddenly Jenny Lind jumped up, saying, "Shall I sing something?"

Of course, every one was wild to hear her. She went to the piano and accompanied herself in "Qui la voce," of "I Puritani." We were all enchanted, clapping our hands with enthusiasm. Then Gounod played and sang, or rather hummed, a new song of his, saying to Jenny Lind, when he took his place at the piano, "I am not worthy to succeed you."

We thought him much too modest.

He *hummed* deliciously!

They asked me to sing, and, though I really hated to sing after these great artists, I did so to please Auber, who accompanied me in "Les Djins," of which he is very proud, because it has the same bass all the way through. How little it takes to please genius!

After this Jenny Lind and I performed the duo from "Le Premier Jour de Bonheur" we had practised at my house. She put her arm around my waist while we were singing, as if we were two school-girls.

Prince Metternich played one of his brilliant Austrian waltzes, which was so bewildering that if any man had dared to put his arm round Jenny Lind's matronly waist I am sure she would have skipped off in the dance.

For *la bonne bouche* she gave us a Swedish peasant song, which was simply bewitching. Her high notes were exquisitely pure, the lower ones I thought weak; but that might have been owing to the good dinner she had eaten—at least she said so.

There is a musical phenomenon here just now in the shape of an American negro; he is blind and idiotic, but has a most extraordinary intelligence for music. All his senses seem to have been concentrated in this one sense. Prince and Princess Metternich, Auber, and ourselves went to his concert. Auber said, "Cet idiot, noir et aveugle, est vraiment merveilleux." Blind Tom had learned his *répertoire* entirely by ear; therefore it was very limited, as he could only remember what he had heard played a few days before. His memory did not last long. He was wonderful. Not only could he execute well, but he could imitate any one's mannerisms and their way of playing. The impresario came forward, saying, "I am told that Monsieur Auber is in the audience. May I dare to ask him to come up and play something?" Auber said he thought he should die of fright. We all urged him, for the curiosity of the thing, to play something of his new opera, which no one as yet had heard, therefore no one could have known it.

Auber mounted the platform, amid the enthusiastic applause of the audience, and performed his solo. Then Blind Tom sat down and played it after him so accurately, with the same staccato, old-fashioned touch of Auber, that no one could have told whether Auber was still at the piano. Auber returned and bowed to the wildly excited public and to us. He said, "This is my first appearance as a pianist, and my last."

Prince Metternich, inspired by Auber's pluck, followed his example, and mounting the stage rattled off one of his *own* fiery, dashing waltzes, which Blind Tom repeated in the Prince's particular manner. After the concert we went into the artist's room to speak with the impresario, and found poor Tom banging his head against the wall like the idiot he was. Auber remarked, "C'est humiliant pour nous autres."

PARIS, *June, 1867.*

DEAR M.,—The famous pianist Liszt, the new Abbé, is pervading Paris just now, and is, I think, very pleased to be a priestly lion, taking his success as a matter of course. There are a succession of dinners in his honor, where he does ample honor to the food, and is in no way bashful about his appetite.

He does a great deal of beaming, he has (as some one said) "so much countenance."

He dined with us the other night, the Metternichs,

IN THE COURTS OF MEMORY

and twenty-five other people, among whom were Auber and Massenet.

In the boudoir, before dinner, he spied a manuscript which Auber had brought that afternoon. He took it up, looked at it, and said, "C'est très joli!" and laid it down again. When we went in to dinner, and after his cigar in the conservatory (he is a great smoker), he went to the piano and played the "*joli*" little thing of Auber's. Was that not wonderful, that he could remember it all the time during the dinner? He seemed only to have glanced at it, and yet he could play it like that off from memory. He is so kind and good, especially to struggling artists, trying to help them in every way. He seemed extraordinarily amiable that evening, for he sat down at the piano without being asked and played a great many of his compositions—quite an unusual thing for him to do! One has generally to tease and beg him, and then he refuses. But I think, when he heard Massenet improvising at one of the pianos he was inspired, and he put himself at the other (we have two grand pianos), and they played divinely, both of them improvising. He is by far the finest pianist I have ever heard, and has a very seductive way of looking at you while playing, as if he was only playing for you, and when he smiles you simply go to pieces. I don't wonder he is such a lady-killer, and that no woman can resist him; even my father-in-law stayed in the salon, being completely hypnotized by Liszt, who ought to consider this as one of his greatest triumphs, if he only knew.

I sang some of Massenet's songs, accompanied, of course, by Massenet. Liszt was most attentive and most enthusiastic. He said Massenet had a great future, and he complimented me on my singing, especially my phrasing and expression.

I wonder if the story be true that he was engaged to be married to Princess Wittgenstein, and on the day of the wedding, when the bridal-dress was ready to be put on, she got a letter from her fiancé (can any one imagine Liszt as a fiancé) saying that he had taken holy orders that very morning.

They say that she bore it very well and wrote a sweet letter to him. It sounds rather unnatural; but one can believe anything from a person who was under Liszt's influence. He has the most wonderful magnetism. His appearance is certainly original as you see him in his *soutane*, his long hair, and his numerous moles, that stand out in profile, whichever way he turns his broad face.

But one forgets everything when one hears him play. He is now fifty-five years old. I invited him to go to the Conservatoire with me in the box which Auber had given me for last Sunday's concert. I inclose his letter of acceptance. (See page 164.)

Auber often gives me his box, which holds six people, and I have the pleasure of making four people happy. Auber sits in the back and generally dozes. We are all crowded together like sardines. Auber, being the director of the Conservatoire, has, of course, the best box, except the Imperial one, which is always empty.

The orchestra played Wagner's overture to "Tannhäuser." The applause was not as enthusiastic as Liszt thought it ought to be, so he stood up in the box, and with his great hands clapped so violently that the whole audience turned toward him, and, recognizing him (indeed, it would have been difficult not to recognize him, such a striking figure as he is), began clapping

Madame,

Permettez-moi de venir vous remercier demain au Conservatoire d votre gracieuse invitation dont je serai charmé d profiter

Mille respectueux hommages

F. Liszt

Samedi matin.

LISZT LETTER

their hands for him. He cried, "Bis!" And the audience in chorus shouted, "Bis!" And the orchestra repeated the whole overture. Then the audience turned again to Liszt and screamed, "Vive Liszt!"

Auber said such a thing had never been seen or heard

before in the annals of these severe and classical concerts. People quite lost their heads, and Auber, being afraid that there would be a demonstration at the *sortie*, advised us to leave before the end.

I think Liszt was very pleased with his afternoon.

The sovereigns are working themselves to death, and almost killing their attendants. Prince Radzivill said, speaking of the King of Prussia: "I would have liked him better if he had stayed at home. He has to be ready every morning at half-past eight, and is often up till three in the morning." Radzivill and the others not only have to go to all the balls, but they must attend all the various civil, military, and charitable functions, and then the Exposition takes a lot of time and energy.

Prince Umberto is here from Italy. When Princess Metternich asked him how long he was going to stay he answered, with a toss of his head toward Italy, "Cela dépend des circonstances. Les affaires vont très mal là-bas."

Aunt M—— says she wishes you had been at a matinée which Baroness Nathaniel Rothschild gave this afternoon at her beautiful new palace in the Faubourg St.-Honoré. At the entrance there were ten servants in gorgeous livery, and a *huissier* who rattled his mace down on the pavement as each guest passed. There was, besides all the élite of Paris, an Archduke of Austria. I sang the "Ave Maria" of Gounod, accompanied by Madame Norman Neruda, an Austrian violiniste, the best woman violinist in the world. Baroness Rothschild played the piano part.

IN THE COURTS OF MEMORY

DEAR M.,—The Metternichs' big ball last night was a splendid affair, the finest of the many fine balls. We were invited for ten o'clock, and about half-past ten every one was there.

The Emperor and Empress came at eleven o'clock. Waldteufel, with full orchestra, was already playing in the ballroom of the embassy, which was beautifully decorated. At twelve o'clock the doors, or rather all the windows that had been made into doors, were opened into the new ballroom, which the Princess Metternich, with her wonderful taste and the help of Monsieur Alphand, had constructed in the garden, and which had transformed the embassy into a thousand-and-one-nights' palace.

The ballroom was a marvel; the walls were hung with lilac and pink satin, and the immense chandelier was one mass of candles and flowers; from each panel in the room there were suspended baskets of flowers and plants, and between the panels were mirrors which reflected the thousands of candles.

One would never have recognized the garden; it was transformed into a green glade; all the paths were covered with fresh grass sod, making it look like a vast lawn; clusters of plants and palms seemed to be growing everywhere, as if native to the soil; flower-beds by the hundreds; mysterious grottos loomed out of the background, and wonderful vistas with a cleverly painted perspective. At the same moment that their Majesties entered this wonderful ballroom, which no one had dreamed of, the famous Johann Strauss, brought

166

from Vienna especially for this occasion, stood waiting with uplifted baton and struck up the "Blue Danube," heard for the first time in Paris.

When their Majesties approached the huge plate-glass window opening into the garden a full-fledged cascade fell over the stucco rocks, and powerful Bengal lights, red and green, made a most magical effect: the water looked like a torrent of fiery lava *en miniature*. It was thrilling.

No one thought of dancing; every one wanted to listen to the waltz.   And how Strauss played it!... With what fire and *entrain!* We had thought Waldteufel perfect; but when you heard Strauss you said to your-self you had never heard a waltz before.   The musicians were partly hidden by gigantic palmettos, plants, and pots of flowers arranged in the most attractive way. But he!—Johann Strauss!—stood well in front, looking very handsome, very Austrian, and very pleased with himself.

Then came the *quadrille d'honneur*. The Emperor danced with the Queen of Belgium, the Crown Prince of Prussia with the Empress, the King of Belgium with the Princess Mathilde, the Prince Leuchtenberg with the Princess Metternich.

The cotillon was led by Count Deym and Count Bergen, and they led it to perfection; there was not a hitch anywhere.   Every one was animated and gay; certainly the music was inspiring enough to have made an Egyptian mummy get out of his sarcophagus and caper about.   I danced with a German *Durchlaucht*, who, though far in the sear and yellow leaf, danced like a school-boy, standing for hours with his arm around my waist before venturing (he could only start when the tune commenced), counting one—two—three under his breath, which made me, his partner, feel like a perfect fool. When at last he made up his mind to start nothing short of an earthquake could have stopped him. He hunched up his shoulders to his ears, arched his leg like a prancing horse, and off we went on our wild career, lurching into every couple on the floor, and bumping into all the outsiders. When we were not careering together, he sat glued to his chair, refusing to dance. If any lady came up with a favor he would say, "I am a little out of breath; I will come and fetch you later." And then he would put the favor in his pocket and never go near her. He seized everything in the way of favors that came his way; some he gave to me, and the rest he took home to his small children.

I was glad, all the same, to have him for a partner, as, being a *Durchlaucht*, he was entitled to a seat in the front row, and I preferred prancing about with my *hochgeboren* high-stepper to having to take a back seat in the third row with a minor *geboren*. After my partner and I had bounded about and butted into every living thing on the floor I brought him to anchor near his chair by clutching his Golden Fleece chain which hung around his neck. I felt like singing Tennyson's "Home I brought my warrior (half) dead." He was puffing and blowing, the perspiration glazing his face, his yellow hair matted on his forehead, and his mustaches all out of kilter.

I really felt sorry for him, and wondered why he exerted himself so much, when he could have been quietly seated watching others, or, better still, at home in bed.

The supper was served at one o'clock. Their Majesties the King and Queen of Belgium, Prince Alfred, the Prince and Princess of Prussia, the Prince of Saxe-Weimar, and all the other *gros bonnets*—too many to write about—went up-stairs through an avenue of plants and palms to a salon arranged especially for them where there were two large tables. The Emperor presided at one and the Empress at the other. Besides the *salle à manger* and some smaller salons, two enormous tents were put up in the garden, which contained numerous tables, holding about ten people each, and lighted by masses of candles and festooned with bright-colored Chinese lanterns. Prince Metternich told me later that the candles were replaced three times during the evening.

The favors for the cotillon were very pretty, most of them brought from Vienna. One of the prettiest was fans of gray wood with "Ambassade d'Autriche, 28th May, 1867," painted in blue forget-me-nots.

We danced "till morning did appear," and it appeared only too soon. The cotillon finished at half-past five, and the daylight poured in, making us all look ghastly, especially my sear and yellow leaf, whose children must have wondered why papa *kam so spät nach hause.*

PARIS, *1867.*

Last week, in the beautiful palace built by Egypt for the Exposition, there was arranged a sort of entertainment for the Viceroy, to which we were invited with the Prince and Princess Metternich. This palace is a large, square, white building of oriental ornamentation and architecture, with a courtyard in the center, where we were received by the Khedive and his suite. A fountain was playing in the middle of the courtyard of marble, surrounded by palmettos and plants of every description. A band of Turkish musicians were seated cross-legged in one of the corners playing on their weird instruments, and making what they seemed to think was music. We sat in low basket-chairs, our feet resting on the richest of oriental rugs, and admired the graceful movements of the dancing-girls, who had not more space than an ordinary square rug to dance upon. There were also some jugglers, who performed the most marvelous and incomprehensible tricks with only an apparently transparent basket, from which they produced every imaginable object.

Coffee *à la Turque* was served in small cups with their silver filigree undercup, and Turkish paste flavored with attar of roses, and nauseatingly sweet, was passed about, with a glass of water to wash it down. Also cigarettes of every description were lavishly strewn on all the little tables, and hovering about us all the time were the thin-legged, turbaned black menials with baggy silk trousers and bright silk sashes.

Everything was so Oriental that, had I stayed there a little longer, I should not have been surprised to see myself sitting cross-legged on a divan smoking a *narghile*. I said as much as this to the Khedive, who said, in his funny pigeon-French-English, "Alas! Were it so!"

I cast my eyes down and put on my *sainte-ni-touche*

air, which at times I can assume, and as I looked at his Highness's dusky suite, who did not look over and above immaculate, in spite of the Mussulman's Mussulmania for washing, I thanked my stars that it "were not so."

The interpreter who was on duty said to Prince Metternich: "Mussulmans drink no wine, nor does the Prophet allow them to eat off silver. Therefore, to ease our consciences" (he said, *mettre nos consciences à couvert*), "we tell them that the silver plates on which they eat are *iron* plated with silver. They think the forks are also iron, otherwise they would eat with their fingers."

The interpreter added that Mussulmans did not think the Parisian newspapers very interesting, because they contained so few crimes and no murders worth mentioning. What an insight this gives of the condition of their country and the tenor of their papers!

We took our leave of the amiable Khedive, who expressed the hope that we would soon meet again.

Before his departure from Paris there came a package with the card of one of his gentlemen, begging me, *de la part de Monseigneur*, to accept the "accompanying souvenir." The package contained two enameled bracelets of the finest oriental work in red-and-green, studded with emeralds. He sent an equally gorgeous brooch to the Princess Metternich.

PARIS, *June, 1867.*

DEAR M.,—I must write you about something amusing which happened to-day. Prince Oscar was most desirous of seeing Delsarte, having heard him so much spoken of. I promised to try to arrange an interview, and wrote to Delsarte to ask him to come to meet the Prince at our house. I received this characteristic answer, "I have no time to make visits. If his Highness will come to see me I shall be pleased," and mentioned a day and an hour. Prince Oscar, Monsieur Dué, the Swedish secretary, Mademoiselle W——, and I went at the appointed time, mounted Delsarte's tiresome stairs, and waited patiently in his salon while he finished a lesson.

Monsieur Dué was very indignant at this *sans-gêne,* and apologized for Delsarte's want of courtesy; but the Prince did not mind, and occupied himself with looking at Delsarte's old poetry-books and albums.

Finally Delsarte entered and graciously received his royal visitor. The Prince was most affable and listened to Delsarte's fantastic theories, pretending to be interested in the explanation of the cartoons, and began to discuss the art of teaching, which exasperated Delsarte to the verge of impoliteness.

Prince Oscar offered to sing a Swedish song, a very simple peasant song, which he sang very well, I thought. The Swedish language is lovely for singing, almost as good as Italian. We looked for some words of praise; but Delsarte, adopting regency manners, which he can on occasions, said, in a most insinuating voice: "Your Highness is destined to become a king, one of these days. Is it not so?"

"Yes," answered the Prince, wondering what was coming next.

"You will have great responsibilities and a great deal to occupy your mind?"

"Without doubt."

"You will not have time to devote yourself to art?"
"I fear not."

"*Eh bien!*" said Delsarte, and we expected pearls
to drop from his mouth, "*eh bien!* If ever I am
fortunate enough to visit your country, I hope you will
allow me to pay my most humble respects to you."

"How horribly impolite," said the indignant Monsieur
Dué. "He ought to have his ears boxed!"

Prince Oscar took it quite kindly, and, giving Delsarte a clap on his back which I am sure made his
shoulders twinge, said: "You are right; I shall have
other things to think of. There"—pointing to diagram
six on the wall, depicting horror, with open mouth and
gaping eyes—"is the expression I shall have when I
think of music and music-teachers."

Delsarte, feeling that he had overstepped the mark,
said, "Perhaps, *mon Prince*, you will sing something
in French for me."

Prince Oscar, drawing himself up his whole six feet
and four, glanced down at little Delsarte and said,
"*Mon cher Monsieur*, have you ever read the English
poets?"

Delsarte looked unutterable things; I blushed for
my teacher.

"When I come again to Paris," the Prince continued,
"I will come to see you. Adieu!" and left without
further ceremony.

We followed him down the slippery stairs in silence.

Prince Oscar thought this little episode a great joke,
and repeated it to many people.

That same evening there was a *soirée musicale* given
for him by the Minister of Foreign Affairs (Marquis de

Moustier). The Prince was begged to sing, which he did three or four times. Every one was delighted to hear the Swedish songs. Ambroise Thomas, who was there, said that he thought they were exquisite, especially the peasant song, which he had introduced into his new opera of "Hamlet." The Prince and I sang the duet, "I Rosens duft." He was the lion of the evening, and I think that he was very pleased. I hoped that he had forgotten the unpleasant incident of the morning and Delsarte, of whom Monsieur Dué cleverly remarked, "Qui s'y frotte s'y pique—"

PARIS, *July, 1867.*

The distribution of prizes for the Exposition took place last Thursday at the Palais de l'Industrie. It was a magnificent affair and a very hot one. You may imagine what the heat and glare must have been at two o'clock in the afternoon on a hot July day. I was glad that I was not old and wrinkled, for every imperfection shone with magnified intensity.

There was a vast platform erected in the middle of the building, which was covered with a red carpet, and over which hung an enormous canopy of red velvet and curtains of velvet with the eagle of Napoleon. The Emperor and Empress sat, of course, in the center, and on each side were the foreign sovereigns; behind them were their suites and the Imperial family. The diplomatic corps had their places on the right of the tribune.

The gentlemen, splendid in their gala uniforms, were covered with decorations, and all the ladies present were *en grande toilette* and low-necked, and displayed every jewel they possessed.

The building, huge as it was, was packed full, every available seat occupied.

The Prince Imperial distributed the prizes. He looked very dignified when he handed the victors their different medals, accompanying each gift with his sweet and winning smile.

When Count Zichy, of Hungary, mounted the steps of the throne to receive his medal (he got a prize for his Hungarian wines) there was a general murmur of admiration, and I must say that he did look gorgeous in his national costume, which is a most striking one. He had on all his famous turquoises. His mantle and coat underneath, and everything except his top-boots, were encrusted with turquoises, some of them as big as hens' eggs. They say, when he appears on a gala occasion in his country, his horse's trappings and saddle are covered with turquoises.

The Sultan sat on the right of the Empress. You never saw anything half as splendid! A shopful of jewelry could not compare to him. He had a *collier* of pearls which might have made a Cleopatra green with jealousy. He had an enormous diamond which held the high aigrette in place on his fez and the Great Mogul (I was so told) fastened on his breast. His costume was magnificent, and his sabre—which I suppose has cut off a head or so—was a blaze of jewels. He was the *point de mire* of all eyes; especially when the rays of the sun caught the rays of his diamonds he blazed like the sun itself. The sun did all it could in the way of blazing that day. I know that I never felt anything

175

like the heat in that gigantic hot-house, the sun pouring through each pane of glass and nothing to protect one against it. I felt like an exotic flower unfolding its petals.

It was a very pretty little scene, and I think that every one was impressed when the Prince Imperial went toward the King of Holland to hand him a medal (probably for Dutch cheese). The tall, stately King rose from his seat, and on receiving it bowed deeply with great ceremony. The Prince made a respectful and graceful bow in response, then the King stooped down and kissed his cheek.

I was tremendously interested when the American exhibitors came forward; there were many of them, quite a procession. They looked very distinguished in their simple dress-coats, without any decorations. I was so glad.

When it was all over it was delightful to get out into the fresh air, even if we had to stand and wait patiently about like Mary's little lamb until the carriage did appear, for we had either to wait or to worm our way, risking horses' tails and hoofs through the surging crowd of bedecked men and women, who were all clamoring for their servants and carriages.

The coachmen were swearing and shouting as only French coachmen can do on such occasions as this. The line of carriages reached almost the whole way down the Champs Élysées. We finally did find ours, and I was glad to seat myself in it. I had had the forethought to put my hat and mantle in, as we intended to drive out to Petit Val for dinner. I put my hat over my tiara and my mantle on my bare shoulders, and enjoyed driving through the shady streets.

Prince Metternich came out here the other day. I had not seen him since the tragic death of Emperor Maximilian in Mexico. I never would have believed that he could be so affected as he seemed to be by this. He cried like a baby when he told us of the Emperor's last days, of his courage and fortitude. It seems that, just as he was going to be shot, he went to each of the men and gave them a twenty-franc gold piece, and said, "I beg you to shoot straight at my heart."

How dreadful it must have been!

Prince Metternich was most indignant at Rochefort, and says he can never forgive him because, in an article in *La Lanterne*, he called the royal martyr "the Arch-dupe." Auber said:

"You must not forget that Rochefort would rather sell his soul than lose an occasion to make a clever remark."

"Yes, I know," moaned the Prince. "But how can one be so cruel?"

"C'est un mauvais drôle," Auber answered (don't think Auber meant that Rochefort was droll; on the contrary, this is a neat way that the French have of calling a man the *worst kind of a scamp*), and added, "Rochefort's brains are made of *pétards*," which is the French for firecrackers.

Auber told many anecdotes. I fancy he wanted to cheer Prince Metternich up a little. One of them was that, on taking leave of the Emperor, the Shah had said:

"Sire, your Paris is wonderful, your palaces splendid, and your horses magnificent, but," waving his hand toward the mature but noble *dames d'honneur* with an expression of disapproval, "you must change all that." Imagine what their feelings would have been had they heard him.

PARIS, *August, 1867.*

DEAR M.,—I thought there would be a little rest for me after the distribution of prizes and before going to Dinard; but repose is a thing, it seems, that I am destined never to get.

Monday morning I received a letter from Princess Metternich saying that the Minister of Foreign Affairs had sent her his box for that evening, to hear Schneider in "La Belle Hélène," adding that Cora Pearl was to appear as Cupidon as an extra attraction, and asked if we would dine with them first, and go afterward to the theater.

I could not resist an invitation from these two delightful people, therefore we drove into Paris and reached the embassy at half-past six, the hour named for dinner.

Prince Metternich told us that he had had a visit in the afternoon from Monsieur Dué, the Swedish secretary, who had been on the verge of desperation on account of his not having been able to secure a suitable box for King Charles XIV. of Sweden, who arrived last night to spend a few days here. He wished to see Schneider in "La Belle Hélène." Monsieur Dué had gone to the Minister of Foreign Affairs and suggested that the Minister offer his box; but that had already been given to the Metternichs. When Prince Metternich was informed of this he did not hesitate to place the box in question at the King's disposal; but, not to disappoint the Princess and me, he had taken an ordinary box opposite. The King was already in his *loge* when we arrived. He is a large, handsome man with a full, black beard, and has a very pleasant face.

Between the first and second acts Monsieur Dué came to Prince Metternich and told him that the King desired to see him. Of course the Prince went directly, and returned delighted with the King's affability, and to our great surprise brought us a message from the King, asking us all to come to his box and join him, and proposing to send Monsieur Dué and his gentleman-in-waiting to take our places in our box.

We accepted with pleasure, and passed the rest of the evening in the charming society of the most amiable of kings. He said to me that "Oscar," as he called his brother (Prince Oscar, the hereditary Prince), had spoken about me and our singing the duet written by his brother, Prince Gustave, and asked how I managed about the Swedish words. I replied that Prince Oscar had taught them to me during the dinner preceding the singing.

"Could you understand the words?" he asked.

"No," I replied. "I only know that it was something about London and Emma."

The King laughed most heartily, and said, "I shall tell that to Oscar when I go home, and he will see how well you profited by his lessons."

We were all immensely amused at Cora Pearl's appearance; it was her début as an actress. I never saw any one look so sheepish as she did, in spite of her paint and powder and beautiful legs. She wore high-heeled slippers, so high that she could hardly walk, which made her even more awkward than she naturally was. She only had a few lines to sing, and this she did so badly that people nearly hissed her.

She was evidently engaged as a drawing-card; but the only thing she drew was ridicule on herself.

During the second act Lord Lyons came into the box. He had known the King before, and, having heard from the Minister of Foreign Affairs that the King was at the theater, went there to pay his respects. The King, noticing that he had a decoration on, said in French: "Please take that off; I am here incognito. To-morrow I shall be official; then you can put it on." So Lord Lyons took off his star and put it in his pocket. He wanted to go after the second act, but the King said: "Monsieur Dué has arranged a supper for us at *La Maison d'Or*. You must come also." Of course Lord Lyons did not refuse.

Monsieur Dué left the box in advance of the rest of us, in order to arrange everything before the King's arrival. The King called to him, as he opened the door, "Don't forget the *écrevisses à la Bordelaise;* I have been looking forward to them for a long time."

After the performance, with which the King was delighted (especially with Hortense Schneider's song, "Dis-moi, Vénus, pourquoi," etc.), we drove to the *Maison d'Or*, where we found Monsieur Dué awaiting us. We asked at what time the carriages should come back. He said: "Not before two o'clock. His Majesty never retires before." We were then shown into a salon, where the Princess Metternich and I were asked by the King to take off our hats. "It is so much more cozy," he said. So off our hats came. We had not been seated ten minutes when we heard some very loud talking and much discussion in the corridor outside. Lord Lyons, who was nearest the door, jumped up to see what the matter was, opened the door, and peeped out.

"Oh!" said he. "It is the Duke of Brunswick making a row; he is half-seas over!" The King turned to Monsieur Dué (the King does not speak English) and said, "What did Lord Lyons say?" Monsieur Dué's English did not go very far, but he translated into Swedish what he had understood Lord Lyons to say.

The King seemed very puzzled and, addressing Lord Lyons, said:

"Was not the Duke of Brunswick obliged to leave England for fear of being arrested?" Lord Lyons coughed discreetly, and the King went on: "If I remember rightly, the Duke, who was in the royal box, shot at and killed a *danseuse* who was on the stage! And did he not leave England in a balloon? It always seemed such an extraordinary thing. Was it true?" Lord Lyons cautiously answered that people had said all that; but it was some time ago, and added, diplomatically, that he had forgotten all the details.

"And I understood," said his Majesty, "that he can never go back there again."

"You are right. He cannot go back to England, your Majesty."

"Oh! don't Majesty me. To-night I am a simple bourgeois," the King interrupted, smilingly shaking his finger. "But tell me, how can the Duke dare return there now?"

"He does not dare," repeated Lord Lyons. "He can *never* go back."

"But," insisted the King, "my good Monsieur Dué says that he is on his way there at this moment."

Lord Lyons replied, "I think Monsieur Dué must be mistaken, for the Duke is out there in the corridor making all this [I am sure it was on his lips to say "devil of a row," but he politely said] *noise*."

Monsieur Dué then remarked, "Did I not hear you say that he was half way across the channel?"

"I certainly did not say *that*. What I did say was that he was 'half-seas over,' which is a slang expression we use in England instead of saying tipsy, or *dans les vignes du Seigneur*, so prettily put by the French.

The King laughed very much at this *quid pro quo* and, looking at Monsieur Dué, said, " I thought your English more up to the mark."

The King was immediately fired with a desire to see the famous Duke who had dared to cross the channel in a balloon rather than run the risk of being shut up in prison, and we all waited with impatience to see whether Lord Lyons's persuasive powers went so far as getting the Duke to show himself. Well, they did, and both the gentlemen came into the salon. The Duke bowed low and did not lose his balance. In fact, for a man half-seas over, I thought he looked as if he could get to the end of his journey without disgrace. He said, very politely, "I am afraid I have disturbed you, but this is the salon which has always been put aside for me every night, and I was surprised to learn that it was occupied."

The Duke is, or rather would have been, a very handsome man if he had not such watery eyes and such a weak mouth; and then he wore the funniest-looking wig I ever saw. It was made out of black (the blackest) sewing-silk and plastered down over his ears. I wonder if it was a disguise, or if he thought any one would ever really take it for his own hair.

The King was very nice to him, and did not seem in the least to mind his being *dans les vignes*. I fancy, from what Monsieur Dué said, that in Sweden people are used to see their friends *always* in *Seigneurial* vineyards—they never see them anywhere else! But he exaggerates, no doubt.

The King said to the Duke of Brunswick, "Will you not sup with us to-night?"

"I thank your Majesty, but I must crave permission to return, for I have some ladies supping with me, including the Cupidon of to-night."

"Tell her," said the King, "if she wears such high heels she will come to grief."

"It will not be the first time," answered the Duke, with a laugh. "But don't ask me to say anything like that to her; she would box my ears!" Seeing the waiter making signs to him, the Duke then made a profound bow and, stroking his sewing-silk locks, left us.

The universal verdict on him was *Quel crétin!*

We had a very pleasant supper, and a most unceremonious one, as much so as is possible where there is royalty.

The King said that he was going to be official all the next day, but that he would like to go to the Exposition. Prince Metternich proposed a cup of tea and the delicious hot rolls they turn out at the Vienna restaurant. The King was delighted to accept, and named the hour of half-past four in the afternoon. We were also bidden, for which I was much pleased. King Carl is the most delightful and fascinating of monarchs, and quite worthy to be his brother's brother. To-morrow he is going to be still more official, for he dines at the Tuileries, and there is a gala performance at the opera; Christine Nilsson is going to sing "Faust" with Nicolini and Faure.

To-morrow we leave for Dinard, where there will be no majesties nor Exposition; just plain bread and butter and Brittany cider, which is as hard as a relentless parent.

COMPIÈGNE, *November 27, 1868.*

When the inclosed invitation came my father-in-law wet-blanketed the whole thing, and I was broken-hearted. The Duke de Persigny, who happened to be at Petit Val at that moment, sympathized with me and tried to change the paternal mind; but the paternal mind was obdurate, and all pleadings were, alas! in vain.

MAISON   *Palais des Tuileries, le 2 9ᵇʳᵉ 1868.*
DE L'EMPEREUR

Premier Chambellan

Monsieur,

Par ordre de l'Empereur, j'ai l'honneur de vous prévenir que vous êtes invité, ainsi que Madame Ch. Moulton, à passer 9 jours au Palais de Compiègne, du 27 9ᵇʳᵉ au 5 décembre.

Des voitures de la Cour vous attendront le 27, à l'arrivée à Compiègne du train partant de Paris à 2 heures ½ pour vous conduire au Palais.

Agréez, Monsieur, l'assurance de ma considération très distinguée.

Le Premier Chambellan,
Vᵗᵉ de Laferrière.

Monsieur Ch. Moulton.

My father-in-law thought it cost too much—my toilettes, the necessary outlay, and especially the *pourboires*. He said that it was a lot of money, and added, in his most choice French, "Le jeu [he pronounced it 'jew'] ne valait pas la chandelle." He was right from his point of view, for he had none of the *jeu* and all of the *chandelle*. I pined and pouted the whole day, and considered myself the most down-trodden mortal in existence.

Imagine my delight, a few days later, to receive a second document, informing us that our names had been re-entered on the list, and that we were expected, all the same, on the 27th to stay nine days. At the same time there came a note from the Duke de Persigny, in which he said, "Their Majesties desired us particularly to come." And he added: "Tell your father-in-law that the question of pourboires has been settled now and forever. No more pourboires to be given nor taken at Compiègne."

Then Mr. M—— gave his consent, and I was blissfully happy.

It seems that the Emperor's attention had been called to the many very disagreeable articles in the newspapers on the subject of the extravagant *pourboires* exacted at Compiègne. The Emperor was very much annoyed, and gave immediate orders to suppress this system, which had been going on for years without his knowledge.

Last night we stayed in Paris, to be ready at half-past two this afternoon. To describe our departure, arrival, and reception would only be to repeat what I have already written last year. Among the fifty or sixty guests there were many who were here then. In addition there are Duke d'Albe, with his daughters; Baron Beyens, the Belgian Minister; Mr. Mallet, of the English Embassy; Mr. Dué, of the Swedish Legation; the poet, Prosper Mérimée; and many, of course, I do not know.

Singularly enough, we were shown into the same apartment we had before, which made us feel quite at home. We found tea, chocolate, and cakes on the table, of which I partook with enthusiasm, and then enjoyed an hour's rest before dressing for dinner.

We met at seven o'clock in the *Salle des Fêtes*, the only room in this huge château large enough to contain all the party here (I suppose there must be one hundred and twenty people), for which reason it serves both as reception and ballroom.

The Empress looked superb in a gown of an exquisite shade of lilac; she wore her beautiful pearls and a tiara of diamonds and pearls. When she approached me she held out her hand, and said she was very glad to see me. The Emperor was kind and gracious, as usual.

The Baron Gourgaud was told to take me in to dinner, and we followed the procession to the dining-room, passing the *Cent Gardes*, who looked like an avenue of blue and glittering trees. The Baron Gourgaud and I are neighbors in the country, their place, La Grange, being not far from Petit Val. His conversation is not absorbing; but as he knows he is dull he does not pretend to be anything else. I was thankful for this, as I felt that I did not need to make the slightest effort to entertain him.

I cast my eyes round the table, and if I had not known that this was *la série amusante* I should never have guessed it—every one seemed so spiritless and "sans le moindre entrain," as my neighbor remarked.

No excitement this evening but the dance. Waldteufel is suppressed! They say that the Emperor, who has a horror of publicity in private life, was very displeased last year by the indiscretions and personal anecdotes, and especially the caricatures made by Gustave Doré, which appeared in the *Figaro*. The Emperor vowed that no outsiders should be invited again; therefore poor Waldteufel has to pay *les pots cassés*, and we must make our own music.

Looking for a substitute for Waldteufel, a clever chamberlain discovered the "Debain piano" (mechanical piano).

You remember I had one in my youth. How I loved it! How I used to love to grind out all the beautiful music those ugly boxes contained! And how I used to wonder that those common wooden slides could reproduce such perfect imitations of the real thing.

I was so glad to see one again, and envied the perspiring chamberlain, who looked bored to extinction having to turn the crank, instead of joining the dance and turning the heads of the ladies. It took two of them to manage the complexities of the piano, and as neither possessed a musical turn of the wrist, and as neither had the remotest idea of time or measure, it was very hard for us poor dancers!

When one of the martyrs wanted to explain to the other what to do he would stop and forget to turn the crank. The dancers were thus obliged to pause, one foot in the air, not knowing when to put it down, and when they did put it down they did not fall in measure, and had to commence all over again. This spasmodic waltzing almost made us crazy. As for me, I could not bear it any longer. No chariot nor horses could have kept me away from that piano; to feel again (after so many years) the delight of playing it! And then I wanted to show how it should be played; so I went to the piano and took the crank out of the tired hands of the chamberlain and ground out a whole dance.

I flatter myself that the dancers enjoyed at least this one. His Majesty walked up to the piano while I was playing and said, "But, Madame, you will tire yourself; you really must stop and let some one take your place."

I replied: "If your Majesty only knew what a pleasure it is for me to play this piano! I had one like it when I was a little girl, and have never seen one since."

"Are these pianos not something quite new?" he asked. "I was told that they were the latest invention."

"They may be," I answered, "the latest improvement on an old invention; but the pianos are older than I am."

"That," answered the Emperor, smilingly, "does not make them very old."

He called one of the chamberlains, and I reluctantly gave up my place. The Count d'Amelot was summoned, and as we were about to waltz off the Emperor said, "If I danced, I should like to dance with you myself; but I do not dance."

"Then," I said, "I must dance without you."

He laughed: "Vous avez toujours la réplique," and stood there watching us with those peculiar eyes of his.

I never received so many compliments on pianoplaying as I did to-night.

188

Here is the list of my dresses (the cause of so much grumbling):

MORNING COSTUMES. Dark-blue poplin, trimmed with plush of the same color, toque, muff to match.
Black velvet, trimmed with braid, sable hat, sable tippet and muff.
Brown cloth, trimmed with bands of sealskin, coat, hat, muff to match.
Purple plush, trimmed with bands of pheasant feathers, coat, hat to match.
Gray velvet, trimmed with chinchilla, chinchilla hat, muff and coat.
Green cloth (hunting costume).
Traveling suit, dark-blue cloth cloak.

EVENING DRESSES. Light green tulle, embroidered in silver, and for my locks, what they call *une fantaisie.*
White tulle, embroidered with gold wheat ears.
Light-gray satin, quite plain, with only Brussels lace flounces.
Deep pink tulle, with satin ruchings and a lovely sash of lilac ribbon.
Black lace over white tulle, with green velvet twisted bows.
Light-blue tulle with Valenciennes.

AFTERNOON GOWNS. Lilac faille.
Light café au lait with trimmings of the same.
Green faille faced with blue and a red Charlotte Corday sash (Worth's last gasp).
A red faille, quite plain.
Gray faille with light-blue facings.

Do you not think there is enough to last me as long as I live?

SUNDAY, *November 28th.*

The mass is at ten o'clock on Sunday, and one meets in the grand salon before going to the chapel.

Madame de Gallifet and I, being Protestants, were

not expected; but, as we wanted to go, we decided to don a black lace veil and follow the others.

The chapel is not large, but it is very richly decorated.

The Empress sat in a tribune facing the altar with a chosen few and her *dames d'honneur*.

The Emperor was not present.

It seemed to me that the mass was very hurried and curtailed. The chorus boys swung their censers nonchalantly, as though they were fanning themselves; probably they were impatient for their breakfast.

The curé did not preach any sermon; he only made an exhortation against the pomps and vanities of this wicked world, and told us that we had better be prepared for death, as it might come at any moment. This was nothing new; any one could have said it. He advised us to have our lamps trimmed, for, when our time came we would be cut down like grass and gathered in the garners. Perhaps he meant we ought to make our hay while the sun was shining. I wondered to myself, if some of those old gentlemen sinners who had sown so liberally would not be gathered in as oats. The curé was going on to say that we should not indulge too freely in the good things of this world; but pulled himself up in time, remembering, no doubt, that he was going to breakfast, as he did every Sunday, at the Imperial board and partake of its luxuries.

And before we knew it the mass was finished.

When we returned to the salon it was eleven o'clock, and every one was assembled for *déjeuner*.

The Marquis d'Aoust happened to sit next to me at table (I say happened, but I believe he manœuvered so as to do so), and, taking me unawares between two

IN THE COURTS OF MEMORY

mouthfuls of *truites saumonées*, decoyed me into accept-
ing a stupendous proposition of his, which was to help
him to get up an operetta which he had had the courage to compose. He said the idea had just come into
his head; but I thought, for an impromptu idea, it was
rather a ripe one, as he had brought the music with him,
and had already picked out those he thought could help,
and checked them off on his lean fingers. He said the
operetta had one act only, which I thought was fortunate, and that it needed only four actors, which I thought
was still more fortunate.

The next thing to be done, he said, was to get the
singers' consent. I should have said it was the first
thing to be done; but he was so bubbling over with enthusiasm that he was sure every one would jump at
the chance of taking part.

He seized the first moment after their Majesties had
retired to pounce upon those he had selected, and having
obtained their consent he proposed a walk in the long,
so-called Treille or Berceau. Napoleon I. built this
walk, which is one thousand meters in length and reaches
to the edge of the forest, for the Queen Marie Louise.
I must say I pitied her toes if she walked there often
on as cold a day as to-day; I know mine ached as we
paced to and fro while the Marquis explained the
operetta. It was really too cold to stay out-of-doors,
and we turned back to the little salon, called the *Salon
Japonais*, to finish the séance there.

"What part am I to take?" asked Prince Metternich.

As he could not be anything else, he accepted the
rôle of prompter, and promised all the help he could give.

When I went to the Empress's tea this afternoon I took those questions Aunt M—— sent me from America. You know them. You have to write what your favorite virtues are, and if you were not yourself, who you would like to be, and so forth.

I was glad to have something new and original which might amuse people. The Empress, seeing the papers in my hand, asked me what they were. I told her that they were some questions: a new intellectual pastime just invented in America.

"Do they invent intellectual pastimes in America?" she asked, looking at me with a smile. "I thought they only invented money-making."

"They do that, too," I replied; "but they have also invented these questions, which probe the mind to the marrow and unveil the soul."

She laughed and said, "Do you wish me to unveil my soul, *comme cela, à l'improviste?*"

I answered: "Perhaps your Majesty will look at them at your leisure. I hardly dare to ask the Emperor; but if he would also look at them I should be so happy. "

"Leave them with me, and to-morrow we will see; in any case my soul is not prepared to-day."

So I left the papers with her.

It is the fashion this year for ladies to wear lockets on a black-velvet ribbon around their necks. The more lockets you can collect and wear, the finer you are. Each locket represents an event, such as a birthday, a bet, an anniversary of any kind, and so forth. Any excuse is good for the sending of a locket. The Empress had seventeen beautiful ones to-day (I counted them). They have a rather cannibalish look, I think.

A. Quelle qualité donnez vous la...

Quelle sont vos auteurs favo...

Quelle sont vos occupations f...

Que voudriez vous être?

Quelles personnes de l'histoir...

Pour quelles fautes avez-vous...

préférence ?
                    la persévérance
: ?   de Mérimée

oiles ? faire des châteaux en
                                    Espagne

                Napoléon III

détestez vous le plus ? -
                    Mazarin
plus d'indulgence ?
        La Gourmandise

            P. Mérimée

Is it not in Hayti (or in which country is it?) that the black citizens wear their rivals' teeth as trophies on their black necks?

Who should offer me his arm for dinner to-night but Prosper Mérimée, the lion of lions, the pampered poet, who entrances all those who listen to him whenever he opens his lips.

He looks more like an Englishman than a Frenchman; he is quite old, and I fancy older than he looks (he may be fifty). He is tall and *dégagé*, with a nice smile and pleasant eyes, though sometimes he gives you a sharp and suspicious glance. He speaks English very well. I told him (stretching a point) that I had never heard a foreigner speak such good English as he did.

He replied, without a blush: "I ought to speak it well. I learned it when I was a child." And he added, complacently, "I can even write better than I speak."

I asked him if he could write poetry in English.

He answered: "I do not think I could. My English goes just so far and no farther. I have what is strictly necessary, but not what is superfluous." ("J'ai, le stricte nécessaire, mais pas le superflu.")

"To make rhymes," said I, "I should think one would have to know every word in the dictionary."

"Oh!" he said, "I don't attempt rhymes; they are far beyond me."

When he talks French he is perfectly delightful. He creates the funniest words, and gives such an original turn to his phrases that you are—at least I was—on the *qui vive* not to lose anything he said. It is like listening to a person who, improvising on the piano, makes unexpected and subtle modulations which you hate to have escape you.

He told me he had been in correspondence with an English lady for over thirty years.

"Were you in love with her, that you wrote to her all those years?" I inquired.

"I was in love with her letters," he replied. "They were the cleverest things I ever read—full of wit and humor."

"Was she in love with you or only with your letters?" I was tactless enough to ask.

"How can you ask?" he said. I wondered myself how I could have asked so indiscreet a question.

"Did she write in English, and did you write in French?"

"Yes, she wrote in English," he answered, and looked bored.

"Is she dead?" I asked, getting bolder and bolder; but he would not talk any more about this clever lady, and we drifted into other channels of conversation. Too bad! I would have liked to have known if the lady was still living.

I wish I could remember all the pearls which fell from his lips; but alas! one cannot, like Cleopatra, digest pearls. But I do remember one thing he said, which was, "If I should define the difference between men and women, I should say, 'Que les hommes valent plus, mais que les femmes valent mieux.'"

I wondered if this was one of the pearls he let drop in his letters to the wonderful English *bas-bleu*.

In the evening we danced to the waltzes of the Debain, and were obliged to tread a very spasmodic measure. The Prince Imperial asked me for a polka, and I had to clutch his shoulder with one hand and beat time with the other on his arm to keep any kind of rhythm in his evolutions. It is nice to see him circulating about and chatting with all the ladies.

November 29th.

A message came to my room this morning, to the effect that I was to sit next to the Emperor. I suppose they thought it best to let me know in time, in case I should go wandering off sight-seeing, like last year; but no danger! Once caught, twice warned, as the saying is.

Therefore, when we descended to the grand salon, I knew what my fate was to be. The Duc de Sesto, who had recently married the widow of the Duc de Morny, gave me his arm and deposited me at the side of his Majesty.

The Emperor was in the most delightful spirits, and full of *bonhomie* and fun. Glancing across the table at a certain diplomat (Baron F——), he said, "I never knew a person more impervious to a joke than that gentleman is." And then he went on to say that once he had told the Baron the old time-worn joke which any child can understand.

(You have heard it many times, I am sure, dear mama.)

One begins by saying, "Vous me permettez de vous tutoyer (You will permit me to use the thee and thou)?" And then one says, "Pourquoi aimes-tu la chicorée (Why dost thou like chicory)?" To which the answer is, "Parce qu'elle est amère (ta mère) (Because it is 'bitter' or 'your mother')."

But I had better tell the story in the Emperor's own language:

"The Baron was making a call upon the Duchess de Bassano, one of the ladies-in-waiting of the Empress, a severe and formal person, as you know, and in deep mourning for her mother. He wished to make himself agreeable and told her this story, saying that it was the most amusing thing he had ever heard. But he forgot to ask her permission to use the thee and thou, and said, point-blank, 'Pourquoi aimes-tu la salade?' The Duchess did not understand, and he, bursting out laughing, continued, without waiting for her to speak, 'Parce qu'elle est ta mère.' The Duchess arose, indignant. 'Monsieur, I beg you cease. My poor mother died three months ago. I am still wearing mourning for her!' With which she burst into tears and left the room.

"The Baron, nothing daunted, tried a second time to relate this anecdote, this time addressing Baronne Pierres, another of the *dames d'honneur*, entirely forgetting to use the thee and thou. 'Madame, pourquoi aimez-vous la salade?' Naturally she had not the slightest idea what he meant, and he rejoined triumphantly, 'Parce qu'elle est Madame votre mère.' What annoys me beyond measure," continued the Emperor, "is that he goes on telling the anecdote, saying, 'The Emperor told it to me.'"

The Emperor laughed heartily, and I did, too. Then he told me another amusing thing:

At a ball at the Tuileries he said to a young American whose father he had met: "J'ai connu votre père en Amérique. Est-ce qu'il vit encore?" And the young man, embarrassed and confused, answered, "Non, sire;

pas encore." "It is so good," the Emperor said, "to have a laugh, especially to-day. All the afternoon I shall be plunged in affairs of state."

I did not forget to tell the Emperor that Delsarte was wildly excited on receiving the present his Majesty had sent him last year. I wandered considerably from the truth, as, in reality, Delsarte, who is not Napoleonic in his politics, had said when I gave it to him, "Comment! c'est Badinguet qui m'envoit cela. Que veut-il que j'en fasse?" with a dark frown. But I noticed he smoked *le bon tabac*, all the same; and I am sure he said (even to his best friend), "Tu n'en auras pas."

Of course the Emperor had quite forgotten that such a person as Delsarte had ever existed.

This was a perfectly delightful *déjeuner*, and I shall never forget it.

The numerous chamberlains were busy arranging the different amusements for the guests, putting horses, carriages, shooting, and excursions at their disposal; but we, unlucky ones, were in duty bound to abide by the Marquis, who had now completed his troupe to his satisfaction. He had enticed the two young Mesdemoiselles Albe and two of their admirers to undertake the chorus; he was very grateful to them, as otherwise it would have had to be suppressed—perhaps the best thing that could have happened to it.

The Princess Metternich asked us to come to their salon (they have the beautiful apartments called *les appartements d'Apollon*), in order that we could try the music with the piano which her husband had hired, as usual, for his stay at Compiègne, and which he had put at the disposition of the Marquis.

The Marquis was in ecstasy, and capered about to collect us; and at last we found ourselves stranded with the manuscript and its master, who was overjoyed to embark us on this shaky craft. He put himself at the piano, played the score from beginning to end, not sparing us a single bar. My heart sank when I heard it; it was worse than I thought, and the plot was even worse than the music—naïf and banal beyond words.

A lord of the manor (Vicomte Vaufreland, basso) makes love to a humble village maiden (myself, soprano); the lady of the manor (Madame Conneau, contralto) becomes jealous and makes a scene with her husband; the friend and adviser (Count d'Espeuilles, tenor) steps in and takes his friend's part and kindly says that it was he who had loved the village maiden. The wife is satisfied, and everything ends beautifully.

It would be very uphill work for the poor Marquis and I wondered if he would really have the patience to go on with it, after realizing how unmusical the men were. D'Espeuilles stood behind the Marquis's bald head and reached over to put his finger on the note he wanted to sing, and then banged on that, until, after singing every note in the scale, he finally fixed it in his brain.

Could anything be more despairing?

Our next thought naturally was our costumes.

The operetta was laid in the time of Louis XV.

Would we be able to find anything in the various trunks in the gallery next to the theater?

When we went there we found everything we did not want—costumes, odds and ends of all sorts, which belonged to all other periods than Louis XV. The contents of the trunks were in a very chaotic state; each article which once had formed one of a complete costume was without its better half; the unprincipled things had meandered off and got mixed up in other sets.

To be sure, there was a Louis XV. coat, with embroidered pockets and satin-lined coat-tails, but nothing more suitable for *culottes* could be found than a pair of redplush breeches, trimmed with lace (I think one calls them "trunk hose"), of Henry II.'s time.

When they were urged upon the Vicomte, he absolutely refused them, saying he would not mix up epochs like that, and, after pulling over everything, he decided to send to Paris for a complete costume.

Count d'Espeuilles was less difficult to satisfy, and was contented with a black-velvet Hamlet costume, with a plumed hat, which suited no epoch at all, but suited his style of beauty.

Madame C—— thought her maid might arrange out of a ball-dress some sort of attire; with powdered hair, paint, and patches, she could represent the lady of the manor very well. My Tyrolean dress of last year would do quite nicely for me, when my maid had put the customary bows on the traditional apron.

We all separated, carrying our carefully written rôles under our arms, and in the worst of tempers.

Monsieur Dué was my neighbor at dinner. He is very musical, and was much interested in hearing about the operetta. He does not think the Marquis has any talent; neither do I! But I don't wish to give any opinion on the poor little struggling operetta before it has lived its day, and then I am sure it will die its natural death.

Monsieur Dué has composed some very pretty things for the piano, which he plays on the slightest encouragement.

Nothing else was talked of in the evening but the operetta, and the Marquis was in the seventh heaven of delight.

Their Majesties were told of the Marquis's interesting intention. I could see, across the room, that the Empress knew that I was going to take part, for she looked over toward me, nodding her head and smiling at me.

There was some dancing for an hour, when one of the chamberlains came up and said to me that the Empress would be pleased if I would sing some of my American songs. I was delighted, and went directly into the *salle de musique*, and when the others had come in, I sat down at the piano and accompanied myself in the few negro songs I knew. I sang "Suwanee River," "Shoo-fly," and "Good-by, Johnny, come back to your own chickabiddy." Then I sang a song of Prince Metternich's, called, "Bonsoir, Marguerite," which he accompanied. I finished, of course, with "Beware!" which Charles accompanied.

The Emperor came up to me and asked, "What does chickabiddy mean?"

I answered, "'Come back soon to your own chickabiddy' means 'Reviens bientôt à ta chérie,'" which apparently satisfied him.

Their Majesties thanked me with effusion, and were very gracious.

The Emperor himself brought a cup of tea to me, a very unusual thing for him to do, and I fancy a great compliment, saying, "This is for our chicka-biddy!"

Their Majesties bowed in leaving the room; every one made a deep reverence, and we retired to our apartments.

November 30th.

The old, pompous, ponderous diplomat (what am I saying?)—I should have said, "the very distinguished diplomat"—the same one the Emperor told me yesterday was so impervious to a joke, honored me by giving me his baronial arm for *déjeuner*. I can't imagine why he did it, unless it were to get a lesson in English gratis, of which he was sadly in need. He struck me as being very masterful and weighed down with the mighty affairs of his tiny little kingdom. I was duly impressed, and never felt so subdued in all my life, which I suppose was the effect he wished to produce on me.

We sat like two gravestones, only waiting for an epitaph. Suddenly he muttered (as if such an immense idea was too great for him to keep to himself), "Diplomacy, Madame, is a dog's business." ("La diplomatie est un métier de chien.")

I ventured to ask, "Is it because one is attached to a post?"

He gave me such a withering look that I wished I had never made this silly remark.

All the same, he unbent a little and, with a dismal twinkle in his eye, his face brightening, and launching into frivolity, said: "The Emperor told me something very funny the other day. (I knew what was coming.)

He asked me why I liked salad." Turning to me he said, "Can you guess the answer?"

I had many ready for him; but I refrained and only said, "No, what was it?"

"Parce qu'elle était ma mère!" he replied, and laughed immoderately, until such a fit of coughing set in that I thought there would not be a button left on him. When he had finished exploding he said, "Did you understand the 'choke'?"

If I had not understood the "choke," I understood the choking, and I thought any more jokes like this would be the end of him then and there.

I answered quite seriously, "I think I would understand better, if I knew what sort of salad his Majesty meant."

He shook his head and said he did not think it made any difference what sort of salad it was. And we became tombstones again.

I could hardly wait till we returned to the salon, I was so impatient to tell the Emperor of the Baron's latest version.

As his Majesty was near me, talking to some lady during the *cercle*, I stepped forward so as to attract his attention.

He soon moved toward me, and I, against all the rules of etiquette, was the first to speak.

"Your Majesty," said I, "I sat next to the Baron at breakfast and was not spared the salad problem."

"How did he have it this time?" asked the Emperor.

"This time, your Majesty, he had it that you had said he liked salad because it was his mother."

The Emperor burst out laughing and said, "He is hopeless."

It would seem as if Fate had chosen the Baron to be the butt of all the *plaisanteries* to-day.

Later in the afternoon we drove in *chars-à-bancs* to St. Corneille, a lovely excursion through the woods. The carriages spun along over the smooth roads, the postilions cracked their whips and tooted their horns, the air was cold and deliciously invigorating, and we were the gayest party imaginable. One would have thought that even the worst grumbler would have been put in good spirits by these circumstances; but no! our distinguished diplomat was silent and sullen, resenting all fun and nonsense. No wonder that all conspired together to tease him.

At St. Corneille there are some beautiful ruins of an old abbey and an old Roman camp. When we came to the "Fontaine des Miracles" Mr. Mallet (of the English embassy) pulled out of his pocket a Baedeker and read in a low tone to those about him what was said about the miracles of the fountain. The Marquis de Gallifet, not wishing any amusement to take place without helping it on and adding some touches of his own, thereupon interposed in a stage whisper (evidently intended to be heard by the Baron), "The waters of this fountain are supposed to remove [then raising his voice] barrenness."

"Baroness who?" asked the diplomat, who was now all alert.

Mr. Mallet, to our amazement (who ever could have imagined him so jocose), said quite gravely, "Probably the wife of the barren fig-tree."

"Ah!" said the Baron, "I don't know them," thus snubbing all the fig-trees.

"A very old family," said Mallet, "mentioned in the Bible."

This seemed to stagger our friend, who evidently prided himself on knowing every family worth knowing. The Marquis de Gallifet, seeing his chance, hurried to tell the story of the d'Albe family, which the crestfallen Baron drank in with open mouth and swallowed whole. As the Duke d'Albe was there himself, listening attentively and smiling, the story must have been true! The Marquis de Gallifet said, when Noah was ready to depart in the ark he saw a man swimming for dear life toward the boat, waving something in the air. Noah called out to him:

"Don't ask to be taken in. We can't carry any more passengers, we are already too full."

The man answered, "I don't want to be taken in; I don't care for myself; but, pray, save the papers of the family."

The Baron looked very grave, and turning to the Duke asked, in an extremely solemn tone, "Is this really true?"

"Perfectly," answered the Duke, without moving a muscle. "The saying, 'Après moi le déluge,' originated in our family; but we say, 'Nous d'abord, et *puis* le déluge!'"

"How interesting!" said the Baron.

Then Monsieur Dué, not wishing to be outdone, said *his* family was as old (if not older), having taken the name of Dué from the dove [in Swedish "dué" means dove] which carried the olive-branch to the ark.

By this time the poor Baron, utterly staggered and bewildered in presence of such a concourse of ancient nobility, did not know on which leg to stand. How could he and his family ever hold up their heads again?

We returned to Compiègne by St. Périne, where there was a most enchanting view, and drove straight through a long avenue and entered *La cour d'honneur*. It was almost half-past five when we reached our rooms.

I thought I had had enough of fossils and ruins for one day, from breakfast onward, so when old General Changarnier came to offer me his arm for dinner I said to myself, "This is the climax!"

But, on the contrary (the unexpected always arrives), he was so delightful and genial that my heart was warmed through, which, indeed, it needed, after the ice-chest I had had for *déjeuner*. He did not try to raise me to his level, but simply let himself down to mine, and talked small talk so youthfully that I felt we were about the same age. He was a charming man.

Monsieur de Laferrière arranged a sort of ball for this evening. There was an unusual flutter, for everything was going to be extra fine, and we put on our prettiest dresses. Programmes with dangling pencils were lavished on us, on which regular dances were set down—quadrilles, waltzes, polkas, and lancers.

The usual *cercle* was curtailed, in view of the ball.

The chamberlains, to facilitate matters, had arranged the boxes of music for the mechanical piano very methodically on a table, so there should be no mistakes or fumbling with the slides.

The ladies were so agitated, fearing they would not get any partners, that they made very transparent efforts to attract the attention of the gentlemen. One would have thought they had never been to a ball in all their lives. The gentlemen, just as agitated, rushed about to secure the ladies, whom they could have had *without* the rushing on other evenings. The Empress looked exquisitely beautiful. The Emperor stood in the doorway, smiling at this whirlwind of gaiety and animation. The Prince Imperial danced untiringly with all the ladies.

Flowers were distributed about, and, wonder of wonders! ices were served at intervals, as if it were a real ball. My old general was chivalry itself. He even engaged a partner for the lancers, and skipped about telling everybody he did not know how to dance them, which was unnecessary, as one could see for oneself later.

There are four kinds of people in society:

Those who know the lancers.

Those who don't know the lancers.

Those who know the lancers and say they don't.

Those who don't know the lancers and say they do.

My old and venerable warrior belonged to class number two, and really did not know the lancers, but tripped about pleasantly and let others guide him. When we came to the *grande chaine* he was completely intoxicated with his success. Every eye was on him. Every one was occupied with his doings, and his alone. All the ladies were pulling him first one way and then the other, trying to confuse him by getting him into another set, until he found himself quite at the other end of the room, still being pulled about and twirled in every direction, never knowing where he was or when he was going to stop. At last, utterly exhausted and confused, he stopped short and placed himself in the middle of the ballroom, delighted to be the center of all eyes and to make this effective *finale*. But no one could compare with him when he made his Louis-Quinze reverence; the younger men had to acknowledge that he scored a point there, and he might well be proud of himself. All this made us very gay, and almost boisterous. Never before had the evening finished with such a burst of merriment, and we all retired, agreeing that the ball had been a great success, and that Monsieur de Laferrière could sleep on his laurels as soundly as we intended to sleep on our pillows.

December 1st.

Count Niewekerke offered me his arm for *déjeuner* this morning. He is a Dutchman (*Hollandais* sounds better) by birth, but he lives in Paris. As he is the greatest authority on art there, the Emperor has made him Count and Director of the Galerie du Louvre. He is very handsome, tall, and commanding, and has, besides other enviable qualities, the reputation of being the great lady-killer *par excellence*.

As we stood there together the Empress passed by us. She held up her finger warningly, saying, "Take care! Beware! He is a very dangerous person, *un vrai mangeur de cœur!*" "I know, your Majesty," I answered, "and I expect to be brought back on a litter."

She laughed and passed on.

Monsieur Niewekerke looked pleasantly conscious and flattered as we walked to the dining-room, and I felt as if I was being led to the altar to be sacrificed like poor little Isaac. His English is very cockney, and he got so mixed up with "heart" and "art" that I did not know half the time whether he was talking of the collection of the Louvre Gallery or of his lady victims. He did not hesitate to call my attention to the presence of some of them at the table, which I thought was very kind of him, in case I was unaware of it.

He is as keen about the good things of the table as he is about art; in fact, he is a great epicure. As he thought well of the menu, I will copy it for you:

> *Consommé en tasses.*
> Œufs au fromage à l'Italienne.
> Petites truites.
> Cailles au riz.
> Cotelettes de veau grillées.
> Viande froide, salade.
> Brioches à la vanille, fruits, dessert, café. . . .

"Well," said the Empress, as she stopped in front of me after *déjeuner*, "are you alive?"

"I am, your Majesty, and, strange to say, my heart is intact."

"Wonderful!" she said, "you are an exception."

We had the choice between going to a *chasse à tir* (without the Emperor), and a drive to Pierrefonds.

I had enough of the *chasse à tir* last year, and I still see in my dreams those poor birds fluttering in their death-agony. Anything better than that!

I preferred Pierrefonds, with its gargoyles and its hard, carved chairs.

I was glad Monsieur de Niewekerke went with us, for he was more interesting and did not go into so many details as Viollet-le-Duc.

The restoration has progressed very much since the

LA SALLE DES PREUX—CHÂTEAU DE PIERREFONDS

last time we were here, though far from being completed yet. In the huge hall Niewekerke told me the statues about the chimney were portraits of the wives of the *preux chevaliers* of that time.

I thought the frescos of this hall were very crude in color; but Monsieur de Niewekerke said they were excellent copies of the ancient style of decoration.

The castle is such a magnificent ruin one almost wishes that it was not restored.

I would like to see it in summer, not in this season, when one perishes with cold and longs, in spite of its beauty, to be out of it and in a warmer place.

There was a dense fog on the lake and a mist in the forest when we left, and it was dreadfully damp and cold. The postilions took a shorter cut and carried us through La Brévière and St. Jean aux Bois.

I should think both must be charming in summer; but now—ugh!

What was my delight at the Empress's tea this afternoon to see Auber, my dear old Auber! He had been invited for dinner, and had come with the artists who are to play to-night. He looked so well and young, in spite of his eighty-three years. Every one admires him and loves him. He is the essence of goodness, talent, and modesty. He is writing a new opera. Fancy writing an opera at eighty-three!

I asked what the name of it was. He answered: "'Le Rêve d'Amour.' The title is too youthful and the composer is too old. I am making a mistake, but what of that? It is my last!"

I said I hoped he would live many more years and write many more operas.

He shook his head, saying, "Non, non, c'est vraiment mon dernier!"

Monsieur de Lareinty said to the Empress at tea that there was an unusual amount of musical talent among her guests—a real galaxy of stars seldom to be found in amateurs.

The galaxy may have existed—but the stars! The Milky Way seen through the wrong end of an opera-glass was nothing to the smallness of their magnitude.

The Empress caught at the idea directly, and the decree went out that there should be a concert to-morrow evening; not mere desultory singing, but singers and songs in regular order.

Auber said he was sorry he could not be there to applaud us. He accompanied us when we went to our rooms, and then he had no idea how to find his own. After having seen him handed over successively to three different valets, we left him to his fate, hoping he would arrive at his destination eventually. When we entered the salon for dinner Auber was already there. If he had not brought his own servant with him, he never would have been in time.

The troop of the Comédie Française played "La Joie fait Peur," by Musset. The theater was brilliantly lighted; the guests, from the environs and the *fine fleur* of Compiègne, filled all the boxes. The gentlemen and the officers were in the parquet. The Court and Imperial guests sat with their Majesties in the Imperial box. It was a magnificent sight!

Madame Favart was most touching in her part, and everybody, I think, wept. Coquelin was excellent; but I do not like him so much in his pathetic rôles; his squeaky voice and nasal tones do not belong to the sentimental style. After the play he gave a monologue, which was the funniest thing I ever heard, "Les Obsèques de Madame X——." The whole house was laughing, and most of all the Emperor. I could see his back shaking, and the diplomatic and apoplectic Baron condescended to explode twice.

The representation lasted till half-past ten. The artists did not change their toilettes, but came into the salon as they were dressed for the play. They were received with great cordiality by their Majesties. The Chamberlain gave them each a little package containing, I suppose, a valuable souvenir from the sovereigns. A special train took them back to Paris.

Auber bid me good-by, saying, "Au revoir until Paris, if you are not too absorbed in these grandeurs to receive a poor, insignificant bourgeois like me."

"You can always try," I answered with a laugh. "Bon soir et bon voyage!"

December 2d.

What a day this has been! A storm of rain and hail raged all night, and when I looked out of the window this morning I saw everything deluged in water. The park looked dismal; all the paths were full of puddles; the trees were dripping with rain, and, to judge from the dark skies and threatening clouds, it seemed as if worse was to follow and there might be thunder and lightning. On the programme for to-day there stood *chasse à courre;* but of course *cela tombait dans l'eau*, as would have been its natural end anyway in this weather. None of the ladies donned their green costumes, as every one was so sure that the day would be passed indoors.

At *déjeuner* I was fortunate enough to sit between Prince Metternich and the Marquis de Gallifet. Certainly I could not have two more delightful companions, each so different and yet so entertaining. The Marquis was very aggressive and grumpy; but very amusing.

In French one says, "On a le vin triste," or "On a le vin gai." The Marquis has "le déjeuner grincheux (grumpy)," I think.

He began by attacking me on the English language. He said it was utterly absurd and illogical, and though he ought to know it, as he had an English wife, he felt he never could learn it.

"Apropos of to-day's weather, you say, 'It never rains but it pours'—au fond qu'est-ce que cela veut dire? 'Il ne pleut jamais, mais il pleut à verse'; cela n'a pas le sens commun—you might as well say, 'It never pours but it rains.'"

I had to confess that it did sound senseless, and tried to explain the meaning; but he grumbled, "Why don't they say what they mean?" He told me he was once traveling in England and put his head out of the carriage window to see something, and some one inside cried, "Look out!" He put his head still farther out, when the person continued to scream, "Look out!" He answered, "I am looking out," at which a rude hand seized him by the coat-collar and jerked him inside, saying, "Damn it, look in then!"

"How can any one conquer a language as stupid as that?"

I told him I felt humiliated to own such a language, and I ought to apologize for it, though I had not invented it and did not feel responsible for it; but he would not listen to me.

Prince Metternich asked, "What shall we do indoors this awful day?"

I proposed tableaux; but he objected to tableaux.

Then I suggested that one might have a fancy-dress tea-party. At last, after many wild propositions, he said, "Why not charades?"

Of course he had intended charades all the time. He asked the Marquis de Gallifet if he would help us.

"No, I won't," answered the Marquis, "but you are welcome to my wife; she loves dressing-up and all that nonsense;" adding, "It is the only thing she can do with success."

"But we want her to act. Can she?"

"Act!" said the amiable husband. "She can act like the devil!"

By the time we had returned to the salon the Prince had not only found a good word for a charade, but had decided in his resourceful mind all minor details. He thought it would amuse the Prince Imperial to join us, and he asked permission of the Prince's *gouverneur* to allow him to do so. The permission was readily given.

Prince Metternich begged Vicomte Walsh to obtain the Empress's gracious consent to honor the performance with her presence. She was very pleased at the idea of seeing her son's *début* as an actor, and promised to come, and even said she would have the tea, usually served in her salon, brought to the little theater.

Prince Metternich gave us a sketch of what he wanted us to do, and gave us general instructions as to our costumes, and bade us meet again in an hour. He would see to everything else: light, heat, scenery, powder, paint, etc., all the accessories, would be ready for us. We ladies were to be *pierrettes* and dancers of Louis-Quinze period; the gentlemen were to represent the *talons rouges*, and to have red cloth pasted on the heels of their low shoes. We could paint our faces and powder our hair after our own ideas. "But, ladies, above all, do not be late," were the parting words of the Prince.

We followed his instructions as well as we could, and reappeared in the theater to hear the now fully matured plans of our impresario.

The Empress was seated before we were ready, Prince Metternich was so long painting the Prince Imperial. We could hear her saying, "Allons! Allons!" clapping her hands in her eagerness for us to commence.

The word was PANTALON.

The first syllable, PAN, was represented by the Prince Imperial as a statue of Pan.

His body was visible to the waist above a pedestal. Over his flesh-colored undershirt he wore a wreath of green leaves across his shoulders, and his head was also covered with a wreath. He held the traditional flute before his mouth. No one could have recognized the delicate features of the Prince Imperial, as Prince Metternich had painted his lips very large and very red, and had added a fantastic mustache. His eyebrows (black as ink) had an upward tilt, in true Mephistophelian style.

à quelle qualité donnez vous

Quelles sont vos occupations favor...

Quelles sont vos couleurs favor...

Que voudriez vous être?

Quelles personnes de l'histoire
détestez vous le plus?

Pour quelles fautes avez
vous le plus d'indulgence?

La preference   La verité

?   servir, travailler   vaudreux

Heine Musset et Napoléon
Le grand Mohul!
Pilate se lavant les mains

Pour toutes qui resultent d'une
mauvaise éducation.

Metternich

It was a sylvan scene. Prince Metternich had ordered from the greenhouse some orange and other trees to be moved on to the stage, which made a very pretty effect.

The Princess Metternich, in a quaint costume, was the Harlequine to her husband's Harlequin. They made a very funny love scene, because, being man and wife, they could make all their kissing real, and so ridiculously loud, that one could hear it all over the theater. Every one laughed till they cried, and particularly as Pan was rolling his eyes about in a very comical manner.

Her other lover (Pierrot) came in unawares; but she had time to throw a shawl over Harlequin, who put himself on all fours, thus making a bench, on which she demurely sat down. In order to throw dust in Pierrot's eyes, she took from her basket a hammer and some nuts and began cracking them (to the audience's and Pan's horror) on poor Harlequin's head, eating them with great *sang-froid*.

Prince Metternich had prudently provided a wooden bowl, with which he covered his head so that his ambassadorial skull should be spared. Pan smiled a diabolical smile, and had, of course, a great success.

TALON was the next syllable. This was a sort of pantomime. The actors were grouped like a picture of Watteau. Count Pourtalès was a dancing-master, and was really so witty, graceful, and took such artistic attitudes that he was a revelation to every one. Prince Metternich (his bosom friend) exclaimed:

"Who would ever have thought it? How talent conceals itself!"

The whole word PANTALON was a combination of

Columbines, Harlequins, and Louis-Quinze cavaliers dancing in a circle, and all talking nonsense at once.

The statue of Pan in knickerbockers, his wreaths still on his head and shoulders, joined in the dance.

The Empress led the vociferous applause, and Prince Metternich came forward on the stage and said, "Ladies and gentlemen, we are deeply flattered at your approval. There will be a second performance before his Majesty, the Emperor of the French, and I hope you will accord us your patronage."

There was great laughter at this.

Count Pourtales took me in to dinner. We were very glad to be neighbors. He was resting on his laurels, and I wanted to rest before getting mine (if I got any) this evening. We exchanged views on nervousness. He said he had been dreadfully nervous in the afternoon. I told him I was always nervous when I had to sing, and when I sang the first song I was hot and cold all over.

"Like Alboni," he said; "she has had to give up singing in opera, she had such stage-frights."

We thanked each other after finishing dinner for having been kind enough to have let the other alone.

The rain was still pouring in torrents when we returned to the salon. In spite of the many voices, we could still hear it pattering against the windows of the terrace. It was lucky there were some stars among us, as Monsieur de Lareinty had said, otherwise we would have seen none to-night.

At ten o'clock the "galaxy" went into the *salle de musique*, and the planets began to shine. First came Baroness Gourgaud, who attacked the "Mi—bémol

IN THE COURTS OF MEMORY

Polonaise," of Chopin. Their Majesties settled themselves in their chairs with a look of heavenly resignation on their faces, which was reflected on those of most of the guests.

However, she played beautifully, more like an artiste than an amateur. The Empress went forward to her, holding out her hand, which the Baroness, bowing to the ground, kissed gratefully, feeling that she had covered herself with glory, as she really had.

Then Monsieur de V—— (our basso) sang "O Marguerite," from Faust, without the slightest voice, but with excellent intentions. Next, having the music under his hand, he continued and sang "Braga's Serenade," which he thought was more suited to his voice, though it is written, as you know, for a soprano. He sang the girl's part in a mysterious, husky, and sepulchral voice, and the angel's part weaker and feebler than any angel ever dreamed of.

I looked at the beautiful ceiling painted by Girodet, and to keep myself from going to sleep counted the legs of the angels, and tried to calculate how many legs belonged to each. Monsieur de V—— said his idea was to make the contrast very strong between the girl and the angel; he certainly succeeded!

Monsieur Dué played some of what he calls his "Sketches." "Il est si doué (gifted)," exclaimed Princess Metternich.

Every one was pleased; so was he.

I sang "Le Rossignol," of Alabieff, in which is the cadenza Auber wrote for me. Princess Metternich played the accompaniment.

Madame C—— (our contralto) sang "Lascia che

pianga," which suited her beautiful voice better than it did the audience's taste. Then she sang "Ah! Mon Fils," of "Le Prophète," with great effect, accompanying herself.

But this was not the kind of music to please our audience.

Count E—— (our tenor) was asked to add his Milky Way tenor to the rest of the planets, but begged to be excused on the plea of a sore throat. No one questioned this, and he was allowed to remain unheard.

Later I sang "Oh! that We Two were Maying," by Gounod, a much too serious song; but the Empress said she thought it was the most beautiful one she had ever heard. I think so, too. I also sang one of Massenet's, "Poème d'Avril." They asked for "Beware!" which I sang. The Emperor came up to me (each time he gets up from his chair every one gets up and stands until he sits down again), and said, "Won't you sing the song about the shoe?"

What did he mean? I had no idea.

"The one you sang the other night," said the Emperor.

What do you think he meant?

Well, he meant "Shoo-fly!" I sang it, as he desired. I don't believe he knows yet what its true meaning is. There is an end to all things, and our concert came to an end at last. Their Majesties, with gracious smiles and repeated thanks, retired, the Milky Way faded from view, and the planets went to bed.

I know I deserved mine, and I appreciated it when I got it.

December 3d.

The *chasse à courre* is generally fixed for the last day of the *série;* but their Majesties, at the suggestion of the thoughtful Vicomte Walsh, ordered it to be changed to this afternoon, in order that the operetta should arrive at a riper stage of perfection. Would it ever be near enough? We had never had a moment yet when we could rehearse all together. Vicomte de V——'s costume had not come from Paris, and he was bordering on brain-fever, in a state of expectancy and impatience. Neither he nor d'Espeuilles knew their songs, and the chorus needed much drilling. The Princess Metternich put her salon at the Marquis's disposal, and he spent half his time teaching some of his pupils.

The days of the *chasse à courre* the gentlemen appear in red coats and the ladies in green-cloth dresses. Those that had *le bouton* put it in their buttonhole. You may be sure I wore mine!

All the carriages, the horses, and grooms were before the terrace at two o'clock, and after the usual delay we drove off to the forest. Their Majesties and the Prince Imperial were on horseback. The Duchess de Sesto invited me to drive with her, and in the same *char-à-banc* with us were Baronne de la Poeze, Comtesse Pourtales, and four or five others. The Duchess looked very dainty, wrapped in her chinchilla furs. I had had so little time to learn the talking part of my rôle that I took it with me in the carriage, hoping to be able to study it. They all sympathized with me, as they knew the operetta was to be given to-morrow evening.

The roads were full of mud; but we splashed through

them regardless of such minor details as dirt. Fortunately it did not rain, and the sun made a few spasmodic efforts to come out; but it was far from being the ideal day of last year.

This *chasse* varies but little, and I described my first acquaintance with it in a letter last year, so I will spare you the repetition of details. I fancy the route we took was the same; but I am not quite sure, for all the roads and avenues resemble one another.

Once, as we halted at an *étoile*, we saw a beautiful stag bound past us, full of life and strength, with enormous horns (they said it was a *dix cors*). Every one in the carriage stood up in their excitement to look after it. How I wished he would escape and live his free and happy life in the forest. I hate this *chasse;* I hate to write about it; I hate to be present at it. It is all so pitiful and painful to me! How can any one find pleasure in such cruel sport?

To kill a living creature, to take the life of an animal that has done you no harm, seems horrible to me. But I will say no more on this subject. It always puts me in a bad temper, and makes me disgusted with my fellow-creatures.

We followed the other part of the cavalcade and arrived at the *carrefour* in time to see the death of one stag. The others saw it, but I was occupied with my manuscript.

There were two stags taken, two beautiful creatures that ought to have lived.

It was so cold and bleak I longed to get back to warm rooms, cheerful fire, and a hot cup of tea, which I was sure to find awaiting me, and I was heartily glad when we turned homeward.

Six o'clock had just struck when we drove up to the front of the Grand Escalier, and I was able to get a little rest before dressing for dinner.

All the ladies who owned diamond crescents, or any crescent suggestive of Diana and her pastimes, put them on. The Empress had a gorgeous crescent on her lovely hair.

The worn-out Marquis took me in to dinner. It was fortunate, for there were some vital points which we had to discuss. On my other side was the Count de Grammont, a sportsman, who wanted to talk only of the hunt; but I was able to turn a deaf ear to his marvelous exploits, thanks to the Marquis's incessant explanations.

There was a little dancing, to fill up the time before the *curée*. It is a pity that this is our last dance. The chamberlains are beginning to show a good deal of talent in their playing *le piano méchanique*, and they can play almost in time.

The *curée* was at ten o'clock. The long gallery was soon alive with an eager public. All the windows were occupied by the ladies. The courtyard was filled, in spite of the cold weather, with the populace of Compiègne; the *piqueurs* waved their torches; the dogs howled and yelped; the *gardes* blew their long *cors de chasse*, and it was just like last year, except that on this occasion there were two stags — therefore, two sets of entrails to be devoured.

Tea and cakes were passed about. Those who had come from the neighboring châteaux took their leave, those who were to return to Paris drove off to the station, and the privileged guests retired to their apartments.

IN THE COURTS OF MEMORY

December 4th.

At ten o'clock this morning I was surprised at hearing a timid knock at my salon door. Who should it be but the Marquis d'Aoust. He begged my pardon for disturbing me; but he wished to consult me about something he considered of great importance.

He looked disheveled and careworn, even at this early hour, as if he had not slept all night. Would I be willing to help Count d'E—— in our duet, and sing a part of his music? Otherwise, he was sure it would never go.

I told him it would not be easy to sing tenor; but I would see at the rehearsal what I could do. He was in despair. I tried to tranquilize him, my compassion triumphing over my forebodings, and assured him that all would go well. I did not tell him that I had had a succession of nightmares last night, where I saw myself stranded on the stage, having forgotten both words and music.

He said that he had been on the stage at work with the carpenters since I don't know when this morning. They had first put up the scenery as he had ordered; but he saw that there would not be space for the eight performers (there are two scenes where we are all on the stage at once). Accordingly, he had ordered the carpenters to change it.

I ate my *déjeuner* sandwiched between the tenor and the basso. We rehearsed our dialogues, although we pretended to discuss other matters.

The Empress went directly to the Marquis after *déjeuner* and said, "We are looking forward to your

222

A Quelle qualité donnez vous la
préférence —?

Quels sont vos auteurs favoris?

Quelles sont vos occupations favorites?

Qui voudriez vous être?

Quelles personnes de l'histoire détestez
vous le plus.? —

Pour quelles fautes avez vous le plus
d'indulgence? —

NAPOLEON'S SIGNATURE AND ANSWER

à la ~~gratitude~~

~~Décité~~

chercher la solution du problème
insoluble

~~petit g'e~~

2 ~~comtesse de Bourbon~~

~~pour cacher~~ 1 ~~par~~ ~~proposé à~~

Napoléon Louis

operetta to-night with real pleasure, and we are sure that it will be a great success." The Marquis was radiant.

When we met later in the theater for our first and only rehearsal we were delighted to find there the grand piano from the *salle de musique*. The curtain rose on a very pretty garden scene, with trees on either side, green linen on the floor representing grass, a village with a church-steeple in the background, and for stage properties a garden bench and a vase placed just before the footlights, so that it would not interfere with our movements, but would show us where *not* to fall off.

The Marquis was, of course, at the piano, and Prince Metternich, as prompter, squeezed into a prompter's box, looking wretchedly uncomfortable. We commenced the rehearsal, which, on the whole, went off better than we expected.

The basso is the first to appear. He sings a melancholy song, in which he makes known his love for the humble village maiden. His voice gets more dismal and lower as he becomes despondent, and higher and more buoyant as his hopes rise. At the end, when he sings "Elle sera à moi," his voice, though very husky, was almost musical. Then I, as the village maiden, enter with a basket, suggestive of butter and eggs, and sing a sentimental ditty telling of my love for the friend of the lord. The music of this is mediocre beyond words. The Marquis tries to show, by a few high soprano notes, how high my wildest flights of aspirations fly before I could ever reach the subject of my love. "Mes tourments" and "le doux plaisir d'aimer" get so mixed that I don't know myself what I am singing about.

The lady of the manor hears my lament, and, believing me to be in love with her husband, berates me in a dramatic duet. The friend and adviser now appears, and we get through an incomprehensible trio. He cannot convince her (the lady) of the innocence of her husband. She insists upon thinking him a traitor, leaves us in a fury, and we have the floor to ourselves when we sing the famous duet on account of which the Marquis had qualms this morning. In it there is a minor phrase which is quite intricate, and I saw that unless I came to d'E——'s rescue he could never manage it.

The lord and the lady reappear, while the friend and I retire in the background and lean up against the village steeple and whisper. The lady is violent and the lord is indifferent. The music sounds like an everlasting grumble, because her voice is contralto and his is bass. The village maiden is called to the front, and denies everything she has been accused of. The husband makes amends in a phrase miles too high for his voice. The friend takes all the blame on his black-velvet shoulders, and says he has loved the maiden all along. The maiden is overcome with emotion and faints for joy.

The final quartette is a sad affair, musically speaking, constructed on the Marquis's own ideas of thorough-bass. All the singers start on the same plane, the soprano soars heavenward, the contralto and the bass grovel in their deepest notes, while the tenor, who ought to fill up the gap, stands counting the measures on his fingers, his eyes glued to the prompter, until he joins me and we soar together.

To use a metaphor, one might say that the contralto and bass were in the lower regions, the soprano floating in heaven, the tenor groping about on earth for his note; then we all meet on the same place we started from, which is the signal for the chorus to unite their forces with ours.

The Marquis was dreadfully put out with me because I refused to faint on the stage (in the text it says *Rosette tombe évanouie*). He said nothing was easier. I had only to put my arms out to break the fall and—fall. He thought that with a little practice between the afternoon and the evening I should be able to do it.

I could see myself covered with bruises tumbling about over sofas and chairs, and I could see the bewilderment of any one coming into my room while I was practising this part of my rôle.

I said, "I absolutely refuse to risk my neck." He thought it was very selfish of me. One would have thought that the whole success of the operetta depended on my fainting. He said he could show me how to fall without hurting myself, and in trying to do so he tripped over the vase and bumped his head against the garden bench. Fortunately he did not damage himself, but the argument ended then and there.

At half-past four my maid came to the theater to tell me that the Empress expected me to tea. I had thought she would, as she had promised the answers to those questions; and so it was. As soon as I appeared (I had had time to change my dress) the Empress called me to her and said:

"Here are the answers to your American soul-probing questions! These are mine (giving me hers) and here are the Emperor's. He was very pleased to write them, as it was you who asked him; besides, I think they amused him. He spent a long time pondering over each answer. You see," she added, with her lovely smile, "nous vous aimons bien."

I was very glad to have the answers. I copy them for you.

À quelle qualité donnez-vous la préférence? À la gratitude.
Quels sont vos auteurs favoris? Tacite.
Quelles sont vos occupations favorites? Chercher la solution de problèmes insolubles.
Qui voudriez-vous être? Mon petit fils.
Quelles personnes de l'histoire détestez-vous le plus? Le Connétable de Bourbon.
Pour quelles fautes avez-vous le plus d'indulgence? Pour celles dont je profite.   NAPOLÉON LOUIS.

À quelle qualité donnez-vous la préférence? Au dévouement.
Quels sont vos auteurs favoris? Calderon, Byron, Shakespeare.
Quelles sont vos occupations favorites? Faire le bien.
Qui voudriez-vous être? Ce que je suis.
Quelles personnes de l'histoire détestez-vous le plus? Lopez.
Pour quelles fautes avez-vous le plus d'indulgence? Pour celles que la passion excuse.   EUGÉNIE.

I add the answers of Prosper Mérimée:

À quelle qualité donnez-vous la préférence? La persévérance.
Quels sont vos auteurs favoris? Pr. Mérimée.
Quelles sont vos occupations favorites? Faire des châteaux en Espagne.
Qui voudriez-vous être? Napoléon III.
Quelles personnes de l'histoire détestez-vous le plus? Mazarin.
Pour quelles fautes avez-vous le plus d'indulgence? La gourmandise.   PROSPER MÉRIMÉE.

I think the Emperor's are very clever.
"And the operetta?" inquired the Empress.

A quelle qualité donnez vous la p...

Quels sont vos auteurs favoris ?

Quelles sont vos occupations fav...

Qu. Voudriez vous être ?

Quelles personnes de l'histoire détestez vo...

Pour quelles fautes avez vous le plus...

EMPRESS EUGÉNIE'S SIGNATURE AND ANSW

"I hope your Majesties will be indulgent," I replied.
Monsieur de Laferrière was next to me at dinner.
He was as much interested in the operetta as other
people seemed to be. I took advantage of his being
my neighbor to ask him to manage it so that we could
leave the salon before the *cercle* commenced, as we had
to dress, and if any of us were late I dared not think
what the effect would be on the nervous Marquis.

The Emperor raised his glass during dinner, though
I sat very far down the table. I suppose he wanted to
inspire me with hope and courage.

Monsieur de Laferrière arranged everything for us
most amiably. We rushed off to our rooms to dress.
I, for one, was not long over my toilette, and, followed
by my maid, hurried through the long corridors to the
theater.

We were all there except Monsieur de V——, who was
no doubt still pottering over his raiment. The artist
he had ordered from Paris was already there, brush in
hand, ready to paint us. The result was very satisfactory. When we looked at ourselves in the glass we
wondered why one should not be beautiful every day
with so simple an art.

We were rather taken back when Monsieur d'Espeuilles appeared in a wig and a false mustache; but
he hastened to say there was nothing like being disguised to put one at one's ease. The gentlemen of the
chorus, not willing to go to any extra expense, had
culottes courtes and white stockings; the ladies had tried
to be more in harmony, but they thought that with rakes,
spades, and basket they had quite enough *couleur locale*.

The chamberlain came to ask whether their Majesties should come now. Prince Metternich answered that we were waiting for them. A tedious delay occurred before the audience had settled into their places in accordance with their rank, to the great annoyance of Prince Metternich, shut up in the small prompter's box, and the Marquis d'Aoust, fidgeting at the piano, and driving us almost to distraction by his repeated questions and exhortations: "Do you think you know your part? Don't forget to"—etc.

At last! at last! No retreating now. *Coûte que coûte!* we must take in the plank and embark on our shaky craft.

The Marquis attacked the overture by playing some vigorous arpeggios and pompous chords. The curtains were drawn aside and the lord of the manor entered. After his monologue, which he did very well, he hesitated a moment. This agitated the Marquis to such a degree that he stood up and waved his hand as a signal to him to commence his song, and gave him the note on the piano. Monsieur de V—— started in all right and sang his song with due sentiment, and very well. I even think as far back as the sixth row of seats they were conscious that he was singing. His acting and gestures were faultless. All Frenchmen can act.

I thought, when I came in, the public was chilly, and I felt cold shivers running down my back. My courage was oozing out of me, and when the lord of the manor said to me, "Rosette, que fais-tu ici?" and I had to answer, "Ce que je fais, Monsieur; mais vous voyez bien, je ne fais rien," I thought I should die of fright and collapse on the spot. However, I pulled myself together and began my silly little song.

The moment I began to sing I felt at ease, and I

flatter myself I gave a certain glaze to the emptiness of the music. Madame Conneau sang her dramatic aria beautifully, and created quite a *furore*. I only wish the music had been more worthy of her. The love duet between the friend and myself was, much to my surprise, a great success. It was encored, and we sang it again.

When we came to the minor passage (the stumbling-block) the Marquis, who was perspiring at every pore in his dread that I should not hit the right note, pounded it on the piano loud enough to be heard all over the theater. I gave him a withering look, which he pretended not to see. Perhaps he did not, for his attention, like mine, was startled by seeing the false mustache of Monsieur d'Espeuilles ungluing and threatening to drop into his mouth. The Marquis began wagging his head and making frantic signs. Monsieur d'Espeuilles was horribly confused, and I feared for the success of our *da capo;* but he patted the now limp offender back on his lip, and we continued the duet. During the applause the Marquis took the occasion to wipe the perspiration from his bald head.

In spite of our qualms the final quartette was not so bad after all. When it was time for me to come down from my upward flight in order to help the tenor, the Marquis again waved his right hand in the air to attract my attention, while he thundered a tremolo with his left, to keep the accompaniment going until he was sure that everything was right. The chorus came on in due order, and flourished their rakes and spades as though they were waving flags, in participation of the joy and gladness of the reconciliation. There was one moment of genuine hilarity, when the little fox-terrier belonging to the Empress's niece rushed on to the stage to join his mistress, who, with great *sang-froid*, picked him up and went on singing, to the immense amusement of the audience.

It was suffocatingly hot in the little theater, and we were glad to think that we had arrived at the end of our perilous journey. The red on our cheeks was getting paler; the powder was becoming paste; the black on the eyebrowless actors began to run down their cheeks; Monsieur d'Espeuilles's wig and mustache were all on one side.

All these details mattered little, now that the end had come, and the performance had concluded with great *éclat*.

The happy Marquis (though I think he aged ten years that hour at the piano) was radiant with his success. Every emotion had swept over him: ambition, vanity, hope, pride, forbearance, patience, long-suffering.

The curtain fell amid great applause, as spontaneous as it was persistent and, I hope, genuine.

We stayed in our costumes for the tea in the Emperor's salon.

Both their Majesties complimented the Marquis, and thanked us all separately for the pleasure they had had and the trouble we had given ourselves. The Emperor said to me, "Vous vous êtes surpassée ce soir." I courtesied and asked him what he thought of the music.

He hesitated before answering. "I don't know much about music; but it seems to me, as Rossini said of the music of Wagner: 'Il y a de jolis moments, mais de mauvais quarts d'heures!' All the same, it was very pretty."

Every one praised the Marquis to the skies, and he
was really in the seventh heaven of delight.

I am only afraid his head will be turned, and that he
will write another *chef-d'œuvre*.

I was glad when their Majesties bade us good night,
for I was completely exhausted.

PARIS, *December 5th.*

It seems nice, all the same, to be at home again. We
arrived in Paris at six o'clock, and at half-past seven I
was in my bed, completely worn out. However, I must
tell you how our visit ended the day before yesterday.
Was it only the day before yesterday? It seems months
ago. At *déjeuner* the Princess Metternich sat on the
right of the Emperor, and the Empress's brother-in-law,
Duke d'Albe, gave me his *avant-le-déluge* arm, and put
me on the left of his Majesty.

I thought the Emperor looked tired and ill, and I
noticed he frequently put his hand on his back, as if he
was in pain. The Princess Metternich engrossed the Emperor's attention. She is so witty and lively that every
one must listen when she talks. All the same, the Emperor talked with me a good deal, and thanked me for
having done so much to amuse them. Never would
they forget the pleasure they had had.

When we went up to our rooms to put on our cloaks
there was no pretentious majordomo demanding his fee,
and our particular valet looked sad, and did not meet
my eye when I tried to catch his to give a smile of adieu,
and persistently fixed his gaze on something at the other
end of the corridor. I rather liked the old way better,

as one felt that in a measure one had made some little compensation for all the delightful days spent there.

I asked my maid how the servants felt about this change. She said that in their *salle à manger* almost all the maids and valets belonging to the guests gave *pourboires*.

After we had made our adieux, and taken our seats in the different carriages, their Majesties came out on the balcony to see us depart. They waved their hands in farewell as we drove off.

The journey back to Paris was a silent one. Every one was occupied with his own thoughts. Prince Metternich sat in a corner talking with the impervious diplomat; I wondered if he were relating the salad's complicated relationships. We all bade one another good-by, adding, with assumed enthusiasm, that we hoped to meet soon again, when perhaps we were rejoicing in the thought that we would not do so for a long time to come.

What insincere creatures we are!

May, 1870.

We were invited to a picnic at Grand Trianon, given by the Emperor and Empress for the Archduke of Austria.

The rendezvous was to be at St. Cloud, and we were asked to be there at four o'clock. On arriving we found the Metternichs, Édouard Delesert, Duperré, and Count Dehm, the Austrian Secretary. Their Majesties and the Prince Imperial joined us when we were all assembled. We then mounted the two *char-à-bancs* which were waiting for us in front of the château, with their postilions and four horses; the *piqueurs*, in their saddles, were all ready to precede us. The Emperor, Empress, the Prince Imperial, Princess Metternich, and the Archduke were in the first carriage; the rest of us were in the second—about fourteen people in all. We drove through the lovely forest of Marly, the long, tiresome avenues of Versailles, and through many roads known probably only to the postilions, and perhaps used only on rare occasions such as this royal excursion, for they were in such a bad condition, ruts and stones everywhere, that our heads and shoulders were bumping continually against our neighbors'. Finally we reached Petit Trianon, where we left the carriages and servants, who were ordered to meet us at Grand Trianon later, bringing our extra wraps with them. The air was deliciously balmy and warm, and was filled with the perfume of lilacs and acacias.

We wandered through the park, admiring the skill of the artist who had laid it out so cleverly, just like Petit Val. This is not surprising, as it was the same person who planned them both. All the surroundings recall the charming life which Marie Antoinette must have lived in the midst of this pastoral simplicity.

I wondered if the same thought passed through the Empress's mind which passed through mine. Could history ever repeat this unfortunate queen's horrible fate? We continued our walk to Grand Trianon, and found the table spread for our dinner under the wide *charmille*, near the lake. The Princess Metternich sat on the right of the Emperor, and I on his left.

The Emperor was in excellent spirits, and bandied repartees with Monsieur Delesert, who surpassed himself in wit, and told many and sometimes rather risky stories, which made every one laugh. The Prince Imperial could hardly wait till the end of the dinner, he was so impatient to get to the rowboat which was ready waiting for him on the lake. The Empress was quite nervous, and stood on the edge of the lake all the time he was on the water, calling to him, "Prends garde, Louis!" "Ne te penches pas, Louis!" and many other such counsels like any other anxious mother, and she never took her eyes from the little boat which was zigzagging about under the hands of the youthful prince.

It was after nine o'clock when we started to return to St. Cloud by another route. The *piqueur*, finding the gate locked through which we had to pass, knocked on the door of the lodge-keeper, who, awakened from his slumbers, appeared in a *déshabillé* more than hasty, intending to administer a *savon* (scolding) to such tardy comers. But on hearing from the *piqueur* that the monarch of all he surveyed was waiting in the carriage, he flew to open the gate, disclosing his scanty night-attire. The funniest part of it was that, as soon as he realized the situation, he thought it his duty to show his patriotism, so he stood on the steps of his lodge and, as we passed through the gate, he chanted a hoarse and sleepy! "Vive l'Empereur!" and waved his smoking candle.

The Emperor was convulsed with laughter. I, who sat behind him, could see his shoulders shaking.

The ball of the *plébiscite* was the most splendid thing I ever saw. The architects and decorators had outdone themselves. The gardens of the Tuileries beyond the fountain had been hedged in by orange-trees, and other large trees moved there in their tubs. The whole *parterre* of flowers was festooned with lanterns and little colored lamps, making this fairy scene as bright as day. The ballroom and adjoining salons, of which the windows had been removed as well as the iron railing outside of them, led on to a large platform which occupied the space of six such windows or doors; these gave out into two colossal staircases which descended into the garden. It was such a beautiful night, so warm that we ladies could walk about in our ball-dresses without any extra wraps; there were about six thousand people invited, they said. It seemed as if all Paris was there.

After the *quadrille d'honneur* their Majesties circulated freely about. Every one was eager to offer congratulations to the Emperor. Was it not the greatest triumph of his reign to have the unanimous vote of all France—this overwhelming proof of his popularity? As he stood there smiling, with a gracious acknowledgment of the many compliments, he looked radiantly happy to thus receive the homage of his country. As the Emperor passed near me I added my congratulations, to which he replied, "Merci, je suis bien heureux."

Their Majesties stood on the dais with the members of the Imperial family, and after watching the dance they all went in to the *Pavillon de Flore*, where supper was served for the notabilities.

For the others there was arranged a supper in the theater; an orchestra on the stage played all the time; the balconies were festooned with flowers and filled with guests; there were supper-tables in the parquet and in the largest *loges*, and plants and shrubs placed in every available spot.

IN THE COURTS OF MEMORY

LONDON, *June, 1870.*

DEAR M.,—What will you think of your dissipated daughter? Do you not think that she is insatiable? I am sure that you will say that I ought to be contented after the long season of gaiety and excitement in Paris, and settle down in lovely Petit Val, where the lilacs and the violets call one with scented voices.

However, we decided to go to London.

Did I write to you of our breakfast at Armenonville? After Lord Lyons's ball, which lasted until six o'clock in the morning, Prince Metternich and several others thought that it would be a good idea to go home, change our ball-dresses for morning-dress, and go out to the Bois for our morning coffee. We did it.

I confess that it was a crazy thing to do after dancing all night; but the beautiful May morning, the glorious sunshine, and our spirits inspired us to carry out this wild whim, much to the disgust of our sleepy coachmen. This excursion was not a success; we were all tired and longed for bed. One cannot be amusing or *en train* at seven o'clock in the morning. And as for the family, when we returned home all the comment they made was, "What fools!" They did not see any fun in it; neither did we, to tell the truth.

The Rothschilds, Lord Lyons, and Prince and Princess Metternich gave us what must have been very powerful letters, for we had hardly been in London more than a few days before we knew every one worth knowing, and all doors worth opening were opened to us, and I found myself what one calls *lancée*.

We took rooms in Park Street; that is, we had the

236

two stories of the house. The landlady lived down-
stairs, and gave us our meals when we were at home.
As soon as we got settled we left our cards and letters
of introduction.

Invitation followed invitation in the most bewildering manner, sometimes several for the same day.

I could not begin to tell you all that we have already
done. Writing letters seems to be the one thing which
I have no time for. It is a perpetual push and rush
from morning till night.

Our first dinner was at Baron and Baroness Rothschilds', where the Prince and Princess of Wales and a
great many distinguished people were invited. I sat
next to a Mr. Osbourne—everybody called him Dick.
He told me that he was the most dined-out and tired-
out man in London, and that he had not eaten at home
for six months.

I had not seen their Royal Highnesses since their
visit to Paris during the Exposition. They said that
they remembered me; but I cannot think it possible
that they can have such wonderful memories.

I never saw such a splendid collection of orchids as
there was on the table, and each lady had a bouquet of
orchids and roses by her plate.

I was asked to sing, and was delighted to do it. The
Rothschilds' ballroom was a glorious place in which
to make a début.

Michael Costa, the well-known musician, came after
dinner and accompanied me in the "Cavatina" from
"Rigoletto," and the waltz from the "Pardon de
Ploermel."

Lady Sherbourne, a charming lady whom I fell in

love with at first sight, sang also. She has a beautiful, rich contralto voice, and sang with a great deal of expression an English song called, "Out on the rocks when the tide is low."

In your last letter you wrote, "I am afraid that you are on the way to become conceited." I am afraid myself I am, still I cannot resist telling you, this once, that my audience was very enthusiastic and Mr. Costa said— well, I won't tell you what he said; it might sound conceited. The last thing I sang was "Beware!" which was immensely appreciated.

The Prince of Wales said: "That is a bewitching song. I never heard it before. Who composed it?"

I told him that it was written for me by my husband, and Longfellow had written the words.

The Princess, before leaving, said, "I cannot tell you how much pleasure you have given us this evening; we hope to see you often while you are in London." She is very beautiful, even handsomer than when I saw her last. Baroness Rothschild kissed me, and thanked me for having sung for her.

Call me vain and conceited if you will, my head is turned, and there is nothing more to be said about it!

A luncheon at "Caroline, Duchess of Montrose's," at two o'clock upset me for the whole day. I am not accustomed to those big *déjeuners-dinatoires*. I was sleepy and felt good for nothing the rest of the day; and when we dined at Lady Molesworth's that evening, "to meet their Royal Highnesses the Prince and Princess of Wales," and wanted to be extra up-to-the-mark, I felt just the contrary. However, after dinner the

Prince of Wales asked me to sing, and I did not refuse, and even sang most of the evening. There was a charming Baron Hochschild, the Swedish Minister, who sang delightfully. He is a thorough musician, and accompanied himself perfectly with all the aplomb of an artist. He has a deep, rich barytone, and his *répertoire* consisted of all the well-known old Italian songs. Lady Molesworth is a beautiful old lady, who must have been a great beauty in her youth. She wears curls just like yours, dear mama, which made me love her. I met here Arthur Sullivan; he was full of compliments.

The next day we were invited to a *matinée musicale* at Lady Dudley's, preceded by a luncheon, which Mr. Osbourne called "a snare," because, he said, I could not refuse to sing. I did not want to refuse, either. The piano was in the beautiful picture-gallery, all full of Greuze's pictures bought from the Vatican; it has the most wonderful acoustics, and the voice sounded splendidly in it. Lady Dudley is a celebrated beauty. Lord Dudley—before he succeeded to the title—was Lord Ward. The Duke and Duchess of Sutherland asked us to dine. This was a very imposing affair; the Duke of Cambridge was at the dinner as the *grosse pièce*, and there were many diplomats. After dinner several artists came from Covent Garden, and among them Madame Patti, who sang the "Cavatina" of "Lucia," with flute accompaniment, and how beautifully!

When I was introduced to her I said, "The first time I heard you sing was years ago when I was a little girl and you were in short dresses."

"Where was that?"

"In Rochester," I replied. "I shall never forget how exquisitely you sang 'Ah! non giunge' and 'Ernani.'"

"Yes, I remember quite well. I was singing in concerts with Ole Bull; but that was a long time ago."

"It was indeed," I said; "but I have never forgotten your voice, nor a lovely song you sang which I have never heard since, called 'Happy Birdling of the Forest.' And your trill! Just like the bird itself!"

We became quite good friends, and she made me promise to come to see her. She is charming. Every one was most enthusiastic. Some one said she gets a thousand pounds for an evening. The Marquis de Caux (her husband) looked rather out of place. It seemed queer to see him again, not as the brilliant Marquis of the Tuileries (the "beau" *par excellence*), but simply as the husband of Patti. He did not find a chance to speak to me.

Some days later Lady Anglesey gave a luncheon for me. On the invitations were, "To meet Mrs. Moulton." I read between the lines: to hear Mrs. Moulton sing. They always put on their invitations, "To meet" so and so.

Mr. Quimby said to me, "I liked you from the first moment I saw you, but I had no idea you were going to be such a beast." "Beast!" I echoed. "That is not very complimentary." "A lion is a beast, isn't it?" he jokingly replied.

"Am I going to be a lion? I did not know it."

"Well, you are a lioness, which is better."

He is considered the wit of London, and this is a specimen of his wit. What do you think?

At the luncheon there were Jacques Blumenthal, the

famous pianist and composer, and Arthur Sullivan, who asked me to sing in his little operetta, which some amateurs are rehearsing for a *soirée* at Lady Harrington's; and on my acceptance he brought the music for me to try over with him the next morning. The *soirée* was to be three days later. The music is nothing remarkable; in fact, the whole thing (it is called "The Prodigal Son") is not worthy of him. I have not met any of my fellow-performers yet. Forgive this jerky letter; I have been interrupted a thousand times. Charles thinks it is time to go back to Paris; but we have just received an invitation from Baron Alfred Rothschild to spend Ascot week—a *séjour de sept jours*—with a party at a house he has hired for the race-week there, and I could not resist.

ASCOT, LONDON, *June, 1870.*

DEAR M.,— Viscount Sydney thought that we ought to ask for an audience of the Princess of Wales, and we did it. The audience was accorded, and we presented ourselves at the appointed hour and were received by the lady of honor and shown into the beautifully arranged drawing-room. The Princess was most gracious; she certainly is the loveliest lady I have ever seen. I told her we were going to Ascot for the week, and she said that they were also going there and hoped they would see us. Our interview came to an end, as such interviews do, without anything very interesting happening, and, finally, we backed ourselves out of the royal presence.

That evening there was a ball at Lady Waldegrave's,

who lives at Strawberry Hill, a mile or two out of London. Baron Alfred Rothschild offered to take us out there in his coach-and-four. We dined first with the Baron Meyer Rothschild, and afterward drove out to Strawberry Hill. It is the most beautiful place you can imagine. I never saw anything so grand as the cedar-trees.

The cotillon lasted very late; the Duke of Saxe-Weimar talked a long time with me, mostly about music. He is very musical, and knows Liszt intimately, and told me a quantity of anecdotes about him. He was interested in what I told him about Liszt's going to the Conservatoire with Auber and me, and about the "Tannhäuser" overture incident. It was six o'clock when we drove back to London. We saw the milk-carts on their morning rounds and the street-sweepers at work. One felt ashamed of oneself at being in ball-dress and jewels at this early hour, galloping through the streets in a fine carriage, making such a dreadful contrast to the poor working-people.

I had great fun at Lady Harrington's musical *soirée*, where Arthur Sullivan's "Prodigal Son" was to be sung.

We had been dining at Lady Londonderry's, and arrived rather late at Lady Harrington's. The whole staircase was crowded with people, and even down in the hall it was so full of ladies and gentlemen that there was no question of moving about. However, I made my way as far as the stairs, every one wondering at my audacity, and I murmured gently:

"May I pass?" There was a chorus of "Quite impossible!" "Perfectly useless!" and other such discouraging remarks. I said to a gentleman who sat stolidly on his step:

"Do you think I could send word to Mr. Sullivan that the Prodigal Son's mother cannot get to him?"

"What do you mean?" said he. "Are you——"

"Yes, I am; and if you don't let me pass you won't have any music."

You should have seen them jump up and make a pathway for me. I marched through it like the children of Israel through the Red Sea. I was enchanted to have my little fun. I joined the other performers, and the mother of the Prodigal Son was received with open arms. The Prodigal Son's father was pathos itself, and we rejoiced together over our weak tenor-boy. The only fatted calves that were to be seen belonged to the fat flunkeys.

We had a beautiful time at Ascot. Alfred Rothschild was an excellent host. Among the other guests were the Archibald Campbells, the Hochschilds, Mr. Osbourne, the Duke and Duchess of Newcastle, Hon. and Mrs. Stoner, one of the ladies of the Queen, Mr. Mitford, and others. Lady Campbell had only one dress with her (they must be very poor!); it was a black velvet (fancy, in the middle of summer!). She wore it high-necked for the races in the daytime and low-necked in the evening. We drove to Ascot every day at one o'clock. We had seats in the Queen's stand, and after seeing one race we went to lunch with Mr. Delane, who had open table for one hundred people every day. Mr. Delane belongs to the *Times* newspaper.

Baron Rothschild had *carte-blanche* to bring any guest, or as many as he liked. The Prince of Wales always lunched there, and any one that was of importance was sure to be present. I made many new acquaintances, and you may imagine how I enjoyed this glimpse of a world so entirely unknown to me. The races at Longchamps, Auteuil, and Chantilly I had seen many times; but I never saw anything like this exciting and bewildering scene.

The Prince of Wales gave a ball at Cooper's Hill (the house they had hired for the Ascot week), which was very charming and *sans façon*. I danced the cotillon with Baron Rothschild and a waltz with the Prince of Wales. The supper, which we had in the palm-garden, was an elaborate affair. We drove home in the early morning, just as the day was breaking.

The next day we lunched first at the barracks, and then afterward went to Virginia Water, where the Princess of Wales had arranged a picnic. There was boating on the pretty lake and tents on the lawn; tea was served during the afternoon, and a military band played the whole time. The great attraction was the echo. We all had to try our voices, and the gentlemen made bets as to how many times the echo would be heard. Some loud, piercing voices were repeated as many as eight times.

Here we bid our kind host good-by and took the train for Twickenham. We passed the night with Mr. and Mrs. Hoffman at their villa. The next day we were invited to a croquet - party and dinner by the Count and Countess de Paris.

We arrived at Twickenham Court at four o'clock, and began playing our game directly. Mrs. Hoffman had been praising me to the Countess de Paris to such a degree that she was fired with ambition to play against a "champion" of the first water, When we appeared on the ground I noticed that the Countess had a small ivory mallet. "This," I said to myself, "is a foregone conclusion; any one who plays with a fancy mallet, and that of ivory, is sure to be beaten." And in my conceit I thought I need not give myself much trouble about the game. Alas! I never appreciated the saying that "pride has a fall" until that day. At first I played with utter indifference, I was so sure of winning, and even when the Countess de Paris walked triumphantly over the ground, carrying everything before her, I smiled inwardly, saying to myself, "Just wait." But though I played my very best I never scored a game, and I could not even make a decent stroke. I felt so discouraged, and I was beaten all to pieces. The dinner was solemn and impressive, the whole Orléans family being present.

The Prince de Joinville, the Duke de Chartres, and the Count de Paris, with their wives; in all, about twenty at table. I was disgusted with myself, provoked at my silly self-assurance, and mortified that I had been beaten *à plate couture*, which in English means that all my seams had been turned down and ironed, and all my feathers were drooping.

We were (at least I was) glad to escape at ten o'clcock. I don't think I ever was so tired. The week at Ascot, the picnic at Virginia Water, the balls, and the late sitting-up at night, all told on my nerves, and instead of resting at the Hoffmans', I passed a miserable and restless night.

The following day we returned to London in time to

drive out, at one o'clock, with the Lionel Rothschilds to their country-place. It is the most magnificent estate; the cedar-trees are particularly beautiful, and the broad lawn, which stretches out in front of the house, is the finest I have ever seen. Baron Rothschild himself drove the coach and four horses, and we spun along the fine road, passing Richmond and all the pretty villas and gardens, which were full of roses. It was my birthday, and I had many splendid presents. From Baroness Rothschild I received a superb traveling-bag, all the fittings of silver gilt, with my initials. Baron Alfred Rothschild gave me a smelling-bottle, with the colors of his racing-stables in enamel. We had a delightful luncheon, and got back to London in time for dinner at Lady Sherbourne's. On hearing it was my birthday, she took a diamond-ring from her finger and gave it to me.

More balls, more dinners, luncheons, and garden-parties followed one another.

We intend to leave London after the ball at Marlborough House. I must go home, as I have nothing more to wear. We had accepted an invitation to the garden-party given by the Princess of Wales at Chiswick (their charming country-place). All the beauty and elegance of London graced the occasion. The Princess looked exquisite in her dainty summer toilette, and had a pleasant smile for every one. The Prince circulated among the guests, speaking to every one in his usual genial manner. The three little Princesses looked like three fluffy pink pin-cushions covered with white muslin. On the extensive lawn, which was like a green-velvet carpet, the ladies strolled about in their pretty, fresh dresses, sometimes sitting at the little tables which were shaded by large Japanese umbrellas placed between the terrace and the walk. It was a garden of living flowers.

The Prince of Wales, in his peculiarly abrupt manner, said to me, "What have you been doing since Ascot?"

"I have been doing a great deal, sir: dining and dancing and enjoying myself generally."

"I am glad to know that. Been singing?"

"Not much, sir. We dined at Twickenham Court, where I played a disastrous game of croquet," I answered.

"Do they play croquet at Twickenham Court?"

"Indeed they do, sir. The Countess de Paris plays a very good game."

"What day did you dine there?"

"On the 17th, your Highness," I replied.

"Are you sure it was the 17th you dined there?"

"Yes, I am quite sure. I *know* it, because it was the day before my birthday."

"Was it a large dinner?"

"It was rather large. The whole Orléans family was there, and some others."

"Did you know that they had had a *conseil de famille* that day?"

"No," I answered; "I heard nothing of it."

The Prince continued: "The whole family signed a petition to the Emperor Napoleon to be allowed to return to France and serve in the army. Can you imagine why they want to go back to France when they can live quietly here and be out of politics?" the Prince said.

"Do you think, sir, that the Emperor will refuse?"

"One never knows," said the Prince. "Qui vivra verra."

The Marlborough ball was very magnificent. The Princess of Wales looked exquisite. She is very lovely, and has gracious, sweet manners. I don't wonder that her people adore her; and I think the Prince is just as good as he can be.

July, 1870.

On our return from London I remained quietly at delightful Petit Val.

On the 10th of July we received an invitation to a dinner at St. Cloud, but unfortunately we had promised Baroness Rothschild to spend some days at Ferrières, and when the invitation came we were obliged to send a telegram to St. Cloud expressing our regrets. There is such a talk of war, and so many rumors afloat, that every one is more than excited. Alphonse Rothschild says that, if there should be a war, it will be a tremendous one, and that Germany is better prepared than France. "But," said he, "you ought to know about that, as your brother-in-law Hatzfeldt is in the secrets of his country."

"That's just it," I answered; "because he is in the secrets of his country he is the last person to learn anything from, and we (the family) would be the last to know. But do you think that, if war were really imminent, the Emperor would think of giving a dinner?" I asked.

"That might be. We don't yet know what the result of Benedetti's interview with the King of Prussia at Ems will be," the Baron answered.

We stayed at Ferrières until the 14th, and returned to Petit Val, where we received another invitation to St. Cloud for the 17th, which we accepted. On the 15th we went to Chamarande, returning to Paris on the following afternoon. The Duke de Persigny was not at Chamarande, otherwise we should have been a little more *au courant* of how desperate things looked in Paris. The Duchess had a word from the Duke the night before, "and he seemed," she said, "very despondent." But I remarked, as I did before, "Things could not be so threatening if they were giving a dinner." "Je n'y comprends rien," she replied, which was her invariable answer to any doubt expressed, or when one wanted a direct response.

We got back to town at half-past five, and I soon began dressing for the dinner. We drove out to St. Cloud, and arrived at the door of the château just before seven o'clock. What was our astonishment at not seeing any of the numerous servants who generally were waiting in the vestibule. There was only one man to be seen.

I began taking off my mantle, still wondering, when Monsieur de Laferrière came quickly out from one of the salons and said excitedly, "Did you not receive my letter countermanding the dinner?"

"Countermanding the dinner! What? Then there is no dinner?"

"No," he rejoined; "it has been countermanded."

As our carriage could not yet have got very far off, nothing was easier than to call it back and return to Paris. And I put on my wrap to depart, and stood there waiting for the coupé. Then Monsieur de Laferrière came out again and said, "Her Majesty says that, now that you are here, you had better stay."

"But," I protested, "it is much better for us to go back."

He looked puzzled and said, "But the Empress desires it; you cannot well refuse, can you?"

"We will do as you advise."

"Then I advise you to stay," he answered.

And stay we did, and I never regretted anything so much in my life.

When we went into the drawing-room their Majesties were already there. The Empress came toward me and said kindly, "How do you do?" The Emperor held out his hand, but did not say a word. He looked so ill and tired. Never had I seen him look like that! The Prince Imperial seemed preoccupied and very serious.

Dinner was announced; the Emperor gave his arm to the Empress, and the Prince gave me his. There was no one beside ourselves and the Household, perhaps twenty in all, and dinner was served in the small dining-room looking toward Paris. On the other side of me was Count d'Arjuson, aide-de-camp to the Emperor.

You may imagine that I wished myself a hundred miles away. The Emperor never uttered a word; the Empress sat with her eyes fixed on the Emperor, and did not speak to a single person. No one spoke. The Emperor would receive telegram upon telegram; the gentleman sitting next to him opened the telegrams and put them before his Majesty. Every now and again the Emperor would look across the table to the Empress with such a distressed look it made me think that something terrible was happening, which was true. I could not learn much from my surroundings, as dead silence reigned. The dinner was very simple. How different from the gorgeous repasts of Compiègne, and how sad every one looked! I was glad when the signal for leaving the table was given and we re-entered the drawing-room.

The Emperor was immediately surrounded by his gentlemen. The Empress moved a little way off, but without taking her eyes from her husband. The Prince Imperial stood by his father, watching him. Then the Empress advanced toward his Majesty and took his arm to leave the room. Just as she neared the door she looked at me, turned back, and coming up to where I was standing held out her hand and said, "Bonsoir." The Emperor stood a moment irresolutely, then, bowing his head, left the room with the Empress on his arm, the Prince following.

We bade the *dames d'honneur* good night and fled, found the coupé before the entrance, and weren't we glad to get in it and drive away? I never in my life felt what it was to be *de trop* and even *deux de trop*. We reached the Rue de Courcelles at nine o'clock. It was too early to go to bed, and so I am sitting in my dressing-gown, while Charles has gone to his club to learn the latest news.

19th July.

This morning war was declared for sure, and they say that the Emperor is leaving soon with the Prince. Every one is very confident of the success of the French Army, and people go about in the streets singing "À Berlin" to the tune of "Les lampions."

PETIT VAL, *28th July*.

The Emperor, with the Prince, left this morning for Metz, to take the command of the army. He did not come into Paris, but in order to avoid demonstrations, noise, etc., had a platform put up on the other side of the station at St. Cloud, where the Empress and her ladies could say their adieux without the crowd looking on. The last words the Empress said to her son were, "Louis, fais ton devoir." She is made the Regent during the absence of the Emperor.

30th August.

It looks now as if there might be war all over France. As it is, the Prussians are near Paris, and the French are trying to regain the ground they have lost. The news we get is very contradictory. According to the French official reports the French Army has been successful all the time. The English papers probably give the untarnished truth, unfavorable as it may be to France. Some people say that at the worst there is only a question of unimportant skirmishes.

We are well out of Paris and safely in Dinard, where Mr. Moulton is building a new house (we have already two). We left Petit Val rather precipitately, leaving everything behind us, clothes in wardrobes and letters in commodes. We shall not be away more than a month.

I can only say that we lead the most peaceful of lives during this time of war. I will not tell you any news, because it won't be news when you read it. We are and have been all the time fed on false reports, great placards

252

pasted up everywhere telling of the French victories, but from our English papers we know the contrary. It is pitiful to see the poor, half-clad peasants being drilled on the beach with sticks in their hands instead of guns. It is the French idea of keeping up the spirits of the army.

I sang in the cathedral last Sunday, and the *quête* (the money taken), they said, was a large sum. I doubt it! I know what the *quêtes* are here. Anything that can rattle in the bag is good. Buttons are particularly popular, as no one can see what you put in, and it does not matter.

There was a tremendous storm last night, and many of the slates of the new villa were blown off. The servants who sleep there thought that the Germans had come at last, and were frightened out of the few wits they own.

Madame Gignoux, our neighbor at Petit Val, who is living in her other château in Brittany, sent a letter to me which I should send to Helen in Berlin, to be sent to Paul, who is in Versailles, to be sent to Mr. Washburn, in Paris, who is to give it to Henry at Petit Val. Rather roundabout way! I can't tell you how much of that sort of thing I am constantly doing for people who are afraid of doing anything for themselves; they think every one is a spy or a traitor.

PARIS, *March 14, 1871.*

DEAR MAMA,—You will be surprised to see that I am in Paris; but you will understand why when I tell you that I received a letter from Mrs. Moulton to this effect: "If you wish to go to Petit Val to look after the things you left there when you went to Dinard last August, you had better come to Paris without delay, as the trains are running regularly now." The trains may have been running regularly (I left Dinard the next day), but they were certainly not running on time, for we missed all connections, and only arrived at Rennes after seven o'clock, too late to catch the evening train for Paris. The fine omnibus at the station made me imagine that it belonged to an equally fine hotel, but the hotel proved to be anything but fine. It was dreadfully dirty and shabby, and filled to overflowing. It was with the greatest difficulty I was able to secure a room for myself. My grumbling maid had to content herself with the sofa. The *salle à manger* was thronged with officers clanking their swords on the brick floor and all talking at once. I passed a sleepless night, being kept awake by the loud and incessant conversations in the corridor and the continual tramping of soldiers under my window. We started for Paris the next morning at eight o'clock. The train was crowded with people who, like myself, were eager to return home after so many months of anxious waiting. In all the stations through which we passed one saw nothing but soldiers, their ragged uniforms hanging on their emaciated forms; their feet—which had been frozen in January (poor things!)—were still bandaged, and hardly any of them possessed shoes. They did look, indeed, the picture of abject dejection and misery.

At Le Mans, the place where we stopped for luncheon, the soldiers were lying about on the brick pavement of the station, too tired and worn out to move, and presenting the saddest sight it has ever fallen to my lot to witness. They were waiting for the cattle vans to take them away. In these they would be obliged to stand until they reached Paris and its hospitals. Every one of the travelers was anxious to alleviate their misery in some way, by offering them cigars, food, and money. My heart bled for the poor creatures, and I gave them all I had in my purse, and my luncheon also. They represented the débris of Faidherbe's army, which of all the troops had seen the most desperate fighting during the war. All the trains we passed were packed tight with soldiers, herded together like cattle, patient misery painted on their pale, tired faces.

Hungry and penniless I arrived at last in Paris, where I was delighted to see a healthy, normal-looking person in the shape of my brother-in-law, Henry, who met me at the station. He had plenty to tell me of his experiences since last September. He had been living at Petit Val throughout the whole campaign, and was still there looking after our interests, *faisant la navette* between Petit Val, Paris, and Versailles at his will. He had free passes for all these places. On my arrival at the Rue de Courcelles I found the family well, Mrs. Moulton knitting as usual, Mademoiselle Wissembourg napping, and Mr. Moulton reading the *Journal des Débats* out loud in his peculiar French.

I thought of the "Brook," by Tennyson: "Men may come and men may go, but I go on for ever." The family had not eaten cats and dogs during the siege as, according to the newspapers, other people had done.

Mr. Moulton having been in Paris at the time of the Revolution of 1848, and knowing about revolutions, had had the forethought to lay in a stock of provisions, such as ham, biscuit, rice, etc., and all sorts of canned things, which he deemed would be sufficient for all their requirements. They had even given dinner-parties limited to a very choice few, who sometimes brought welcome additions in the shape of other canned delicacies.

When the family moved from Petit Val to Paris last September, the French Government had given them permission to keep one or two cows. They also brought a calf, a sheep, and some chickens with them. The cows and the sheep shared the stables with the horses, while the chickens were let loose in the conservatory, and were expected to lay enough eggs to pay for their board. The gardener had cleverly converted the conservatory into a sort of kitchen garden, and had planted some useful vegetables, such as radishes, carrots, salad, etc., so you see the family took good care that it should have enough to eat, and mice and rats only appeared on the table after the repasts.

PARIS, *March 16, 1871.*

DEAR MAMA,—This has been a very fatiguing day for me, so you will only receive a short letter.

Paul [1] invited Mrs. Moulton and me to come to Versailles, and offered us a cup of tea as an inducement. You know Paul is Count Bismarck's private secretary, having been with him and the German sovereign during the entire war. He is still at Versailles, but expects to leave for Berlin one of these first days. He came to fetch us at the station with the fat ponies and the basket-

---

[1] Count Hatzfeldt, my brother-in-law.

wagon (the ponies had escaped the fate of other fat
ponies, and they had not furnished steaks for famished
Parisians, but continued to trot complacently about, as
of old). Fortunately they were not too fat to carry us
through the park at a lively pace, and land us at Paul's
palatial residence. It seemed strange to see German
officers, in their tight-fitting uniforms, strolling leisurely
about in the park, where before I had only seen the
rather slovenly *pious-pious* on holidays, when the fountains played by day and the fireworks by night.

The park looked enchanting in its spring toilette,
and made me think of the last time I was here. Could
it have been only last May? It seems years ago!

Paul had invited some of his German officer friends
to take tea with us. Paul had been with the King of
Prussia and Jules Favre and Bismarck at Ferrières, where
they had met, he said, "with no other result than to see
Jules Favre weep."

Paul had been at Versailles when the King was pro-
claimed Emperor in the *salle de glaces* — the greatest
emotion he had ever experienced, he said. He had also
been witness of the signing of the armistice. The pen
with which it was signed had been given him as a
souvenir, and it was lying on his table.

Paul thought the Emperor Napoleon more to be pitied
than blamed. He had gone into this war without really
knowing the true state of things. He was made to believe that there were four hundred thousand men ready
to take the field, when in reality there were only half
that number, and those certainly not fit to be pitted
against the Germans, who had been provided with better
and newer maps than the French, and knew France and

its army more thoroughly than the French themselves. We could have talked on this subject for hours had not the fat ponies come to take us to the station, where we bade farewell to Paul and the officers, and returned to Paris for the modest repast which we dignified by the name of dinner.

March 17th.

DEAR MAMA,—Such a funny thing happened to-day.

I don't know whether I told you of some Americans, called the O——s, I met in Dinard fresh from America (*via* Southampton). When I bade them good-by, I said, in an offhand way, "When you come to Paris you must come and see me."

"Oh! that will be nice," gushingly replied Mrs. O——. "Where do you live? (Every one of the O——s' phrases commenced with "Oh!")

"I live in the Rue de Courcelles," I answered.

"Oh! Roue de Carrousel," she repeated. "What number?"

"Rue de Courcelles," I replied, correctingly; "twenty-seven."

Mrs. O——'s next question was, "Oh! have you a flat?"

"A flat!! No," I said, "we have a hotel. Every one knows our hotel in the Rue de Courcelles."

I then proceeded to forget the O——s and everything concerning them. This morning, when we were at luncheon, the *concierge* came rushing in, the tassels on his *calotte* bristling with agitation.

"Madame," he gasped, "there is a fiacre full of people with a lot of trunks asking to come in to Madame. I

258

can't understand what they want." His emotion choked him.

We all said in unison: "Ask for their cards. Who can they be?"

The *concierge* came back with Mr. O——'s card.

I recollected my impulsive invitation and thought it very polite of them to be so *empressés*. I went into the salon, followed by Mademoiselle W——, where we found Mr. O—— seated at his ease in a *fauteuil*, his feet reposing on the white-bear rug.

I apologized for having kept him waiting, but explained that we had been at luncheon.

He (complacently), "Oh, that's all right; we have just arrived in Paris and we came straight to you."

I felt overwhelmed at such a keen appreciation of my politeness.

"How is Mrs. O——?" I said.

He answered with the inevitable "Oh!" "Oh! she's all right. She's outside in the cab."

"Indeed!" I said, and wondered why she had not sent her card in with his, though I supposed she was waiting to be asked to come in, if he found me at home.

"We thought before trying anywhere else we would see if you could take us in."

This staggered me considerably. I tried to take *him* "in" as he stood before me with traveling cap and umbrella.

"Are you full?" he went on. Mademoiselle and I wondered if we showed signs of a too copious luncheon.

"Why, what a nice place you have here!" looking about. "Well," he continued, nothing daunted, "you see, we only want one bedroom, for us, with a room next for baby, and one not too far off for Arthur."

What was he driving at? Mademoiselle W——
thought he was either a spy or a burglar who had come
to take a survey of the hotel. Her bracelets and bunch
of keys rattled ominously as the thought of burglars
entered her brain.

He, familiarly settling himself down for a chat, "Do
you think you could pick up a maid for Mrs. O——?"

Mademoiselle and I exchanged a glance of intelligent
indulgence and thought: All our friends wanted, probably, was a few addresses before settling themselves in
Paris. How stupid of us not to have thought of this
sooner! I hastened to promise all sorts of names and
addresses of tradespeople, thinking he would take his
departure.

Not he! On the contrary, he tucked his umbrella
more firmly under his arm, and turned to Mademoiselle
W——: "Have you got a register?" taking her, no
doubt, for *la dame du comptoir.*

Mademoiselle draped herself in her most Rachel-like
attitude and glanced knowingly at the hot-air flue which
she had been told was a register.

"We have," she answered curtly, wondering if this
extraordinary creature could be suffering from cold on
this warm spring day.

"I had better write my name down!" This was too
much! Mademoiselle thought now that he was not only
a burglar, but a lunatic.

"I think," I said, "I can give you the address of a very
nice maid," trying to lead him back into the paths we
had trodden before.

"Oh! that'll be all right. You have perhaps a maid
in the house?"

"Certainly we have," answered Mademoiselle with asperity, giving her velvet bow an agitated pat.

"Money is no object," continued he; "I'm always willing to pay what one asks." Mademoiselle now thought he was drunk and was for sending for the servants.

I asked him, "How is the baby?"

"Oh! baby's all right. The nurse has been a little upset by the journey. You might give us the address of your doctor."

"Yes, yes." I gave him the name instantly, hoping he would go.

"We don't need him right off; he can come here later, and you can talk to him yourself. Maria does not speak French."

Mademoiselle gasped for breath, while he looked about him approvingly.

"Real nice house you have, Madame, not very central, but we don't mind being in a quiet part of Paris, as Maria wants to learn French"; and seeing the conservatory, he remarked: "Arthur can play in there. That'll do splendidly." After an awkward pause: "Well, if the rooms are ready, we can come right in. Maria will be wondering why I have been so long." *I* also wondered why he had been so long!

To cap the climax, he handed Mademoiselle a five-franc piece, saying: "I guess this will cover the cab. The coachman can keep the change."

A light dawned on me! He thought this was a hotel!

I said, "When you get settled in your hotel I will come and see you."

"What! Can't you take us in? We counted on coming to your hotel."

I laughed outright. Mademoiselle raised what she is pleased to call her eyebrows and shrugged her shoulders.

I explained to my guest his mistake. Instead of saying, "Oh! that's all right," he said, "Well, I'll be blessed," and without wasting any more time than for a hasty good-by he marched out to join the tired Maria, the baby, the nurse, and Arthur. We watched them as they drove off, all gazing out of the window at the hotel which was *not* a hotel.

May Allah protect them!

March 19th.

DEAR MOTHER,—The day before yesterday Henry and I decided to go to Petit Val. I looked forward with delight to seeing my beautiful home again. Mrs. Moulton promised to drive out and bring me back to Paris late in the afternoon. We drove to the Gare de la Bastille and took our tickets for La Varenne. The station was so horribly dirty, it looked as if it had not been swept or cleaned since the commencement of the war, and as for the first-class compartment we entered I really hesitated to sit down on the shabby and dilapidated cushions.

We traveled very slowly, and stopped at every station mentioned in the time-table. Although these were devoid of travelers, the conductor opened the doors of all the carriages, and after waiting the allotted time shouted mechanically, "En voiture," though there was absolutely no one to get in.

I thought we never would arrive!

All the little towns, once so thrifty and prosperous, are now hardly more than ruins. It is no wonder that this part of the country (Vincennes, St. Maur, Chenvières, etc.) is so destroyed, because it was all about here that the French, shut up in Paris, had made the most frequent sorties. Everything was terribly changed.

Now my beautiful bridge is a thing of the past. There is one arch half in water and débris of stone and mortar on the shore.

Henry and I, having no alternative, were obliged to walk from the station to the pontoon bridge, made, Henry said, in one night. I don't know about that; but what I do know is that the French blew up my bridge *in one night*. Then we made the whole distance to Petit Val on foot, passing by the châteaux of Ormesson, Chenvières, Grand Val, and Montalon.

All the châteaux we passed are utterly abandoned, some quite in ruins; one can see, for instance, right through beautiful Grand Val, bereft of windows and doors.

But worse was awaiting me! My heart sank within me when we came in sight of the *potager*, the glory of Petit Val, so renowned in its day for its fruits and vegetables. Now it is frightful to see! Its walls torn asunder; cannon put in its crenelated sides, dilapidated and destroyed; the garden filled with rubbish of all description. But, as though nature were protesting against all this disorder and neglect, the cherry-trees were placidly blossoming; the almond-trees, with their delicate pink flowers, filled the air with perfume: everything, in short, doing its part in spite of war and bloodshed. Your heart would ache if you could see the place as it is now. The porter's lodge is completely gutted, windowless and doorless, open to wind and weather.

It seems strange to see a sentry-box stationed at the entrance of the park and a sentinel pacing to and fro. Henry gave the password, and we walked up the avenue toward the château. I will not weary you by trying to depict my feelings, but will leave you to imagine what they must have been. I looked in vain for the beautiful Lebanon cedar which, you remember, stood where my nightingale used to sing, on the broad lawn. Henry said that it had been the first tree that the Germans had cut down, and it had been lying there on the lawn just as it fell, where the soldiers could conveniently cut their fuel. Henry called my attention to a white flag flying on the château, which, at Paul's request, Count Bismarck had ordered to be put there.

Henry said it signified in military language that only staff officers were to occupy the château, and that no unnecessary damage should be done "if we are quiet." Did Bismarck think we were likely to be unruly and go about shooting people? The one thing in the world we wanted was to be quiet. The flag also signified that the château should be protected. Henry had once complained to Bismarck of the damage done by the German soldiers at Petit Val, and Bismarck had replied, "À la guerre comme à la guerre," adding, "The German Government will hold itself responsible for private losses, with the exception of those which are consequences of a state of war . . . there is always a certain amount of unavoidable destruction."

"Unavoidable destruction!" cried Henry; "this can cover a multitude of sins."

"The exigencies of war, if you like that better," rejoined Bismarck.

Paul Hatzfeldt wrote to Helen last September that the King of Prussia had promised to put Petit Val under special protection. He even wished to go there himself; but Paul thought Petit Val looked so spoiled that he was glad the King did not go. If it was spoiled in September last, imagine what it must have been six months later, with six months of soldiers to spoil it!

When we arrived at the château itself the officers, who had evidently just been lunching, came out to meet us, wondering, apparently, who this courageous lady (poor trembling me!) could possibly be. Henry knew their names, and presented them all to me; they clanked their heels together and made the most perfect of military salutes.

The commanding officer in charge of Petit Val is Count Arco, a major of a Bavarian regiment. I hastened to explain my presence among them, saying that I wished to collect the various things I had left in the château when I went away last August, and I had taken advantage of the first occasion which offered itself of coming here.

Count Arco held a short conversation with Henry, who told him I would like to go to my apartment. "Do not trouble to have anything disarranged for me," I said, "as I shall only be here for a short time. My mother-in-law is driving out later in the afternoon to take me back to Paris."

While we were talking Count Arco informed me that

there were twenty-six officers in the château itself and one hundred and twenty soldiers quartered round in the different pavilions, farm-houses, *ateliers*, and—I think he said—about fifty in the *orangerie*.

Presently an orderly appeared and conducted me to my rooms, which had evidently been hurriedly evacuated, but they looked quite nice and clean. I was agreeably surprised to find my writing-desk and commodes pretty nearly as I remembered to have left them. At any rate, letters, trinkets, and so forth seemed undisturbed. I wish I could say the same for my wearing apparel, which had considerably diminished since my departure. Waists without their skirts, and skirts without their waists, and I found various female articles unknown to me; but never mind! *Honi soit qui mal y pense!*

It was said in France that no German could resist a clock, and that the dearth of clocks after the war is quite noticeable. To prove the contrary, and to applaud the officers who had lived in Petit Val (and there had been many hundreds of them), my clock was ticking away as of old on my mantelpiece.

Having finished packing the things to take with me, I wished to have a look at *protected* Petit Val.

The "unavoidable destruction" had been interpreted in a very liberal sense.

The salon was a sight never to be forgotten. The mirrors which paneled the whole of the east wall were broken, as if stones had been thrown at them; every picture had been pierced by bayonets. The beautiful portrait of the Marquis de Marigny (the former owner of Petit Val and brother of Madame de Pompadour) had vanished. Instead of the Aubusson furniture we had left, which, I suppose, has been transferred to other homes, I found two pianos, one grand (not ours), two billiard-tables (not ours), some iron tables, and some very hard iron chairs (certainly not ours), annexed, I should say, from a neighboring café.

The library, formerly containing such rare and valuable books, is now a bedroom—the shelves half empty, the books scattered about, some of them piled up in a corner and used as a table. Henry said that, when any one wanted to light a fire or a pipe, they simply tore a page out of a book. What did they care? Was it not one of the "exigencies of war"? The frames and glasses of the engravings were broken; but, fortunately, all the engravings were not ruined.

You remember Mrs. Moulton's boudoir, where all was so dainty and complete? The soldiers had converted it into a kitchen, and at the moment we were there they were cooking some very smelly cabbage *à la tedesco*.

My pretty pavilion! If you could have seen it!

Evidently the all-powerful flag had not protected this, for it was without doors, windows, and parquets. The only thing in it was a dear little calf munching his last meal before being killed. To make it look more like a slaughter-house, there were haunches of beef hanging on the Louis XV. appliques, which had been left on the walls to serve as nails. Fresh blood was dropping from them on the sacks of potatoes underneath.

The officers had coffee served under the *charmille*.

I was glad to get something to sustain my sinking heart. Henry and I took a sad walk through the park. The once beautifully kept lawn is now like a ploughed field, full of ruts and stones.

The lake was shining in the sun, but on it there were no boats. The grotto over which used to trickle a little waterfall was completely dry, showing the ugly stucco false rocks. It seemed dismal and forlorn. I wondered how I ever could have thought it beautiful! The *rivière* was without its pretty rustic bridge; the picturesque pavilions were filled with soldiers; some were sitting on the porches mending their clothes.

Five o'clock came before we realized how late it was. We expected the carriage every moment; but there was no sign of it, though we scanned the length of the long avenue with the Count's field-glasses.

Why did Mrs. Moulton not come? Something must have happened! But what? Henry and I were seriously alarmed. Noticing our looks of dismay, Count Arco asked me if I was anxious. I replied that I naturally was anxious, because if my mother-in-law could not come or send the carriage she certainly would have telegraphed. He then inquired if I wished to send a telegram. No sooner had I said "yes" than an orderly appeared on horseback to take the telegram to the station. He returned, while we still stood in the avenue looking for the longed-for carriage, with the astounding news that all the telegraph wires were cut.

To take the train was our next idea, and the wondering orderly was again sent back to find out when the next train would start. This time he returned with still more astounding news.

There were no trains at all!

Count Arco seemed to be most agitated, and I could see, by the expression of the faces of the other officers, that they were more disturbed than they wanted us to notice.

What should I do? Everything was in ruins in the village. There was not even an *auberge* of the smallest dimensions. All the neighboring châteaux were abandoned. Of whom could I ask hospitality? Count Arco, seeing my embarrassment, proposed my staying the night at Petit Val. Henry's living there made it easier for me. So I accepted his offer; besides, there was no choice. The soldiers arranged my room according to their ideas of a lady's requirements, which included a boot-jack, ash-trays, beer-mugs, etc. Their intentions were of the best.

At seven o'clock Henry and I dined with the officers. It seemed strange to me to be presiding at my own table surrounded by German officers, Count Arco being my *vis-à-vis*.

Do you want to know what we had for dinner? Bean soup, brought from Germany. Sausages and and cabbage, put up in Germany. Coffee and zwiebacks, I suppose also from Germany.

The evening passed quickly, and I must admit very pleasantly. Any one who had pretensions to music played or sang. Henry performed some of his compositions; one officer did some card tricks. They all had an anecdote of their experience from the past months, which they told with great relish. Henry whispered to Count Arco: "My sister-in-law sings. Why don't you ask her for a song?" I could have pinched him!

Although I was very tired and did not feel like it, I reflected that almost anything was preferable to being begged and teased. And, after all, why not be as amiable as my companions, who had done their best to amuse me?

I seated myself at the piano and commenced with one

of Schumann's songs, and then I sang "Ma Mère était Bohémienne," of Massé, which had a great success, and at the refrain, "Et moi! j'ai l'âme triste," there was not a dry eye in the little circle. Graf Waldersee, one of the oldest warriors, wept like an infant while I was singing, and coming up to me, after blowing his nose, said, in his delightfully broken English, "You zing like an angle [I hope he meant angel]. It is as if ze paradise vas opened to us." Then he retired in a corner and wiped his eyes. I sang "Ein Jüngling liebt ein Mäd-chen," of Schumann, and when I came to the line, "Und wem das just passieret, dem bricht das Herz entzwei," I heard a mournful sigh. It came from the Benjamin of the flock, a very young officer, who sat with his hands over his face sobbing audibly. What chord had I struck? Was *his* the heart that was breaking *entzwei?*

I had sung to many people, but I think I never sang to a more appreciative audience than this one.

Henry accompanied me in "Beware!" Their en-thusiasm knew no bounds. They all gathered around me, eager to thank me for the unexpected pleasure. I really think they meant what they said.

When I returned to my room I looked out of my window and saw the sentinel pacing to and fro in the moonlight. I realized *for the first time* that the château was protected!

I mourned the beautiful and stately Lebanon cedar!

March 18th.

It seemed so strange to wake up and find myself in my room. An orderly brought me a very neatly arranged tray, with tea and buttered toast and a note from Henry announcing the terrible news that Paris was under arms —a revolution (*rien que ça*) had broken out, and all approaches to the city were barricaded. This was news indeed! I understood now why no carriage came last night, why trains were stopped, why telegraph wires were cut, and why no mother-in-law appeared.

Henry was waiting to communicate with me as soon as I was out of my room. Indeed, a more stranded mortal than I was could hardly be imagined! However, there seemed nothing for me to do but to await events.

The officers met us in the salon, and we discussed the situation and different possibilities, but without any practical result.

Every one was much excited about the news. The officers pretended not to know more than *we* did; perhaps what they did know they did not care to tell. We saw messengers flying in all directions, papers handed about, more messengers galloping down the avenue, agitation written on the faces around us. All I knew was that there was a revolution in Paris and *I was here*.

Going out to the stables, we found the soldiers grooming their horses unconcernedly. From there we went to the *orangerie*, which presented a queer sight. The soldiers, of whom there must have been sixty, had arranged their beds all along the walls on both sides, and to separate them one from another had placed a tub with its orange-tree. The aviary had been converted into a drying-ground for their *lingerie;* they had suspended ropes from side to side, and thereon hung their *week's wash* amid all its "unavoidable destruction." Henry told me that when the Germans first came to

Petit Val they begged old Pérault (the butler) to hand them the key of the wine-cellar, and on his refusing they had tied the old man to a tree in the park, and left him there the whole of one cold night to consider the situation. Needless to say, the next day the Germans had the key. After they had taken all the best Château-Lafitte and all the rare wines Mr. Moulton had bought during the Revolution of 1848, they emptied the casks containing the *Petit Bleu, made on the estate!* The result was disastrous, and could Mr. Moulton have only seen the poor creatures doubled up with torture he would have felt himself amply revenged.

We ascended the hill behind the château to the high terrace, from where one can see Paris. We saw no smoke, therefore Paris was not burning. But what was happening there? We returned to breakfast, where the military band was playing on the lawn (a superfluous luxury, I thought, but I did not realize that so trivial a thing as a revolution could not interfere with military order). We were treated to the eternal sausage and something they called beefsteak; it might as well have been called "suprême de donkey," it was so tough. However, the others ate it with iron jaws and without a pang. Count Arco suggested I should take a drive, *en attendant les événements*, and see the neighborhood. I acquiesced, thinking anything in the way of distraction would be a welcome relief. Imagine my feelings when I saw our *calèche*, a mere ghost of its former self, dragged by four artillery horses and postilioned by two heavy dragoons.

"The exigencies of war" had obliged the soldiers to remove the leather, the carpet, the cushions, and all the cloth; only the iron and wood remained to show that once this had been a carriage.

This ancient relic drew up with a thump on what had been flower-beds, and the Count opened the door for me to enter, but on observing my look of dismay when I saw the hard, cushionless seats, despatched an officer to try to find a cushion for me. Apparently, however, cushions were souvenirs our friends had forgotten to bring with them from other residences. Judging from the time we waited, the officer must have ransacked the whole house, but had found nothing better than a couple of bed-pillows, with which he appeared, carrying one under each arm, to the great amusement of the beholders. I mounted this grotesque equipage, the Count and Henry following, and sat enthroned on my pillows of state.

We asked, before starting, if there was any news from Paris, and receiving an answer in the negative, we drove off. Up hills, over lawns and flower-beds, zigzagging through vineyards and gardens, never by any chance keeping to the proper road, we made the tour of the environs.

To give you an idea how completely the châteaux had been ransacked, I can tell you that I picked up about a yard and a half of handsome Brussels lace in the courtyard of the château of Sucy. We drove hastily through the adjoining estate of Grand Val, which looked even more deplorable than Sucy. I began to wonder if the artillery horses and the carcass of the vehicle in which we sat would be capable of carrying me to Paris, or at least within walking distance of it. You see, I was beginning to get desperate. Here was I, with the day almost over, without any apparent prospect of getting away. But, as the Psalmist puts it, "Sorrow endureth for a night, but joy cometh in the morning." My joy came late in the afternoon, on returning to Petit Val, where I found the landeau of the American Legation, my mother-in-law, and (hobnobbing with the German officers) the American Minister himself, the popular and omnipotent Mr. Washburn.

They were overjoyed to see me, as they had been as anxious as I had been, having tried every means in their power to reach me. To telegraph was impossible; to send a groom on horseback equally so. Finally, as a last resource, they had written to Mr. Washburn to see if he could not solve the difficult question, which he did by driving out himself with Mrs. Moulton to fetch me.

As soon as the horses were sufficiently rested (my hosts and I being profuse in our mutual thanks), we started for Paris, passing through Alfort, Charenton, and many villages, all more or less in ruins. There were plenty of people lounging about in the streets. We reached Vincennes without difficulty; but thenceforth our troubles commenced in earnest.

Mr. Washburn thought it more prudent to close the carriage, cautioning the coachman to drive slower. We were stopped at every moment by soldiers and barricades; then Mr. Washburn would show his card and his *laissez passer*, after which we were allowed to pass on, until we came to more soldiers and more barricades. Omnibuses turned over, paving-stones piled up, barrels, ladders, ropes stretched across the streets, anything to stop the circulation. Poor Mr. Washburn was tired out popping his head first out of one window then out of the other, with his card in his hand.

ELIHU WASHBURN
United States Minister to France during the Commune

The men who accosted us were not discourteous, but spoke quite decidedly, as if they did not expect to be contradicted. We did not care to contradict them, either.

"We know you, Monsieur, by reputation, and we know that you are well disposed toward France. How do you feel toward *la Commune?*"

Mr. Washburn hesitating a moment, the man added, cynically, "Perhaps you would like to add a stone to our barricades." He made as if he would open the door of the carriage; but Mr. Washburn answered, holding back the door, "I take it for granted, Monsieur, that I have your permission to drive on, as I have something very important to attend to at my Legation," and gave the man a defiant look, which rather frightened him, and we drove through the crowd. All along the Rue de Rivoli we saw the soldiers massing together in groups, *La Garde nationale* (Mr. Washburn said they so called themselves since yesterday), a miserable-looking set of men, talking very loud and flourishing their guns as if they were walking-sticks.

In passing the Rue Castiglione we saw. it was full of soldiers, and looking toward the Place de la Concorde we saw more barricades there.

This was a sight to behold! The space around the Column was filled with paving-stones and all sorts of débris (strange to say, my eyes saw more brooms than anything else); and cannon pointing everywhere. A very impertinent, common-looking *voyou* said, on looking at Mr. Washburn's card, "Vous êtes tous très chic . . . mais vous ne passerez pas, tout de même."

We shook in our shoes.

But Mr. Washburn, equal to the occasion, said something which had the desired effect, and we passed on.

All along the Rue de Rivoli the yesterday-fledged soldiers were straggling about, glad to have a day of leisure. They brandished their bayonets with a newly acquired grace, pointing them in front of them in such a reckless way that people made a large circle around them, frightened to death.

As we passed the Hôtel de Ville we saw the red flag of the Communards waving over the Palace. Barricades and cannon filled the space between that and the Rue de Rivoli. Here we were stopped again, and tired Mr. Washburn, annoyed to death, answered more stupid questions, showed his card and documents, and gave a little biography of himself.

I thought we should never get on.

I could have cried when I saw the Tuileries; it was only last August I had had a delightful half-hour with the Empress (she asked me to take tea with her). Then she was full of confidence in the triumph of the Emperor (who could have doubted it?), pleased that her son should have received *le baptême du feu*, as the Emperor telegraphed—oh, the pity of it all! and that was only last August—seven months ago.

As we drove by I thought of the famous ball given at the Tuileries last May (*Le bal de Plébiscite*), the most splendid thing of its kind one had ever seen.

And now! The Tuileries deserted, empty, the Emperor a prisoner, the Empress a fugitive! All France demoralized! All its prestige gone! One wonders how such things can be.

Mr. Washburn said he was not sorry to have remained

RUE DE RIVOLI, WHERE THE HÔTEL CONTINENTAL NOW STANDS

in Paris (an experience he would on no account have missed). He thought he had been of service to his own country and also to France.

Mrs. Moulton remarked, "What would those shut up in Paris have done without you?"

"Oh! I was only a post-office," he answered.

"The only *poste restante* in Paris," I said under my breath; but I did not dare utter anything so frivolous at the moment.

In the Faubourg St.-Honoré things were much quieter, though there were numbers of soldiers slouching about with their muskets pointing every which way. When we arrived at last in the Rue de Courcelles (it had taken us four hours) all was as quiet as Sunday in Boston.

Mr. Moulton had been almost crazy with anxiety; but the thought that we were sailing under the American colors had calmed him somewhat, and his past emotions did not prevent him from reading the *Journal des Débats* to us. I slipped off to bed tired out, but thankful not to be any longer "under protection."

March 20th.

Louis asked permission to go and assist at the proclamation of the Commune, which was to be read at the Hôtel de Ville.

There was a platform built in front of the façade, which was decorated with many red flags and covered with a red carpet, and all the new members of the committee wore the symbolical red sashes over their worthy shoulders. The statue of Henry II. was duly draped with red flags and ragged boys. Louis stood first and foremost among many of his old comrades, the famous and plucky Zouaves. Henri d'Assy read the proclamation out in a loud voice, and informed the public that the Commune (this new and charming infant) was baptized in the name of *Liberté, Égalité,* and *Fraternité.* There was great enthusiasm, and a salvo of artillery underlined the big words, and there arose a mighty shout of "Vive la Commune!" from thousands of hoarse throats which shook the very earth. Louis's account was worth hearing; but mine is only the truth with variations. He was most impressed, and I fancy it would not have taken much persuasion to have made him a red-hot Communist then and there.

Great excitement prevailed all Sunday. The Communists remained in possession of all the public buildings. The red flag was hoisted everywhere, even from the palace of the Princess Mathilde, who, as you know, lives directly opposite us. The Princess had left Paris last September. All the world knows how our clever American dentist, Dr. Evans, helped the Empress safely out of Paris, and of her flight; and after the catastrophe of Sedan it would have been dangerous for any member of the Imperial family to have remained here. As I look from my window across to the Princess's palace, and see all the windows open and the courtyard filled with shabby soldiers, I realize that we are *en pleine Commune,* and wonder when we shall come out of all this chaos, and how it will all end.

To-day there was a great demonstration in the streets.

A young fellow named Henri de Pène thought if he could collect enough people to follow him he would lead them to the barricades in the Place Vendôme, in order to beg the Communards, in the name of the people, to restore order and quiet in the city. He sent word beforehand that they would come there *unarmed*.

De Pène started at a very early hour from the distant Boulevards, calling to every one and beckoning to them, in order to make them come from their balconies and from their work, and shouting to all in the streets, managed to assemble a large crowd to join in his courageous undertaking.

I happened to go at one o'clock to Worth's, in the Rue de la Paix, and, finding the street barred, I left my coupé in the Rue des Petits Champs, telling Louis to wait for me in the Rue St.-Arnaud (just behind the Rue de la Paix), and I walked to No. 7.

I wondered why there were so few people in the streets. The Place Vendôme was barricaded with paving-stones, and cannon were pointing down the Rue de la Paix. I walked quietly along to Worth's, and hardly had I reached his salon than we heard distant, confused sounds, and then the shouting in the street below made us all rush to the windows.

What a sight met our eyes!

This handsome young fellow, De Pène, his hat in his outstretched hand, followed by a crowd of men, women, and children, looked the picture of life, health, and enthusiasm.

De Pène, seeing people on Worth's balcony, beckoned to them to join him; but Mr. Worth wisely withdrew inside, and, shaking his Anglo-Saxon head, said, "Not I." *He*, indeed!

The crowd bore banners on which were written: "*Les Amis du Peuple*," "*Amis de l'Ordre*," "*Pour la Paix*," and one with "*Nous ne sommes pas armés.*" This mass of humanity walked down the Rue de la Paix, filling the whole breadth of it.

One can't imagine the horror we felt when we heard the roar of a cannon, and looking down saw the street filled with smoke, and frightened screams and terrified groans reached our ears. Some one dragged me inside the window, and shut it to drown the horrible noises outside. De Pène was the first who was killed. The street was filled with dead and wounded. Mr. Hottingeur (the banker) was shot in the arm. The living members of *Les Amis* scampered off as fast as their legs could carry them, while the wounded were left to the care of the shopkeepers, and the dead were abandoned where they fell until further aid should come.

It was all too horrible!

I felt terribly agitated, and, moreover, deadly sick. My one thought was to reach my carriage and get home as quickly as possible. But how was I to accomplish it? The Rue de la Paix was, of course, impossible. Worth had a courtyard, but no outlet into the Rue St.-Arnaud. He suggested that I should go through his *ateliers*, which he had at the top of the house, and reach an adjoining apartment, from which I might descend to the Rue St.-Arnaud, where I would find my carriage. He told one of his women to lead the way, and I followed. We toiled up many flights of wearisome steps until we arrived at the above-mentioned *ateliers*. These communicated with another apartment, of which Worth's woman had the key. On her opening the door we found ourselves in a small bedroom (not in the tidiest condition), which appeared to have just been occupied.

We passed through this room and came out to a staircase, where the demoiselle said, "You have only to go down here." I therefore proceeded to descend the five flights of waxed steps, holding on to the wobbly iron railing, my legs trembling, my head swimming, and my heart sick. My only hope was to reach the carriage and home!

When at last I came to the *porte-cochère* I found it closed and locked, and the frightened *concierge* would not open for me. Fortunately, I had a gold piece to make her yield to my demand. She reluctantly unfastened the door and I went out. The street was filled with a terrified mob howling and flying in every direction. I caught a glimpse of the carriage away up the street, and I saw a hand gesticulating above the heads of the crowd, which I recognized as Louis's. It was the only one with a glove on!

I pushed my way through the mass of people, saying, very politely, "Pardon," as I pushed, and very politely, "Merci," after I had passed.

My horse had been unharnessed, and a man was trying to lead him away in spite of Louis's remonstrances. The man had hold of one side of the bridle, while Louis, with a pluck unknown before, kept a firm grip on the other, the horse being tugged at on both sides; and had he not been the angel he was, there would have been trouble in that little street.

The man holding the bridle opposite to Louis seemed a most formidable person to me. Still, I tried to smile with placid calmness, and though I was shaking all over said, "Pardon, Monsieur, will you permit me to have my horse harnessed?" I think he was completely taken off his guard, for, with the intuitive gallantry of a Frenchman, he answered me amiably, throwing back his coat, and showing me his badge, said, "I am the agent of the Committee of Public Safety, and it is for the Government that I take the horse."

I made him observe that it would be very difficult for me to walk to my home in the Rue de Courcelles, and if his government wanted the horse it could come there and fetch it. He looked doubtfully at me, as if weighing the situation, then said, very courteously, "I understand, Madame, and I give you back your horse." And he even helped Louis to reharness the horse, who seemed happy to return to his shafts.

When I arrived home I had to go to bed, I was so exhausted. Mademoiselle W—— administered the infallible camomile tea, her remedy for every ill. Her mind cannot conceive of any disease which is not cured by camomile tea, unless *in extremis*, when *fleurs d'oranger* takes its place.

24th of March.

The American secretary, Mr. Hoffman, and his wife, who are living in Versailles, invited Mrs. Moulton and me to luncheon to-day, saying that Mr. Washburn was also of the party; therefore we need have no fear of being molested or inconvenienced on our way.

There were only two trains to Versailles now. We took the one at midday from Paris, and arrived slowly but surely at the dirty, smoky station, where we found Mr. Hoffman waiting for us with a landau, in which we drove to his house.

We had an excellent luncheon, to which we all did

justice; after which Mr. Hoffman proposed our going
to the *Assemblée*, which has its sittings in the Palace,
and we readily consented. I was particularly glad to
have an opportunity to see the notabilities whose names
and actions had been our daily food these last months.

We sat in Mr. Hoffman's box, who, in his position as
secretary of the American Legation, had been obliged
to attend all these *séances* from the first. He knew all
the celebrities, and most amiably pointed them out to
me. Thiers was in the president's chair; Louis Blanc,
Jules Favre, Jules Grévy, and others were on the platform.

I confess I was rather disappointed; I thought that
this pleiades of brilliant minds would surely overcome
me to such a degree that I should not sleep for weeks.
But, strangely enough, they had just the opposite effect.
I think Mr. Washburn must be writing a book on modern
history, and Mr. Hoffman must be writing one on ancient
history. I sat between them—a drowsy victim—feeling
as if my brain was making spiral efforts to come out of
the top of my head.

While I was trying with all my might to listen to
Thiers's speech, who, I was sure, was saying something
most interesting, Mr. Hoffman, on one side of me, would
say, in a low tone, "Just think of it! Here, in these very
same boxes, the pampered and powdered [or something
like that] Court of Louis XIV. sat and listened to
Rameau's operas." I tried to seem impressed. Then,
on the other side, I would hear, "Do you know, Mrs.
Moulton, that the Communists have just taken seven
millions of francs from the Bank of France?" The
distant, squeaky voice of Thiers trying to penetrate

space, said, "La force ne fonde rien, parce qu'elle ne résout rien." And when I was hoping to comprehend why "La force" did not "fonder" anything I would hear Mr. Hoffman whisper, "When you think that Louis XVI. and Marie Antoinette passed the last evening they ever spent in Versailles in this theater!" "Really," I replied vaguely. My other neighbor remarked, "You know the 'Reds' are concentrating for a sortie to Versailles." "You don't say so!" I answered, dreadfully confused.

There would be a moment's pause, and I caught the sound of General Billet's deep basso proposing that the French nation should adopt the family of General Lecomte, who had been so mercilessly butchered by the mob. Mr. Hoffman, continuing *his* train of thought, remembered that Napoleon III. gave that "magnificent dinner" to Queen Victoria in this theater. Jules Grévy talked at great length about something I did not hear, and when I asked Mr. Hoffman what it was, he answered me, something I did not understand. Jules Favre next spoke about the future glories of *notre glorieux pays* and the destiny of France. These remarks were received with tremendous applause. People stood up, and ladies waved their handkerchiefs, every one seeming very excited; but my American friends were not greatly impressed. "How typical!" says Mr. Hoffman. "What rubbish!" says Mr. Washburn.

When we returned to Paris we found Mr. Moulton in a flutter of agitation. Beaumont (the renowned and popular painter) had been at the house in the afternoon, and had asked Mr. Moulton's permission to bring Courbet (the celebrated artist, *now* a Communard) to see us. Mr. Moulton had no sooner said yes than he regretted his impulsiveness, but he forgot to call Beaumont back to tell him so. The result was that we had the visit of Courbet last evening.

Mr. Moulton put on a bold face and broke the news to us on our arrival; but, contrary to his fears, Mrs. Moulton and I were enchanted. Mademoiselle Wissembourg was not so enthusiastic. A live Communard at such near focus had no attraction for her.

Beaumont's politics are sadly wanting in color, making him supremely indifferent to other people's politics; and, as he has a great admiration for Courbet as an artist, he does not care whether he is a Communard or not.

We waited with impatience for the appointed hour, and lo! Courbet stood before us. Mademoiselle Wissembourg had once remarked that she had great sympathy for the people, who must feel themselves oppressed and degraded by the rich and powerful, and so forth. But I noticed, all the same, that she retired into a corner, probably thinking Courbet was bristling all over with pistols, as behoves a Communard.

Courbet is not handsome; he is fat and flabby (of the Falstaff type), with a long beard, short hair, and small eyes; but he is very clever, as clever as Beaumont, which is saying a good deal.

Of course they talked of "the situation." Who could help it? Courbet belongs more to the fraternity part of the motto than he does to the equality part of the Commune! He is not bloodthirsty, nor does he go about shooting people in the back. He is not that kind! He really believes(so he says) in a Commune based on principles of equality and liberty of the masses. Mr.

Moulton pointed out that unlimited liberty in the hands of a mob might become dangerous; but he admitted that fraternity absolves many sins.

They talked on till quite late. Beaumont showed him his last picture, which he (Beaumont) thinks very fine, but all Courbet said was, "What a pretty frame!" I don't know if Mrs. Moulton and I felt much admiration for the great artist, but he left us convinced that we were all in love with him. We told Mr. Moulton we thought it might get us into trouble if Courbet vibrated between us and the hotbed of Communism. But Mr. Moulton answered, "What does it matter now?" as if the end of the world had come.

Perhaps it has.

March 24th.

Since I have been in Paris I have wished every day to go and see my former singing-master, Delsarte; but something has always prevented me.

To-day, however, having nothing else to do, I decided to make the long-projected visit; that is, if I could persuade Mademoiselle to accompany me. After my experience in the Rue St.-Arnaud the other day I did not venture to drive, so we started off to walk (with Mademoiselle's reluctant consent) to the Boulevard de Courcelles, where Delsarte moves and has his being. Poor Mademoiselle was frightened almost to death, shaking with terror at every sound, and imagining that the Communards were directly behind us, dodging our footsteps and spying upon our actions. At the sight of every ragged soldier we met she expected to be dragged off to prison, and when they passed us without so much as glancing at us I think she felt rather disappointed, as if they had not taken advantage of their opportunities.

Finally we reached the house, and mounted the six stories, the stairs of which are steep, slippery, and tiring. On our upward flight I remarked to Mademoiselle that I wished Delsarte lived in other climes; but she was far too much out of breath to notice any such little joke as this. I saw no change either in him or in any of his surroundings.

He told us that he had suffered many privations and deprivations while the siege was going on. Probably this is true; but I do not see how he could have needed very much when he had the piano to fall back on, with all its resources.

How vividly the scenes of my former lessons loomed up before me when I stood shivering with cold in the never-heated room, my voice almost frozen in my throat, and was obliged to sing with those awful diagrams staring me in the face!

Delsarte asked me many questions about my music: whether I had had the heart to sing *pendant ce débâcle*. I said, "*Débâcle* or no *débâcle*, I could never help singing."

My dear old friend Auber came to see me this afternoon. He had not had much difficulty in driving through the streets, as he had avoided those that were barricaded. We had a great deal to talk about. He had been in Paris all through the war and had suffered intensely, both physically and mentally; he looked wretched, and for the first time since I had known him seemed depressed and unhappy. He is eighty-six years old and now he looks his age. He is a true Parisian, adores his Paris, and never leaves it, even during the summer, when Paris is insufferable. One can easily imagine his grief at seeing his beloved city as it is now. He was full of uneasy forebodings and distress. He gave me the most harrowing description of the killing of General Lecomte! It seems that the mob had seized him in his home and carried him to the garden of some house, where they told him he was to be judged by a *conseil de guerre*, and left him to wait an hour in the most pitiable frame of mind.

The murder of General Clément Thomas was even more dreadful. Auber knew him well; described him as kind and gentle, and "honest to the tips of his fingers." They hustled him into the same garden where poor General Lecomte already was, pushed him against the wall, and shot him, killing him instantly. Then they rushed upon their other victim, saying, "Now is your turn." In vain did Lecomte beg to be judged by his equals, and spoke of his wife and children. But his tormentors would have none of that, and shot him then and there. Lecomte fell on his knees; they dragged him to his feet, and continued firing into his still warm body. When the populace was allowed to come in they danced a saturnalia over his corpse. Auber said: "My heart bleeds when I gaze on all that is going on about me. Alas! I have lived too long."

I tried to make him talk of other things, to divert him from his dark thoughts. We played some duets of Bach, and he accompanied me in some of his songs. I sang them to please him, though my heart was not "attuned to music," as the poets say.

IN THE COURTS OF MEMORY

March 25, 1871.

I have not had the time to write for some days, but I am sure you will forgive me. Mrs. Moulton and I have been going to the ambulances every day this week.

There are many of these temporary hospitals established all over Paris, supplied with army surgeons and nurses.

Mrs. Moulton, like many other ladies, had volunteered her services during the war, and had interested herself in this worthy cause; and as she is about to leave for Dinard one of these days, she wanted me to take up her work in the hospital of the Boulevard la Tour-Maubourg. She knows all the directors and nurses and introduced me to them.

The director asked me if I would like to help in the *section des étrangers.* I replied that I would do anything they wished, hoping inwardly that I might develop a talent for nursing, which, until now, had lain dormant.

It was not with a light heart I entered the ward to which I was assigned, and saw the long rows of beds filled with sick and wounded.

My first patient was a very young German (he did not look more than twenty). He had been shot through the eyes, and was so bandaged that I could hardly see anything but his mouth. Poor little fellow! He was very blond, with a nicely shaped head and a fine, delicate mouth.

His lips trembled when I laid my hand on his white and thin hand, lying listlessly on the coverlid. I asked him if I could do anything for him.

289

He answered me by asking if I could speak German. On my saying that I could, he said he would like to have me write to his mother.

I asked the director if it was allowed for me to communicate with his family. He answered that there would be no objection if the contents of the letter were understood by me.

Therefore, armed with pencil and paper, I returned to my invalid's bedside, who, on hearing me, whispered: "I thought you had gone and would not come back."

"You don't think I would be so unkind as that?" I answered.

I felt that we were already friends. I sat down, saying that I was ready to write if he would dictate.

His lips moved; but I could not hear, and was obliged to put my ear quite close to his poor bandaged face to hear the words, *Meine liebe Mutter*. He went on dictating, and I writing as well as I could, until there came a pause. I waited, and then said, "Und?" He stammered something which I made out to be, "It hurts me to cry," whereupon I cried, the tears rolling fast down my cheeks. Fortunately he did not see me!

This is my first trial, and I have already broken down!

I told him I would finish the letter and send it to his mother, "Frau Wanda Schultz, Biebrich am Rhein," which I did, adding a little postscript that I was looking after her son, and would take the best care of him. I hope she got the letter.

The doctor advised the patient to sleep, so I left him and went to another bed, which they indicated.

This was an American, a newspaper reporter from

Camden, New Jersey. He had joined Faidherbe's army in February, and had been wounded in the leg. He was glad to talk English. "They do things mighty well over here," said he; "but I guess I'll have to have my leg cut off, all the same."

When I put the question to him, "What can I do for you?" he replied, "If you have any papers or illustrated news or pictures, I should like to see them." I said I would bring some to-morrow.

He was very cheerful and very pleasant to talk with.

On reaching the Rue de Courcelles we found Mr. Washburn.

He was utterly disgusted with the Communards. He even became violent when he spoke of their treatment of Generals Lecomte and Clément Thomas. He rather took their defense during the first days of the Commune, saying they were acting in good faith; but now I think he has other ideas about them.

Auber also came at five o'clock; he gets more and more despondent, and is very depressed. He had heard that the Communards had commenced pillaging in the Quartier de l'Odéon, also that the Place Vendôme was being plundered.

To what are we coming?

The next day I found my little German soldier decidedly worse. He had received a letter from the *Mutter*, which he asked me to read to him. I tried my best to overcome the difficulties of the writing and spelling, and made many mistakes, causing the poor little fellow to smile. He corrected me every time very conscientiously.

I did feel so sorry for him; he seemed so gentle and

never complained of his sufferings, which must have been intense. The nurse, feeling his pulse, announced an increase of fever, and thought he had better rest. When I said, in as cheerful a voice as I could assume: "Well, good-by for to-day," he said, "To-morrow you will come?" Alas! there was to be no to-morrow for him.

My other patient, Mr. Parker, appeared very comfortable, and immensely pleased to see that I had not forgotten to bring the newspapers and pictures. I also took a chess-board, thinking to amuse him. The doctor looked dismayed when he saw me carrying a chess-board under my arm. "Madame," he said, "I think that chess is too fatiguing for an invalid; perhaps something milder would be better. I have always understood," he smilingly added, "that chess is a game for people in the most robust health, and with all their mental faculties."

I felt utterly crushed. This was the way my attempts to divert the sick and the wounded were received! I thought how little I understood the character of hospital work. Mr. Parker, evidently feeling sorry for my discomfiture, told the doctor it would amuse him to play checkers if he would allow it. The doctor consented to this, and I sent Louis off to buy a box of checkers. Mr. Parker and I played two games, and he beat me each game, which put him in splendid spirits, and I think did him no harm.

Mrs. Moulton and I drove out to the Bois after the ambulance visit. I had not been there since last August. How changed it was! The broad Avenue de l'Impératrice, where the lovely Empress drove every day in her *calèche à la Daumont*, surrounded by the magnificent *Cent Gardes*, is now almost impossible to drive in. The trees are cut down, and the roads full of ditches and stones.

Rochefort, who was in power while the siege was in progress, suggested some medieval methods too childish for belief—to annihilate the whole German army if they should enter Paris. He had ordered pitfalls in the Avenue de l'Impératrice—holes about three feet deep—in which he intended the German cavalry to tumble headlong. He thought, probably, the army would come in the night and not see them. Rochefort had also built towers, as in the time of the Crusaders, from which hot oil and stones were to be poured on the enemy. Did you ever hear of anything so idiotic? He little dreamt that the German army would take possession of Paris, bivouac in the Champs-Élysées, and quietly march out again.

We visited the Pré Catalan, where last year fashionable society met every day to flirt and drink milk. That is, as you may imagine, minus cows. These had, like all the other animals, been eaten and digested long ago. Thick hides not being at a premium, the hippopotamus and rhinoceros had been kindly spared to posterity.

March 29th.

To-day I went to the ambulances as usual. The doctor greeted me with his usual kindness; he said there was an invalid for whom I was needed, and conducted me to his bedside.

My new patient was a German officer about thirty-

20   293

five years old. He said he came from Munich. I told him about Count Arco (also from Munich), whom he knew, and about Petit Val, in which he seemed interested. We talked music, and he became quite excited when he spoke of Wagner, to whom, according to him, no one could compare. I did not want to discuss this wide subject; I merely remarked that Mendelssohn and Weber had their good points, which he allowed, but replied that they were utterly out of fashion. I did not agree with him, and, to show that Weber was a genius, I hummed the prayer from "Der Freischütz."

There was a visible movement among the white-covered beds, and the nurses frowned, while the doctor came hurriedly toward me, holding up his finger warningly.

I really have no talent for nursing. It seems that everything I do is wrong.

The German officer said, when I went away, "I will convince you to-morrow, when you come, that Wagner is the greatest genius living." I answered that undoubtedly he would, and bade him good-by.

When I reached the carriage I found a small crowd collected around it, and I hurried to get in, and hardly had time to shut the door when Louis whipped the horse, and we were galloping away toward home. Once there, Louis told me that he would respectfully advise me not to go in the carriage with a coachman in livery again. Anything, he said, in the form of luxury or wealth excited the mob, and no one could tell what it might do when excited.

Therefore we decided to abolish the liveries for the future. When we reached home we found that we were

RAOUL RIGAULT

one horse less, the Communards having taken it out of the stables without further ado than a mild protest from the frightened *concierge.* The Comité de Transport promised to return the horse when no longer needed.

March 31st.

DEAR MAMA,—Mr. Moulton thought it better that I should leave Paris. But to leave Paris one must have a passport from the Prefect of Police. He consulted Mr. Washburn about it, who not only consented to give me a card of introduction to Raoul Rigault (whom he knew personally), but offered to send me to the prefecture in his own carriage.

This morning at eleven the carriage was at the door, and with it the promised card of introduction. I noticed that the coachman had no livery, nor did he wear the cockade of the Legation; neither was there any servant. I suppose Mr. Washburn thought it safer for us to drive through the streets without creating any unnecessary notice or running the risk of being insulted.

Mademoiselle W—— accompanied me, and with her the omnipresent bag filled with chocolates, bonbons, etc., for any unforeseen event.

On our way she discoursed on the manner one ought to treat *ces gens-là.* One should (she said) not *brusquer* them, nor provoke them in any way, but smile kindly at them and *en générale* be very polite.

I don't know how many times I had to pull out my *billet de circulation* before we reached the prefecture.

It was a long time since I had been down the Rue de Rivoli, and I was disgusted when I saw the half-clad, half-starved soldiers, in their dirty boots and down-trodden shoes, slouching about with their torn uniforms and carrying their rusty guns any which way.

At last we arrived, and we were about to descend from the carriage, when a ragamuffin of a Communist, shouldering his gun and looking all-important, sprang forward to prevent us; but on showing my "billet," he nodded his head, saying, "C'est bien."

At the mere sight of him Mademoiselle W—— said, "Don't you think, chère Madame, that it is better to return home?" I answered: "Nonsense! Now that we are here, let us go through with it."

A few steps farther an awkward soldier happened to drop his gun on the pavement. At the sound of this, poor Mademoiselle W—— almost sank on her knees with fright.

The small gate next to the large iron one was opened, and we entered the courtyard. This was filled with soldiers. A sentinel stood before the door of the large corridor which led to the Prefect's office. Inside this room stood a guard, better dressed and seemingly a person of more importance. On showing Mr. Washburn's card, I said to him that I had come here for the purpose of getting a passport, and would like to speak to Monsieur Rigault himself.

We went toward the door, which he opened, but on seeing Mademoiselle W—— he stopped us and asked: "Who is that lady? Has she a card also?"

We had never thought of this! I was obliged to say that she had not, but she had come to accompany me.

He said, rather bluntly, "If she has no card, I cannot allow her to enter."

Here was a pretty plight. I told him, in the suave manner which Mademoiselle W—— had recommended to me, that Mr. Washburn would have included this lady's name on my card had he foreseen that there would be any difficulty in allowing her to follow me as my companion.

"Madame, I have strict orders; I cannot disobey them."

I did not wish him to disobey them; but, nevertheless, I whispered to Mademoiselle W——, "Don't leave me, stay close by me," thinking the man would not, at the last moment, refuse to allow her to remain with me.

Alas! the door opened. I entered; the door closed behind me; I looked back and saw I was alone. No Mademoiselle in sight! My heart sank.

I was escorted from room to room, each door guarded by an uncouth soldier, and shut promptly as I passed.

I must have gone through at least seven rooms before I reached the sanctuary in which Monsieur Raoul Rigault held his *audience*.

This autocrat, whom the republicans (to their eternal shame be it said) had placed in power after the 4th of September, is (and was *then*) the most successful specimen of a scamp that the human race has ever produced. At this moment Rigault has more power than any one else in Paris.

When the guard opened the door he pointed to the table where Raoul Rigault was seated writing (seemingly very absorbed). He appeared to me to be a man of about thirty-five or forty years old, short, thick-set, with a full, round face, a bushy black beard, a sensuous mouth, and a cynical smile. He wore tortoise-shell eyeglasses; but these could not hide the wicked expression of his cunning eyes.

I looked about me and noticed that the room had very little furniture; there was only the table at which the Prefect sat and two or three plain chairs. Just such a chamber as Robespierre might have occupied during *his République*. There were two gendarmes standing behind Rigault's chair waiting for orders, and a man (of whom I did not take particular notice) leaning against the mantelpiece at the other end of the room.

I approached the table, waiting like a culprit for the all-powerful Rigault to look up and notice me.

But he did not; he continued to be occupied with what he was doing. So I ventured to break the ice by saying, "Monsieur, I have come to procure a passport, and here is Mr. Washburn's card (the American Minister) to tell you who I am."

He took the card without condescending to look at it, and went on writing.

Getting impatient at his impertinence, I ventured again to attract his attention, and I said, as politely as possible (and as Mademoiselle could have wished), "Will you not kindly give me this passport, as I wish to leave Paris as soon as possible?"

Thereupon he took up the card, and, affecting the "Marat" style, said, "Does the *citoyenne* wish to leave Paris? *Pourquoi?*"

I answered that I was obliged to leave Paris for different reasons.

He replied, with what he thought a seductive smile, "I should think Paris would be a very attractive place for a pretty woman like yourself."

How could I make him understand that I had come for a passport and not for conversation?

At this moment I confess I began to feel dreadfully nervous, seeing the powerless situation in which I was placed, and I saw in imagination visions of prison-cells, handcuffs, and all the horrors which belong to revolutions. I heard the sonorous clock in the tower strike the hour, and realized that only minutes, not hours, had passed since I had been waiting in this dreadful place.

"Monsieur," I began once more, "I am rather in haste, and would thank you if you would give me my passport."

Upon which he took Mr. Washburn's so-much-looked-at card, scrutinized it, and then scrutinized me.

"Are you La Citoyenne Moulton?"

I answered, "Yes."

"American?"

I replied I was, and *in petto*—mighty glad I was to be so.

"Does the American Minister know you personally?"

"Yes, very well."

"Why do you wish to deprive us of your presence in Paris?"

I repeated that my affairs required my presence elsewhere.

I saw he was taking no steps toward making out my passport, and I became more agitated and unnerved and said, "If it is impossible for you, Monsieur, to give me the passport, I will inform Mr. Washburn of the fact, and he will no doubt come to you himself for it."

This seemed to arouse him, for he opened a drawer and took out a blank to be filled for a passport, with an impatient shrug of his shoulders, as if he was bored to death.

Now followed the most hateful and trying *quart d'heure* I ever passed in my life. I fancy Raoul Rigault had never been in the society of a lady (perhaps he had never seen one), and his innate coarseness seemed to make him gloat over the present situation, and as a true republican, whose motto is *Egalité, Fraternité, Liberté*, he flattered himself he was on an equality with me, therefore he could take any amount of liberty. He took advantage of the unavoidable questions that belong to the making out of a passport, and showed a diabolical pleasure in tormenting *la citoyenne* who stood helplessly before him.

When it came to the description and the enumerating of my features, he was more obnoxious than I can express. Peering across the table to see whether my eyes were brown or black, or my hair black or brown, he never lost an opportunity to make a fawning remark before writing it down. He described my *teint* as *pâle*. I felt pale, and think I must have looked very pale, for he said: "Vous etes bien pâle, Madame. Voudriez-vous quelque chose à boire?" Possibly he may have meant to be kind; but I saw BORGIA written all over him. I refused his offer with effusion.

When he asked me my age, he said, *insinuatingly*, "Vous êtes bien jeune, Madame, pour circuler seule ainsi dans Paris."

I answered, "Je ne suis pas seule, Monsieur. Mon mari [I thought it best to tell this lie] m'attend dans la voiture de Monsieur Washburn et il doit être bien étonné de ma longue absence."

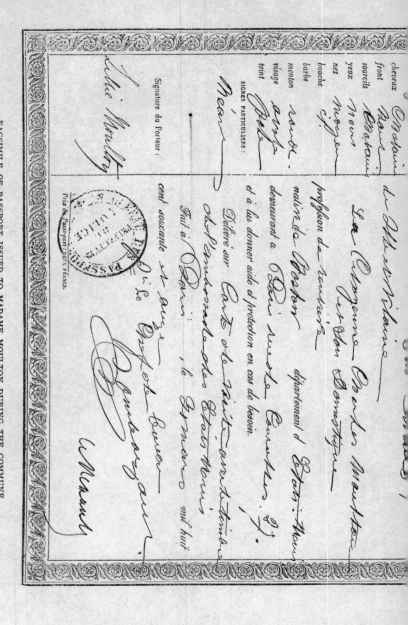

FACSIMILE OF PASSPORT ISSUED TO MADAME MOULTON DURING THE COMMUNE

(P. I.)

PASSE-PORT
à l'Intérieur,

valable pour un an,

DÉPARTEMENT
de la Seine

SOUS-PRÉFECTURE
de Paris

COMMUNE
de Paris

Registre
N° 791

SIGNALEMENT.

Âgé de XX ans

taille d'un mètre

République FRANÇAISE

Passe=port à l'Intérieur,
valable pour un an.

Nous Préfet, Paris

Invitons les Autorités civiles et militaires à laisser passer et
librement circuler de ... à Paris ...
département.

I considered this extremely diplomatic.

Turning to the man at the mantelpiece, he said, "Grousset, do you think we ought to allow the *citoyenne* to leave Paris?"

Grousset (the man addressed) stepped forward and looked at Mr. Washburn's card, saying something in an undertone to Rigault, which caused him instantly to change his manner toward me (I don't know which was worse, his overbearing or his fawning manner).

"You must forgive me," he said, "if I linger over your visit here. We don't often have such luck, do we, Grousset?"

I thought I should faint!

Probably the man Grousset noticed my emotion, for he came to my rescue and said, politely, "Madame Moulton, j'ai eu l'honneur de vous voir à un bal à l'Hôtel de Ville l'année dernière."

I looked up with surprise. He was a very handsome fellow, and I remembered quite well having seen him somewhere; but did not remember where. I was happy indeed to find any one who knew me and could vouch for me, and told him so. He smiled. "I venture to present myself to you, Madame. I am Pascal Grousset. Can I be of any service to you?"

"Indeed you can," I answered, eagerly. "Please tell Monsieur Rigault to give me my passport; it seems to have been a colossal undertaking to get it." I preferred the *Pascal* G. to the *Rascal* R.

Grousset and Rigault had a little conversation together, and presto! my longed-for passport lay before me to sign. No Elsa ever welcomed her Lohengrin coming out of the clouds as I did my Lohengrin coming from the mantelpiece.

I signed my name quickly enough; Rigault put the official seal on it, and, rising from his chair, politely handed it to me.

Before taking my leave of the now over-polite Prefect, I asked him how much there was to pay.

He courteously replied, "Rien, absolument rien," and added he was glad to be of any service to me; and if there was anything more he could do, I had only to command.

I did not say that I thought he had done enough for one day, but I bowed him good-by and turned to go out.

Mr. Pascal Grousset offered me his arm, begging to take me to my carriage. The gendarmes threw open doors, and we retraced our steps through all the different rooms until we reached the one where I had left Mademoiselle W——, whom I expected to find waiting for me in agonizing anxiety.

But what did I see?

Mademoiselle sound asleep on the bench, bag, smile, and all, gazed at and guarded by the dreaded soldiers.

"I am afraid," said Pascal Grousset, "that you have been greatly annoyed this morning. Your interview with the Prefect must have been most painful to you!"

"I confess," I said, "it has never been my fate to have been placed in just such a situation, and I thank you, *de tout mon cœur*, for your assistance. You certainly saved my life, for I doubt if I could have lived another moment in that room."

"Perhaps more than your life, Madame; more than you imagine, at any rate."

As he put us in the carriage, he looked puzzled when he saw *le mari* I had said was waiting for me; but a smile of comprehension swept over his face as he met my guilty glance. He apparently understood my reasons.

On reaching home, tired, exhausted, and oh! so hungry, we found Mr. Washburn. He and Mr. Moulton had been very anxious about me, picturing to themselves all sorts of horrors, and when I told them what really had happened they felt that their anxieties had not been far from the truth. Mr. Washburn laughed at the subterfuges I had used and the lie I had told. They examined my passport as a great curiosity, and noticed it had *Valable pour un an.*

Mr. Washburn said, "Evidently they intend this sort of thing to go on forever."

23d of April.

Mrs. Moulton has decided to leave for Dinard, and starts the day after to-morrow.

We have been assured that the train would make connections as far at least as Rennes; beyond that no one could tell whether they went regularly or not.

Mrs. Moulton had procured a red *billet de circulation* with a date, a white one without a date, Mr. Washburn's card, and different passes. She was certainly well prepared for any emergency. As there was only one day train, she was obliged to take that (it left at seven o'clock A.M.).

A desire to see some of her friends before her departure spurred Mrs. Moulton to invite them to dinner. Our friends are now so few and far between that it is not difficult to know whom to choose or where to find them.

The result was a miscellaneous company, as you will

see: Mr. Washburn, Auber, Massenet, Beaumont, and Delsarte. Our family consisted of Mr. and Mrs. Moulton, Henry, Mademoiselle Wissembourg, and myself.

Mrs. Moulton asked Henry to bring with him some green peas from Petit Val to eke out the chef's meager menu.

With the aid of a friendly officer, Henry managed to pick a "whole bushel" (he always exaggerates), which, with his toilet articles, completely filled his large *sac de voyage*. Besides this, he had a portmanteau with his evening attire, and a package which Count Arco wished to send to Paris.

Count Arco ordered out the "ancient and honorable relic" of our landau (the same I had used on the famous 18th of March) and the artillery horses, with their heavy dragoons, in order to deposit Henry and his bags at the pontoon bridge, where a man was found to take them as far as the station.

To divert himself while tramping along with his *sac de voyage*, Henry shelled the peas, casting the pods behind him, after the manner of Tom Thumb, never dreaming that the peas thus left to chum familiarly with his toilet things might suffer from the contact and get a new flavor. He was surprised to see how the "bushel" had diminished in volume since it started.

Mrs. Moulton had promised to send the carriage to meet *l'envoi extraordinaire;* but Henry, finding none, started to walk toward home, followed by a porter carrying his extra baggage.

What was Henry's astonishment at seeing Louis drive out of the Hôtel de Ville with two strange men in the coupé. Henry hailed Louis, who, though scared out of his wits, pulled up obediently, disregarding the angry voices from inside. Henry opened the door and addressed the strangers politely, "Messieurs, this is my carriage; I beg you to alight."

"Par exemple!" cried the two, in chorus. "Who are you?"

"I happen to be the proprietor of the carriage," replied Henry, assuming an important air, "and if you decline to leave it I shall call the Sergent de Ville." Then turning to the porter, he told him to put the bags in the coupé, which he did.

"Ha, ha!" laughed the two men. "*Faites ça, mon bon!* that would be amusing. Do you know who we are?"

Henry did not, and said he was not particularly anxious to know.

"This is Monsieur Félix Pyat, and I am his secretary. Here is a *bon* for your carriage," handing Henry the card.

"Well," said Henry, pulling out his card, "here is my card, here are my passes, and here [pointing to Louis] is my coachman!"

Félix Pyat said, "How do we know that this is your carriage?"

Henry acknowledged that at the moment he looked so little like the owner of anything except the bag, in which the peas were rattling like bullets, that he forgave the doubt.

Louis was called from the box and the question was put to him. In ordinary moments Louis would have mumbled and stuttered hopelessly; but he seemed to have been given overwhelming strength on this occasion, and surprised Henry by confirming his words with an unction worthy of the great Solomon himself. He waved his whip aloft, pointed to Henry, and putting his hand on his heart (which I am sure was going at a tremendous pace) said, "I swear that this is my master!"

No one but a Communard could have doubted him; but Félix Pyat no more believed Louis's oath than he did Henry's documents.

"*Bien*," said Pyat; "if it is true that you live in the Rue de Courcelles, we will leave you there and continue on our way."

Now followed the most spirited altercation, all talking at once, Henry trying to get in the coupé, and the others refusing to get out.

"À la maison!" shouted Henry.

"À la Place Beauvais!" shouted the Communards. They continued giving these contradictory orders to poor, bewildered Louis until a crowd had collected, and they thought it better to stop quarreling. Henry entered the carriage, meekly taking his seat on the *strapontin* opposite the intruders, and thinking of the peas, which ought to have been in the pot by this time, assented to be left at home, and ordered Louis to drive the triumphant Communards to the Ministry of the Interior, Place Beauvais.

It would be difficult for one who did not know Louis to guess what his state of mind must have been. He was not of the kind they make heroes of; he was good, kind, and timid, though he was an *ancien Zouave* and had fought in several battles (so he said). I always doubted these tales, and I still think Louis's loose,

bulging trousers and the tassel of his red cap were only
seen from behind.

It was as good as a play to hear Louis's tragic account
of yesterday, and it made your hair stand on end when
he recounted how he had been stopped in the Rue de
Castiglione, how two fiery Communards had entered
the coupé and ordered him to drive to the Hôtel de Ville,
where Félix Pyat had mounted the carriage. What
must his account have been in the kitchen?

However, the principal thing was that the harassed
peas were safe in the kitchen and in time to be cooked
and figure on the menu as *légumes* (*les petits pois*).

Our guests' faces beamed with satisfaction at the idea
of these *primeurs*, and evidently anticipated great joy
in eating them; but after they had tasted them they
laid down their forks and . . . meditated! The servant
removed the plates with their *primeurs*, wondering how
such wanton capriciousness could exist in this *primeur-
less* Paris. Only Mr. Moulton ate them to the last pea.
We—the initiated—knew where the peculiar taste of
soap, tooth-wash, perfume, etc., came from! The peas
descended to the kitchen, and ascended again un-
touched to the hothouse, where they finished their wild
and varied career. If they could have spoken, what
tales they could have told! They had displaced the
German Army, they had aided and abetted the cause
of the Commune, and they had cost their bringer untold
sums in *pourboires*, in order to furnish a few forkfuls
for Mr. Moulton and a gala supper for the hens.

We had an excellent dinner: a *potage printanier* (from
cans), canned lobster, corned beef (canned), and some
chickens who had known many sad months in the con-

servatory. An ice concoted from different things, and named on the menu *glace aux fruits*, completed this *festin de Balthazar.*

Mr. Moulton was obliged to don the obnoxious dress-coat, laid away during the siege in camphor, and smelling greatly of the same. He held in his hand *La Gazette Officielle.* The same shudder ran through us all. It was to be read to us after dinner! Coffee was served in the ballroom, which was dimly lighted.

Would it not be too trying for an old gentleman's eyes to read the fine print of the *Gazette?* Alas! no. Mr. Moulton's eyes were not the kind that recoiled from anything so trivial as light or darkness; and hardly had we finished our coffee than out came the *Gazette.* We all listened, apparently; some dozed, some kept awake out of politeness or stupefaction; Mademoiselle Wissembourg, without any compunction, resigned herself to slumber, as she had done for the last twenty-five years.

Delsarte squirmed with agony as he heard the French language, and murmured to himself that he had lived in vain. What had served all his art, his profound diagnosis of voice-inflections, his diagrams on the wall, the art of enunciation, and so forth? He realized, for the first time, what his graceful language could become *nel bocca Americana!*

Delsarte's idea of evening-dress was worthy of notice. He wore trousers of the workman type, made in the reign of Louis Philippe, very large about the hips, tapering down to the ankles; a flowing redingote, dating from the same reign, shaped in order to fit over the voluminous trousers; a fancy velvet waistcoat and a huge tie bulging over his shirt-front (if he had a shirt-front, which I doubt). He asked permission to keep on his *calotte*, which I fancy had not left his skull since the Revolution of 1848.

Massenet, who had come in from the country for the day to confer with his editor, received our invitation just in time to dress and join us. After the *Gazette* we awoke to life, and Massenet played some of the "Poème de Souvenir," which he has dedicated to me (I hope I can do it justice). What a genius he is! Massenet always calls Auber *le Maître*, and Auber calls him *le cher enfant*.

Auber also played some of his melodies with his dear, wiry old fingers, and while he was at one piano Massenet put himself at the other (we have two in the ballroom), and improvised an enchanting accompaniment. I wished they could have gone on forever.

Who would have believed that, in the enjoyment of this beautiful music, we could have forgotten we were in the heart of poor, mutilated Paris—in the hands of a set of ruffians dressed up like soldiers? Bombs, bloodshed, Commune, and war were phantoms we did not think of.

Delsarte, in the presence of genius, refused to sing "Il pleut, il pleut, Bergère," but condescended to declaim "La Cigalle ayant chanté tout l'été," and did it as he alone can do it. When he came to the end of the fable, "Eh bien, dansez maintenant," he gave such a tragic shake to his head that the voluminous folds of his cravat became loosened and hung limply over his bosom.

I sang the "Caro Nome" of "Rigoletto," with Massenet's accompaniment. Every one seemed pleased;

21

even Delsarte went as far as to compliment me on the
expression of joy and love depicted on my face and
thrown into my voice, which was probably correct, according to diagram ten on his walls.

He now felt he had not lived in vain.

It being almost midnight, our guests took their departure.

There were only two carriages before the door, Mr.
Washburn's and Auber's. Mr. Washburn took charge
of the now very sleepy Delsarte, who declaimed a sepulchral *bonsoir* and disappeared, his redingote waving in
the air.

The *maître* took the *cher enfant*, or rather the *cher enfant* led the *maître* out of the salon. The family retired
to rest. The *Gazette Officielle* had long since vanished
with its master, and was no doubt being perused in
the privacy of the boudoir above, the odious dress-coat
and pumps replaced by *robe de chambre* and slippers.
Henry said the next morning he had had a bad night; . . .
he had dreamt that the whole German army was waiting outside of Paris, shelling the town with peas.

April 1, 1871.

Beaumont wished to accompany us to the ambulance
to-day, thinking that he might get an idea for a sketch;
but, though he had his album and pencils with him, he
did not accomplish much.

We sat by the bedside of the German officer, and
Beaumont made a drawing of him. The officer said in a
low tone to me, "Is that the famous artist Beaumont?"

I replied that it was.

"I am so glad to have an opportunity to see him, as I have heard so much of him, and have seen a great many of his pictures in Germany."

This I repeated to Beaumont, and it seemed to please him very much.

When we left, Beaumont said to him, showing him the sketch, "Would you like this?"

The officer answered in the most perfect French, "I shall always keep it as a precious souvenir"; and added, "May I not have a sketch of my nurse?" (meaning me).

Beaumont thought that it was rather presuming on the part of the officer to ask for it, and seemed annoyed. However, he made a hasty drawing and gave it to him, saying in his blunt way, "I hope this will please you." The officer thanked him profusely, and we left. Turning to me he said: "I have not profited much by this visit. I have given, but not taken anything away."

"But the experience," I ventured to say.

"Oh yes, the experience; but that I did not need."

In the evening we had one of our drowsy games of whist, made up of Countess B——, our neighbor opposite, brought across the street in her sedan-chair (she never walks), Mr. Moulton, myself, and Beaumont making the sleepy fourth. Neither of our guests speaks English with anything like facility, but they make frantic efforts to carry on the game in English, as Mr. Moulton has never learned the game in French and only uses English terms.

Mr. Moulton always plays with Countess B——, and I always play with Beaumont; we never change partners.

This is the kind of game we play:

It takes Beaumont a very long time to arrange his

cards, which he does in a unique way, being goaded on by Mr. Moulton's impatient "Well!" He picks out all the cards of one suit and he lays them downward on the table in a pile; then he gathers them up and puts them between the third and fourth fingers of his left hand. With the next suit he does likewise, placing them between the second and third fingers, and so on, until the grand *finale*, when the fingers loosen and the cards amalgamate. During this process his cards fall every few minutes on the floor, occasioning much delay, as they have all to be arranged again.

It is my deal; I turn up a heart. The Countess is on my left. We wait with impatience for her to play, but she seems only to be contemplating her cards.

"Well!" says Mr. Moulton, impatiently.

We all say in unison, "Your play, Countess!"

The Countess: "Oh, what dreadful cards! I can never play. Oh," with a sigh, "how dreadful!"

We are all very sorry for her. She has evidently wretched cards.

Long pause. "Your turn, Countess!" we all cry.

"What are trumps?" she asks.

We show her the trump card on the table and say together, "Hearts."

Another long pause.

She arranges her cards deliberately and then shuts them up like a fan.

"Your play, partner," says Mr. Moulton, tired out with waiting.

With a dismal wail, and looking about for sympathy, she plays the ace of clubs.

Mr. Moulton gathers up the trick.

She has no idea that she has taken anything, but is quietly adjusting her cards again.

"Your turn, Countess!"

"What, my turn again?" She expresses the greatest surprise.

She: "What dreadful cards! Indeed, I cannot play."

Poor thing! That was probably her only good card, and we expected her next would be the two of spades. But no. She pulls out, with the air of a martyr, the ace of spades.

Mr. Moulton: "Well! that's not so bad."

Great astonishment on her part. She can't believe that she has actually taken a trick. She had hoped some one else would have played.

A long, fidgety silence follows.

All: "Your play, Countess!" She plays the queen of hearts.

This has no success, as I take it with my king.

Mr. Moulton: "Why did you play trumps?"

She: "Oh! was that trumps? I must take it back. Pray, let me take it back."

We all recover our cards. (My partner takes this occasion to drop some of his on the floor. He picks them up and arranges them again in order.)

"Your turn, Countess!" we cry, exhausted.

She: "What, again! Why does some one else not play?"

Then out comes the ace of diamonds.

Some one said, "You have all the aces."

She: "Oh! not all; I have not the ace of hearts."

Her partner, aghast, begs her not to tell us what her other cards are, and so the game proceeds to the bitter end.

There were other moments funny beyond words, especially when Mr. Beaumont's English fails to cope with the situation and he will try to discuss the points where the Countess has failed. He says, "Did you not see he put his king on your spade ace-spot?" and, "Madame, you played the third of spades." And when we count honors, Beaumont will cover the table with his great elbows and enumerate his: "I had the ass, the knight, and the dame."

I heard a suppressed chuckle from my father-in-law, and seemed to see a vision of Don Quixote and Sancho Panza pass before me.

24th of April.

DEAR MAMA,—Auber sent a note early this morning by his coachman to ask me to lunch with him at ten-thirty o'clock (of course accompanied by Mademoiselle, my aunt, as he calls her). The coachman says that his master is not feeling well and longs to see a friend.

I am proud to be the friend he longs to see, and was only too happy to accept. Mademoiselle W—— was equally happy, ready, as always, for any excursion where a good repast was in view, and of that we were sure, as Auber's chef is renowned, and is so clever that, though the market is limited, he can make something delicious out of nothing.

Louis appeared in a short jacket and a straw hat, looking rather waggish and very embarrassed to present himself in such a costume.

Driving through the Boulevard Clichy and endless out-of-the-way streets, we finally reached Auber's hotel, which is in the Rue St. Georges.

Louis was glad to find safety under the *porte-cochère*, and to see his bosom companion, Auber's butler, into whose arms he fell with joy.

Auber came to the door to welcome us, seeming most grateful that we had come, and led us into the salon. There is only one way to get into the salon, and that is either through the dining-room or the bedroom; we went through the bedroom, as the other was decked for the feast.

I have never seen Auber look so wretched and sad as he did to-day; I could hardly believe it was the same Auber I have always seen so gay and full of life and spirits.

I brought a tiny bunch of lilies of the valley, which Louis had gathered in the all-producing hothouse.

"Merci, merci," he said. "Les fleurs! C'est la vie parfumée." Waiting for the breakfast to be served, he showed us about in his apartment. In the salon, rather primly furnished, stood the grand piano. The book-shelves contained Cherubini's (his master) and his own operas, and his beloved Bach. A table in the middle of the room, covered with photographs and engravings, completed *son salon de garçon*.

The bedroom was also very primitive: his wooden bed, with its traditional covering of *bourre;* a chiffonier containing his curios, royal presents, and costly souvenirs; his writing-table; and his old piano, born in 1792, on which he composed all his operas.

The piano certainly looked very old; its keys were yellow as amber, and Auber touched them with tenderness, his thin, nervous fingers, with their well-kept nails, rattling on them like dice in a box.

He said: "Le piano est presqu'aussi vieux que moi. Que de tracas nous avons eu ensemble!"

Breakfast was announced, and we three took our places at the beautifully arranged table. I wondered where the butler had found flowers and fruit and *écrevisses*. Mademoiselle and I ate with an astounding appetite; but Auber, who had not eaten a *déjeûner* for thirty years, contented himself with talking.

And talk he did, like a person hungry and thirsty to talk. He told us about Scribe, for whom he had an unlimited admiration. "I wish you had known him," he said; "he was the greatest librettist who ever existed. I only had to put the words on the piano, put on my hat, and go out. When I came back the music was all written—the words had done it alone." ("Je n'avais qu'à mettre les paroles sur le pupitre, prendre mon châpeau et sortir. Quand je revenais la musique était toute écrite, les paroles l'avaient faite toutes seules.")

He related incidents connected with his youth. His father was a banker very well off, rich even, and had destined Auber to be a banker, like himself; but when Auber went to London to commence his clerkship he found he had no vocation for finance, and began to devote himself to music and composition. He was thirty-six years old when he wrote his first opera. He told us that his first ones were so bad that he had given them to the Conservatoire *pour encourager les commençants*.

Breakfast had long since finished; but dear old Auber rambled on, and Mademoiselle and I sat listening.

He said he was going to leave all his music to me in his will. I thanked him, and replied nothing would give me greater pleasure than to have something which had belonged to him.

"Je ne regarde jamais mes partitions sans être gagné par la tristesse et sans penser que de morceaux à retoucher! En composant, je n'ai jamais connu d'autre muse que l'ennui."

"On ne le dirait pas," said Mademoiselle, wanting to join the conversation. "Votre musique est si gaie, si pleine d'entrain."

"Vous trouvez! Vous êtes bien bonne. Je ne sais comment cela arrive. Il n'y a pas de motifs parmi ceux qu'on trouve heureux, que je n'ai pas écrit entre deux baillements. Je pourrais," he went on, "vous montrer tel passage où ma plume a fait un long zigzag parce que mes yeux se sont fermés et ma tête tombait sur la partition. On dirait, n'est ce pas? qu'il y a des somnambules lucides."

We thought Auber seemed very fatigued, and we soon left him, driving back the same way we came, and reached home without any adventures.

7th of May.

I received this morning, by a mysterious messenger, a curious document; it looks like a series of carriage-wheels, but it is a cipher from Prince Metternich, who is in Bordeaux, and is dated the 1st of May. It took me a long time to puzzle it out: "Vous conseille de partir; pire viendra. Pauline à Vienne; moi triste et tourmenté."

Very good advice, but rather difficult to follow now.

Never has Paris led such a sober life; there is no noise in the almost empty and dimly lighted streets;

there are no drunkards, and, strange to say, one hears of no thefts. There are, I believe, one or two small theaters open, most of the small cafés, and a great many wine-shops. The soldiers slink about, looking ashamed of their shabby uniforms and ragged appearance.

Thiers has done all in his power to conciliate the different parties, but has now concluded that Paris must be conquered by the troops of Versailles. Every day there comes more disturbing news. How will it all end? When shall we get out of this muddle? *En attendant*, we live in a continual fright.

A note came yesterday from Mr. Washburn (I don't know if he is in Paris or not). He writes: "Nothing could be worse than the present state of affairs. I wish you were out of Paris; hope you are well," etc.

If we could get a message to him, we would tell him that we are well enough, and have enough to eat; that Mademoiselle Wissembourg and I tremble all day; but that Mr. Moulton has not enjoyed himself so much since the last revolution.

Slippers all day if he likes.

May 8th.

Though I have so much time on my hands (I never have had so much), I really have not the heart to write of all the horrors we hear of and the anxieties of our daily life. Besides, you will probably have heard, through unprejudiced newspapers, all that is happening here, and know the true facts before this dismal letter reaches you. And who knows if letters leave Paris regularly in the chaotic state of disorder and danger we are now in?

I cannot write history, because I am living in it. I can only tell you the news which Louis gathers when he does his errands, coming home with the wildest tales, of which we can only believe the half.

I have read somewhere that some one lived "in a dead white dawn of thought." I have not the slightest idea what "a dead white dawn of thought" can be (I have so little imagination); but whatever it is, I feel as if I was living in it now. I don't remember in all my life to have stagnated like this.

We are glad Mrs. Moulton left Paris when she did, and is now in a bourne of safety at Dinard, taking my place with the children while I take hers in the Rue de Courcelles.

This is no sacrifice on my part; the existence we are leading now interests me intensely, being so utterly different from anything I have ever known, and I do not regret having this little glimpse into the unknown.

I cannot go to the ambulances, as we (Mademoiselle and I) do not dare to walk, and driving is out of the question.

I have not seen Auber for many days; Beaumont has not been here either, and we do not know where he is.

They still go on issuing some official newspapers, though whether what they contain is true, or how far the imaginations of the editors have lured them into the paths of fiction, we cannot tell. If we live through this *débâcle* I count on history to tell us what we really have been living through. However, truth or fiction, I am thankful that we have the newspapers, for how would I ever have a moment's sleep if I did not listen to Mr. Moulton's intoning the *Moniteur* and the *Journal des Débats* (the *Figaro* has been suppressed) to us, and we did not have our three-handed drowsy whist to doze over.

May 9th.

While we were at breakfast this morning the servant came rushing in, pale and trembling, and announced to us that pillage had commenced in the Boulevard Haussmann, just around the corner, and that the mob was coming toward our house. We flew to the window, and, sure enough, there we saw a mass of soldiers collected on the other side of the street, in front of the Princess Mathilde's palace, gesticulating and pointing over at us.

We thought our last day had come; certainly it did look like a crisis of some kind. We gazed blankly at one another. Mademoiselle disappeared, to seek refuge, I fancy, between the mattresses of her bed, and the smile and the urbane language with which she was prepared to face this emergency (so often predicted by her) disappeared with her.

The mob crossed the street, howling and screaming, and on finding the gate locked began to shake it. The frightened *concierge*, already barricaded in his lodge, took care not to show himself, which infuriated the riotous crowd to such an extent that they yelled at the top of their lungs to have the gate opened.

Mr. Moulton sent a scared servant to order the still invisible *concierge* to open not only one gate, but all three. He obeyed, trembling and quaking with fear. The Communists rushed into the courtyard, and were about to seize the unhappy *concierge*, when Mr. Moulton, seeing that no one else had the courage to come forward, went himself, like the true American he is, . . . out on to the *perron*, and I went with him. His first words (in pure Angle-Saxon), "Qu'est-ce que vous voolly?" made the assembled crowd giggle.

The leader pushed forward, and, presenting a paper with the official seal of the *Comité de Transport*, demanded, in the name of the Commune (*requisitioned*, they call it), everything we had in the way of animals.

Mr. Moulton took the paper, deliberately adjusted his spectacles, and, having read it very leisurely (I wondered how those fiery creatures had the forbearance to stay quiet, but they did; I think they were hypnotized by my father-in-law's coolness), he said, in his weird French, "Vous voolly nos animaux!" which sounded like *nos animose*. The crowd grinned with delight. His French saved the situation. I felt that they would not do us any great harm now.

Mr. Moulton fumbled in his pocket, and, judging from the time he took and the depths into which he dived, one would have thought he was going to bring out corruption enough to bribe the whole French nation. But he only produced a gold piece, which he flourished in front of the spokesman, and asked if money would be any inducement to leave us *les animose*. But the not-to-be-bribed Communard put his hand on his heart, and said, in a tone worthy of Delsarte, "Nous sommes des honnêtes gens, Monsieur," at which my father-in-law permitted himself to smile. I thought him very brave.

Raising his voice to an unusually high pitch, he cried, "Je ne peux pas vous refiuser *le* cheval, mais [the pitch became higher] je refiuse *le* vache (I cannot refuse to give you the horse; but I refuse the cow)."

The men before us were convulsed with laughter. Then Mr. Moulton gave the order to bring out the horse, but *not* the cow. The official turned to me. "Madame," he said, "you have a cow, and my orders are to take all your animals. Please send for the cow."

"It is true, Monsieur," I answered, with a gentle smile (like the one reposing under the mattress), "that we have a cow; but we have the permission from your Government to keep it."

"Which government?" he asked.

"The French Government. Is that not yours?"

The man could not find anything to answer, and turned away mumbling, "Comme vous voulez," which applied to nothing at all, and addressed Mr. Moulton again, "Nous avons des ordres, Monsieur!" But Mr. Moulton interrupted him, "Ça m'est égal, je refuse *le* vache."

Some one in the crowd called out, "Gardez *le* vache!" This was received with a burst of applause. I think that these men, rough as they were, could not but admire the plucky old gentleman who stood there so calmly looking at them over his spectacles. The servants were all huddled together behind the glass windows in the *antichambre*, scared out of their wits, while the terrible Communards were choking with laughter.

It was heart-rending to see poor Louis's grief when he led out the dear, gentle horse we loved so fondly; the tears rolled down his cheeks, as they did down mine, and I think a great many of the ruffians around us had a tear of sympathy for our sorrow, for the merriment of the few moments before faded suddenly from their pale and haggard faces.

MINISTÈRE
DE
L'AGRICULTURE
ET
DU COMMERCE.

DIRECTION
DE L'AGRICULTURE.

1" BUREAU.

Monsieur *Moulton,* ————

demeurant à Paris, rue *de Courcelles, 27,*

est autorisé à conserver *ses* vache*s* laitière*s* ,
d'après sa déclaration constatant qu'il a le fourrage
suffisant pour l *es* nourrir pendant un mois au
moins.

Paris, le *14* novembre 1870.

Par autorisation :

Le Chef du 1er bureau
de la direction de l'Agriculture,

FACSIMILE OF THE GOVERNMENT PERMIT TO KEEP COWS

When Louis leaned his kind old face against the nose of his companion of the stable he sobbed aloud, and when he gave the bridle over to the man who was to take the horse away he moaned an adieu, saying, "Be good to her!"

I went down the steps of the *perron* (the men politely making way for me) and kissed my poor darling Medjé, and passed my hand over her soft neck before she left us for her unknown fate. She seemed to understand our sorrow, for, as she was being led out of the courtyard, she turned her head toward us with a patient, inquiring look, as if to say, "What does it all mean?"

I hope she will be returned when "no longer needed," as they promise, and Louis will have the joy of seeing her again.

The now-subdued mob left us, filing out quietly through the gates; they had come in like roaring lions, but went out like the meekest of lambs.

We returned sorrowfully to the salon. I was so unstrung that Mademoiselle, who in the meantime had returned, administered a cup of camomile tea to restore my nerves.

After the fright caused by this last *réquisitionnement*, two of the servants thought it expedient to find safer quarters in the center of Paris, and to live in seclusion, rather than run the risk of being requisitioned themselves.

The forts Mont Valérien, Montrouge, Vanves, and Issy keep up an incessant firing. We would not be surprised if at any moment a bomb reached us, but so far we have escaped this calamity. The "Reds" are fighting all around Paris with more or less success. If one could believe what is written in the *Le Journal de la Commune*, one would say they were triumphant all along the line. We have just heard that General Bergeret has been arrested; no one knows why, except that he did not succeed in his last sortie, and had thereby displeased his colleagues generally. It does not take more than that to arrest people in these days.

The good Archbishop of Paris (Darboy), the curé of La Madeleine (Monseigneur Duguerry), also President Bonjean, and the others who were arrested on the 10th of May, have been kept in Mazas Prison ever since. I saw a letter of marvelous forbearance and resignation, written by the Archbishop to the Sisters of the St. Augustine Convent; and the beloved curé of the Madeleine beseeches people to pray for order to be restored. Poor martyrs! I hope that their prison will not prove to be the antechamber of the scaffold; as Rochefort says, "Mazas est l'antichambre de l'échafaud."

It appears that Félix Pyat really did give his demission as a member of the Commune, but his colleagues would not accept it.

10th May.—While Mr. Moulton was reading this morning's news to us we were startled by a terrible crash. We were paralyzed with terror, and for a moment speechless, fearing that all we had dreaded was about to be realized. After somewhat recovering our equilibrium, we sent for Louis to find out what dreadful thing had happened.

Louis appeared with the *concierge*, both trembling from head to foot, and announced that a portion of a bomb which had fallen and exploded near us had come through the roof, shattering many windows and causing great havoc. On further examination of the disaster we were greatly relieved to hear that it was only a question of a damaged roof, windows, and masonry. No one was killed or even wounded; but all were so completely frightened that no one dares to sleep on the upper floor. Consequently we have moved down on the drawing-room floor, and have abandoned the upper stories to future bombs. Mr. Moulton is located in the salon; Mademoiselle has taken the *salon jaune*, and I the boudoir. Louis has improvised a bedroom in the small dining-room, that he may be near us at night if we should need him. The other servants sleep in the basement.

Our family is now reduced to Mr. Moulton, Mademoiselle, Louis, my maid, and the cook. Louis has proved himself invaluable. He is the man of all work. After milking the cow and doing his farming (in the conservatory) in the early morning, he waits at table, does errands, and gathers whatever news there is in the neighborhood, helps in the kitchen, and aids Mr. Moulton in his toilet and into his slippers. He is never tired; is always ready, early in the morning and late at night, to do anything required of him. He fills all gaps.

The untiring hens have made their nests in obscure corners in the hothouse and dream serenely of future posterity, while the one cock scratches for tired worms to provide for their repasts. I go every morning after breakfast with a little offering of scraps to add to their meager meals.

It is one of my few occupations.

Louis has succeeded in some of his agricultural schemes,

and has raised mushrooms, radishes, and watercresses, which appear quite a luxury in contrast to our usual canned things, and almost make us forget other privations.

This farming of Louis's in the hothouse goes to prove how an unnecessary palm-garden in time of peace can be transformed into a useful kitchen garden in time of war. Louis expends the same energy and water that he used in washing his carriages, much to the detriment of the once fine greenhouse.

The days are very monotonous. I never imagined a day could have so many hours. I, who have always been over-busy, and have never found the days long enough to do all I wanted to do, pass the most forlorn hours listening and waiting and wondering what will happen next. I wait and wait all through the sleepless nights. I am so nervous I cannot sleep. I do not even take off my clothes.

I have my writing-table put in the ball-room, and here I sit and write these sad letters to you. I play the piano; but I have not the heart to sing, as you may imagine.

We know that there are many tragedies going on about us, and we hear, through Louis, awful things; but we only believe the half of what he tells us.

May 11th.

The Minister of Finance has spent in a month twenty-six millions for the war expenses alone.

My two friends, Pascal Grousset and (Rascal) Rigault, spent for their *menus plaisirs* nearly half a million, whereas Jourde, who is Minister of Finance, and could take all the money he liked from the banks, lives in the same modest apartment, and his wife still continues to take in washing as of old, showing that he, at least, is honest among thieves.

Grousset's appeal to the large cities of France is very theatrical. He reproaches them with their lukewarmness and their platonic sympathy, and calls them *aux armes*, as in the "Marseillaise."

We had a very sad experience yesterday. At seven o'clock the *concierge* was awakened from his slumbers, which (if one can judge from the repeated efforts at his bell of persons who come before breakfast) must be of the sweetest and most profound nature.

On cautiously peeping out, he saw a poor fellow leaning against the gate in a seemingly exhausted condition; he had been wounded, and begged to be allowed to come inside our courtyard. The *concierge*, who thinks it wise to be prudent, consulted with Louis; but neither dared do anything until Mr. Moulton had given the necessary orders. Louis ran about to wake up the family, and Mr. Moulton told the porter to take the man directly to the stables and to go for a doctor. The wounded man begged to see a priest, and Louis was despatched to bring one. Securing a doctor seemed to be a great undertaking. The *concierge* had had cramps in the night (so he said), which would necessitate his remaining at home, and made so many excuses that Mr. Moulton lost patience and declared he would go himself; but this I would not hear of his doing alone, and insisted upon going with him. Mademoiselle, issuing from her room, appeared in her lilac dressing-gown, holding a pocket-handkerchief in one hand and a smelling-bottle to her nose with the other. She was told to keep watch over the invalid while we were absent. Mr. Moulton and I walked to the Faubourg St. Honoré, to our apothecary, who gave us the name of the nearest doctor. It was not pleasant, to say the least, to be in the streets. We were in the habit of hearing bombs and shells, so that was no novelty; but to see them whizzing over our heads was a new sensation, and not an agreeable one. We found a doctor, a most amiable gentleman, who, although he had been up all night, was quite ready to follow us, and we hurried back to the Rue de Courcelles, where we found Mademoiselle seated on a water-pail outside the stables and looking the picture of woe. Her idea of keeping vigil!

The doctor made a hasty examination, and was preparing the bandages when Louis arrived with the priest. I left them and went into the house to make some tea, which I thought might be needed; but my father-in-law came in and said that the man had gone to sleep.

Later, about two o'clock, Louis told us that all was over; the poor fellow had received the last sacraments, had turned over on his side, and had breathed his last. We sent for the ambulance; but it was five o'clock before they took him away.

It made us very sad all day to think that death had entered our gates.

15th May.—Thiers's house in the Rue St. Georges was pillaged to-day by the mob, who howled like madmen and hurled all sorts of curses and maledictions on luckless Thiers, who has done nothing wrong, and certainly tried to do good.

Auber, who lives in the same street, must have seen

PLACE VENDÔME AFTER THE FALL OF THE COLUMN

and heard all that was going on. How he must have suffered!

16th May.—The Column Vendôme fell to-day; they have been working some days to undermine it at the base of the socle. Every one thought it would make a tremendous crash, but it did not; it fell just where they intended it to fall, toward the Rue de la Paix, on some fagots placed to receive it. They were a long time pulling at it; three or four pulleys, and as many ropes, and twenty men tugging with all their might—*et voilà.* The figure that replaced the Little Corporal (which is safe somewhere in Neuilly) came to earth in a cloud of dust, and the famous column lay broken in three huge pieces.

I inclose a ticket which Mr. Lemaire obtained somehow, and which, as you see, permitted him to circulate *librement* in the Place Vendôme:

I think it is strange that Auber does not let us hear from him. I fear his heart is broken, like the column.

The weather is heavenly. The two chestnut-trees in our front courtyard are in full flower; the few plants in the greenhouse are all putting out buds. Where shall we be when the buds become flowers?

Last year at this time it was the height of the giddiest of giddy seasons. One can hardly believe it is the same Paris.

My father-in-law feels very bad that I did not leave when I still had the chance. So do I, . . . but now it is too late. I must stay till the bitter end, and no doubt the end will be bitter: battle, murder, and sudden death, and all the things we pray against in the Litany.

Dombrowski has failed in his sortie to St. Cloud.

18th May.—It seems that the Communards wish all France to adopt their gentle methods, and they believe and hope that Communism will reign supreme over the country.

Rigault, to prove what an admirable government France has, yesterday issued the decree to arrest a mass of people. No one knows exactly why, except that he wishes to show how great his power is. He wants the Commune to finish in fire and flame as a funeral pile. I hope he will be on the top of it, like Sardanapalus, and suffer the most. Horrible man!

I received a letter from Mr. Mallet this morning, inclosing an invitation to assist at a concert given by all the *musiques militaires à Paris* on the Place de la Concorde, and offering a ticket for two places on the terrace of the Tuileries. The idea of these creatures on the brink of annihilation, death, and destruction giving a concert! If it were not so tragic it would really be laughable.

DEAR LADY,—I wish I could bring you this extraordinary document *de viva persona;* but I do not like to leave the embassy, even for a short time. Lascelles and I are well, but very anxious. You will notice that this invitation is for the 21st. Our friends evidently think we will be pleasantly attuned to music on that day. They are as mad as March hares; they will be asking us to dance at Mazas next. . . . Hoping you are not as depressed as we are,

Yours,   E. MALLET.

Just as I had finished reading the above we heard a tremendous explosion. Louis said it was *l'École Militaire*, which was to be blown up to-day. What are we coming to?

Louis and I ventured to go up to the third story, and we put our heads out of one of the small windows. We saw the bombs flying over our heads like sea-gulls. All the sky was dimmed with black smoke, but we could not see if anything was burning, though we hear that the Tuileries is on fire and all the public buildings are being set fire to.

An organized mob of *pétroleurs* and *pétroleuses* receive two francs a day for pouring petroleum about and then setting fire. How awful!

Louis assures us that they will not come near us, as their only idea is to destroy public property. My father-in-law says the fever of destruction may seize them, and they might pillage the fine houses and set fire to them. He is having everything of value, like jewels, silver, and his precious bric-à-brac, carried down to the cellar, where there is an iron vault, and has showed us all how to open it in case of a disaster.

May 21st (Sunday evening).—The Versaillais entered Paris by the Point du Jour, led by gallant Gallifet.

May 22d.—Rigault gave the order that all the hostages (*ôtages*) were to be shot. Rigault wrote the order himself. It does not bear any of the fantastic seals they are so fond of, and of which they have an incredible quantity. It has been written on a paper (*une déclaration d'expédition du chemin de fer d'Orléans*). Probably he was trying to get away. It was the last order he gave, and the last fuse to be used to set fire to the funeral pile.

This proclamation, of which I give an exact copy, will give you a little idea of what this horrible brute is capable of:

Floréal, an 79 [the way they date things in republics]. Fusillez l'Archevêque et les ôtages; incendiez les Tuileries et le Palais Royal, et repliez-vous sur la rue Germain-des-Prés.

Procureur de la Commune,
Ici tout va bien.   RAOUL RIGAULT.

In the evening of the 22d the victims—forty of them —the good Darboy, Duguerry, Bonjean, and others— were piled into a transport-wagon with only a board placed across, where they could sit, and were taken to the place of execution.

The Archbishop seemed suffering; probably the privations he had endured had weakened him. Bonjean said to him, "Lean on my arm, it is that of a good friend and a Christian," and added, "La religion d'abord, la justice ensuite." As soon as one name was called a door opened and a prisoner passed out—the Archbishop went first; they descended the dark and narrow steps one by one. When they were placed against the

332

wall Bonjean said, "Let us show them how a priest and a magistrate can die."

Rigault ordered their execution two hours after they were taken; and when some one ventured a remonstrance he curtly replied, "Nous ne faisons pas de la légalité, nous faisons de la révolution." Some ruffian in the mob cried out the word "liberté," which reached Darboy's ears, and he said, "Do not profane the word of liberty; it belongs to us alone, because we die for it and for our faith." This sainted man was the first to be shot. He died instantly; but President Bonjean crossed his arms and, standing erect, stared full in the faces of his assassins with his brave eyes fastened on theirs. This seemed to have troubled them, for of the nineteen balls they fired not one touched his head—they fired too low—but all his bones were broken. The defiant look stayed on his face until the *coup de grâce* (a bullet behind his ear) ended this brave man's life. These details are too dreadful. I will spare you, though I know many more and worse.

Dombrowski had a slight advantage over l'Amiraut the other day, which puffed them all up with hope; but how foolish to think that anything can help now!

May 23d.—Now they have all lost their heads, and are at their wits' end. There are thirty thousand artillery and more cannon than they know what to do with.

Everything is in a muddle; you can imagine in what a fearful state of anxiety we live. The only thing we ask ourselves now is, When will the volcano begin to pour out its flames?

If the troops should come in by the Arc de Triomphe and fight their way through Paris by the Champs-Élysées and the Boulevard there would not be much hope for us, as we would be just between the two fires.

May 25th.—The Arc de Triomphe and the Champ de Mars were captured to-day, and the fighting in the streets has commenced. They are fighting like mad in the Faubourg St. Honoré. When I open the door of the vestibule I can hear the yelling and screaming of the rushing mob; it is dreadful, the spluttering of the fusillades and the guns overpower all other noises. We hope deliverance is near at hand; but who knows how long before we have peace and quiet again?

May 28th.—MacMahon has stormed the barricades and has entered Paris, taking fifty thousand prisoners. Gallifet has ordered thousands to be shot.

We are rescued from more horrors. Thank God! these days of trembling and fear are over.

Pascal Grousset was killed on the barricades. I am thankful to say that Raoul Rigault has also departed this world. Courbet, Regnaud, a promising young painter, and how many shall we know of afterward, have been shot.

We hear that Auber became quite crazy and wandered out on the ramparts, and was killed with the soldiers. He deserved a better fate, my dear old friend! I am sure his heart was broken, and that that day we breakfasted with him was not his first but his last *jour de bonheur*.

Seventy-two days of Communism has cost France 850,000,000 francs.

IN THE COURTS OF MEMORY

Dear Mother,—Our peaceful life here is a great contrast to the bombs of poor dilapidated Paris. I have still the screams and bursting shells of the Faubourg St. Honoré in my ears.

When I wrote of Strakosch's persisting in his idea of my singing in concerts, I did not dream that I should be telling you that I have succumbed to his tempting and stupendous proposition. It is true that I have said *yes*, and *vogue la galère!*

And the most curious thing is that the whole family sitting in council have urged me to do it.

"Why not?" said Mr. Moulton, making mental calculations.

"I would, if I were you," said Mrs. Moulton, overflowing with enthusiasm.

"I agree," said Charles, only seeing the fun of a new experience.

"But," I urged, "I doubt if I can stand on my own merits. Singing in public as an amateur is one thing, and singing as an artist is another." This wise saying was scorned by the council.

I have ordered some fine dresses from Worth, and if my public don't like me they can console themselves with the thought that a look at my clothes is worth a ticket.

Well, the fatal word has gone forth; I shall probably regret it, but it is too late now.

Therefore, dear mother, please break the news gently to the family and the genealogical tree, whose bark, I hope, is worse than its bite.

We leave for America in September. Strakosch goes before, "to work it up," he says.

New York, *October.*

My dear Mother-in-law,—Don't send any more letters to the Barlows'. We thought that it was better not to stay with them (pleasant as it was) any longer. There was such a commotion in that quiet house, such ringing of bells and running about. The servants were worn out attending to me and my visitors.

I don't know where to begin to tell you about this wonderful escapade of ours. I call it my "bravura act." It is too exciting! I copy a letter just received from Strakosch, in answer to a letter of mine, to show you what the process of "working up" is. He writes: "You wonder at your big audiences. The reason is very simple. In the first place, people know that you are thought to be the best amateur singer in Paris—"La Diva du Monde"—besides being a favorite in Parisian society, and that you have not only a beautiful voice, but also that you have beautiful toilettes. This is a great *attraction.* In the second place, I allow (*as a great privilege*) the tickets to be subscribed for; the remaining ones are bought at auction. You see, in this way the bids go *'way up*. . . . I am glad I secured Sarasate to supplement," etc.

We have taken a suite of rooms in the Clarendon Hotel, so as to be near the opera-house, where I go to practise with the orchestra. You cannot imagine how intense the whole thing is.

To feel that I can hold a great audience, like the one that greeted me the first night, in my hand, and to know that I can make them laugh or cry whenever I please—to see the mass of upturned faces—is an inspiring sensation. The applause bewildered me at first, and I was fearfully excited; but one gets used to all things in the end. My songs, "Bel raggio" (Rossini), "Voi che sapete" (Mozart), and "La Valse de Pardon de Ploërmel" (Meyerbeer), were all encored and re-encored.

I said to Strakosch, "I can't go on forever, tripping on and off the stage like that!"

He answered, laconically, "Well, you see people have paid much for their tickets, and they want their money's worth."

I said, "I wish the tickets cost less."

The flowers (you should have seen them!) were mostly what they call here "floral tributes" (what you would call *des pièces montées*), and were brought in by a procession of ushers and placed on the stage. I do not mention the quantities of bouquets handed up to me!

One "floral tribute" received an ovation as it was borne up the aisle by four men, and hauled up on to the stage by a man who came from the side scenes. It was a harp made entirely of flowers, about six feet high. It made quite a screen for me as I went in and out. The card of the harp was brought to me, and I read, "H. P. Stalton, 'Asleep in Jesus,' North Conway." I had no idea what it meant, but mama remembered that some years ago, when she and I were traveling in the White Mountains, we stopped overnight at the little town of North Conway. At the hotel we heard that a lady had died, and her son was terribly grieved. There was to be a funeral service the next morning in the parlor of the inn. I asked, "Do you think that I might sing something?" "Of course, *any* music would be welcome," was the answer. So I chose the hymn, "Asleep in Jesus," which I sang when the time came. As there was nothing but an old piano, I preferred to sing without accompaniment. I was very much affected, and I suppose my voice showed my emotion, because other people were equally affected. As for the young man, he knelt on the floor and put his hands over his face and sobbed out loud. Poor fellow, my heart bled for him!

I sang the hymn through with difficulty. The last verse I sang *pianissimo* and very slowly. The silence was painful; you could have heard a pin drop. The whole scene was very emotional, and I remember feeling that I never wanted to go through such a thing again. The young man had not forgotten, after all these years, either the song or the singer. Hence the beautiful harp of flowers to thank me. I should have liked to have seen him, to thank *him*.

There is a very sad, pathetic, and patriotic song called "Tender and True," by a composer, Alfred Pease, which I sing. Strakosch said, "You must have in your *répertoire* something American." This song is about a young soldier who takes "a knot of ribbon blue" from his lady-love, and who dies on the battle-field with the knot of ribbon on his breast. When I sing "the flag draped over the coffin lid" the whole audience is dissolved in tears. The women weep openly; the men hide behind their opera-glasses and try to blow their noses noiselessly between the verses.

I always finish with "Beware!" and Charles always accompanies me, which pleases him very much. He thinks that American audiences are very appreciative, because they stand up and clap and the women wave their handkerchiefs.

I tell him they stand up because the next thing they are going to do is to go out.

WORCESTER, *December, 1871.*

DEAR MOTHER,—Thanks for your letter. I had hoped to have received better news of Charles.

When he left Thursday he did not look well, but I thought it was owing to the excitement and late hours and the irregular life we have been leading. He wanted to go to Cambridge, where he thought that he could take better care of himself. I would have gone with him, but I felt that I could not leave Strakosch and Worcester in the lurch.

If I don't receive a reassuring telegram from you, I shall start off without delay.

I was dreadfully nervous and unstrung, as you will see, when I tell you how I blundered. I do not like singing in oratorio. Getting up and sitting down all the time, holding and singing from a book, losing my place and having to find it in a hurry, is not what I like. However, I got on very well at first, but there is a place in the score where three angels come forward and sing a trio without accompaniment. Then the soprano (me) steps in front and sings, without a helping note: "Hail, Hail, O Lord God of Hosts!" The orchestra and chorus take up the same phrase after me.

I sang boldly enough, "Hail, Hail, O Lord God of Hosts!" but suddenly felt cold shivers down my back when Zerrahn tapped his baton on his stand, thereby stopping all further proceedings, and turning to me said, in a low whisper, "A half-tone lower."

Good gracious, how could I find the right note! First I had to remember the last tone I had sung, then I had to transpose it in my head, all in an instant. It was a critical moment.

Suppose I did not hit the right note! The whole orchestra and the two-hundred-man-strong chorus would come thundering after me—the *orchestra on the right key* and *the chorus following in my footsteps*.

I turned cold and hot, and my knees trembled under me. You may imagine what a relief it was when I heard things going on as if nothing had happened. *I had struck the right note!* And I finished the oratorio without further disaster. I do not think that any one in the audience remarked anything wrong.

I said to Zerrahn, after: "Could you not have helped me? Could you not have given me the note?"

"No," he answered. "Impossible! I could not ask the nearest violinist to play the note, and I could not trust myself to find it. I was as nervous as you were."

.   .   .   .

[Mrs. Moulton was called to Cambridge the next day. Mr. Moulton had died suddenly.]

CUBA, HAVANA, *January, 1873.*

DEAR MAMA,—We left New York in a fearful blizzard. It was snowing, hailing, blowing, and sleeting; in fact, everything that the elements could do they did on that particular day. We were muffled up to our ears in sealskin coats, furs, boas, and so forth, and were piloted over the wet and slippery deck to our stateroom on the upper deck, which we wished had been on the under deck, as it was continually washed by the "wild waves."

We knew pretty well "what the wild waves were saying"; at least Laura did, and they kept on saying it until well into the next day.

I being an old sailor (not in years but in experience), as I had crossed the Atlantic several times, felt very superior on this occasion, and looked down without sympathy on the maiden efforts of my suffering sister; and, having dressed, goaded her almost to distraction to get up and do likewise, which she obstinately refused to do.

After ordering breakfast I ventured out on deck, to find myself alone, among deserted camp-stools. I realized then that the others preferred "rocking in the cradle of the deep" in their berths and in the privacy of their cabins. I myself felt very shaky as I stumbled about on the deck holding on to the rails, and I, hurrying back to the haven of my stateroom, happened to meet the struggling steward endeavoring to balance the tray containing the breakfast I had ordered, and to make his way through my door.

The steward, the tray, and I all collided. The result was disastrous: the food made a bee-line for the ceiling, the drinkables flooded the already wet floor and our shoes, while cups, saucers, plates, and dishes were scattered to fragments.

All that day we and every one were dreadfully sick; but what a contrast the next day was! A hot, tropical sun blazed down on us; the awnings were put up, the ladies appeared in lighter costumes, the men in straw hats and thin jackets. How odious our warm wraps and rugs seemed! And how completely our discomforts of the day before had disappeared! Laura had forgotten her miseries, and was already planning another sea-trip, and eagerly scanning the menu for dinner, to which she did ample justice.

The third day was still hotter; parasols, summer dresses, and fans made their appearance, and at four o'clock we saw Morro Castle and the lighthouse; and we steamed (literally, for we were so hot) up the exquisite harbor, where white Havana lay like a jewel on the breast of the water.

Hot! It must have been one hundred and ninety in the shade—if there had been any; but there was none. The glare of the whiteness of the city and the reflection on the water, the air thick with perfumes, gave us a tropical tinge, and made us shudder to think what we should have to endure before we could rest in the hotel, which we hoped would be cool.

Young Isnaga, who has just come from Harvard College, where I knew him, and who was now returning to his native land to help his father on the plantation, served us as a guide; in fact, he was our Baedeker. He told us that all those hundreds of little boats with coverings like hen-coops stretched over them, which swarmed like bees about our steamer, did not contain native ruffians demanding our money or our lives, as they seemed to be doing, but were simply peaceable citizens hoping to earn an honest penny.

We dreaded going through the custom-house in this

excessive heat; but Isnaga recognized one of his servants, in a small boat coming toward us, gesticulating wildly and waving a paper; this paper meant, it seemed, authority with the officials, so we had no delay, as Isnaga took us under his wing. I almost wished that the custom-house had confiscated my thick clothes and the fur-lined coat; and as for the boa, it looked like a vicious constrictor of its own name, and I wished it at the bottom of the sea.

Isnaga took us in his boat and landed us on the tropical "Plaza," where we found his *volante* waiting. He insisted on our getting into this unique vehicle, which I will describe later when I have more time.

Our one thought was to reach the hotel, which we did finally, sending the *volante* back to its owner by a sweeping wave of the hand in the direction of the quay, which the black Jehu seemed to comprehend.

Fortunately the proprietor spoke what he thought was English, and we were able to secure very good rooms overlooking the harbor. How delicious the cool, marble-floored room appeared to us! How we luxuriated in the fresh, cold water, the juiciest of oranges, the iced pineapples, and all the delicious fruits they brought us, and, above all, in the balmy air and the feeling of repose and rest! We reappeared in the thinnest of gauzes for the repast called dinner.

Adieu, cold and ice! *Vive le soleil!*

This hotel (San Carlos) is situated right on the bay. The quay in front of us is garnished with a row of dwarfy trees and dirty benches, these last being decorated, in their turn, by slumbering Cubans. There were colonnades underneath the hotel, where there were small shops, from which the odor of garlic and tobacco, combined with the shrieks and the snapping of the drivers' whips, reached us, as we sat above them on our balcony.

The hotel is square, with an open courtyard in the middle, and all the rooms open on to the marble gallery which surrounds the courtyard. This gallery is used as a general dining-room; each person eats at his own little iron table placed before the door of his bedroom.

Our large room contains two iron beds (minus mattresses), with only a canvas screwed on the iron sides, but covered with the finest of linen sheets. An iron frame holds the mosquito-net in place.

Evidently a wash-stand is a thing to be ashamed of, for they are concealed in the most ingenious way. Mine in the daytime is rather an attractive commode; Laura's is a writing-table, which at night opens up and discloses the wash-basin. Otherwise there is little furniture—two cane-bottomed chairs, two bamboo tables (twins); one has a blue ribbon tied on its leg to tell it from its brother. Two ingeniously braided mats of linen cord do duty for the *descente de lit*. Oh yes! there is a mirror for each of us, which in my hurry to finish my letter I forgot to mention; but they are so small and wavy that the less we look in them the better we are satisfied with ourselves.

We have a large balcony, which has a beautiful view of the harbor and the opposite shore, two huge wooden so-called windows, which are not windows, opening on to the balcony. There is a panel in the middle which you can open if you want some fresh air. Glass is never used for windows, so that when you shut your window you are in utter darkness. Opposite is the door which is not a door, but a sort of a gate with lattice shutters, giving the room the look of a bar-room. There is space above the shutters which is open to the ceiling. Any one in the gallery who wanted to could stand on a chair and peer over. Everything that goes on in the gallery, every noise, every conversation, can be clearly overheard, and if one only understood the language it might be very interesting.

The bars and locks on our doors and windows date from the fifteenth century, I should say, and it is with the most herculean efforts that we manage to shut ourselves in for the night; and we only know that the day has broken when we hear the nasal and strident Cuban voices, and the clattering of plates on the other side of the gate. Then we work like galley-slaves unbarring, and the blazing sun floods our room.

I don't know if bells are popular in Havana; but in this hotel we have none. If you want a chambermaid, which you do about every half-hour, you must open your gate and clap your hands, and if she does not come you go on clapping until some one else comes.

For our early breakfast we begin clapping at an early hour, and finally our coffee and a huge plate filled with the most delicious oranges, cut and sugared, are brought to us. We tried to obtain some simple toast; but this seemed unknown to the Cuban cuisine, and we had to content ourselves with some national mixture called rolls.

CUBA, *January 24, 1873.*

The letters of introduction which kind Admiral Polo (Spanish Minister in Washington) gave me must be very powerful and far-reaching, for we are received as if we were Princesses of the blood. The Governor-General came directly to put himself, his house, his family, his Generalship—in fact, all Cuba—*á la disposición de usted*. The Captain of the Port appeared in full gala uniform, and deposited the whole of the Spanish fleet, his person, and the universe in general at my feet, and said, "That no stone should be left unturned to make our stay in Havana illustrious in history."

What could the most admirable of Polos have written to have created such an effect? Then came the General Lliano, a very handsome man, but who I thought was rather stingy, as he only put the Spanish Army at my disposition, and himself (*cela va sans dire*).

Next came Señor Herreras, dressed all in white, with the most perfect patent-leather boots, much too tight for him, and which must have caused him agonies while he was offering to put himself (of course), his bank, and all his worldly possessions in my hands.

I accepted all with a benign smile, and answered that I only had America and my fur-lined coat and boa to offer in return.

We had so many instructions given to us as to what to do and what not to do in this perfidious climate that we were quite bewildered.

Never to go out in the sun. Result—Malaria and sudden death.

Never put your feet on the bare floors. Result—Centipedes.

Never drink the water. Result—Yellow fever.

Never eat fruit at night. Result—Typhoid fever.

If you sleep too much; if you sit in the draught; if

you let the moon shine on you. Result—Lockjaw and speedy annihilation.

These admonitions were very confusing, and we lay awake at night thinking how we could manage to live under these circumstances.

What a delight to look at the view from our balcony! I never imagined anything so beautiful: the distant hills are so blue, the water so sparkling, the sun gilds the hundreds of sails in the harbor. At night the water is brilliant with phosphorescence, and when the boats glide through it they throw out a thousand colors; even the reflection of the stars is multicolored. And then, pervading all, the delicious fragrance of fruit and flowers and tropicality!

When I am not poetical, as above, I notice the ox-carts with their cruel drivers yelling at their poor beasts and goading them with iron-pointed sticks. When they were not striking them, they struck picturesque attitudes themselves, leaning on their carts and smoking endless cigarettes. The cabmen are also picturesque in their way. After their return from a "course," tired out from whipping their forlorn horses into the sideling trot which is all they are equal to, and after flicking their ears until they are too lazy to continue, they hang their hats and stockingless feet over the carriage lamps and chew sugar-cane, looking the picture of contentment.

Cabs are cheap; twenty-five cents will take you anywhere *à la course*. But if you go from one shop to another, or linger at a visit, fancy knows no bounds, for there is no tariff and the coachman's imagination is apt to be vivid; and as you can't trust anything else, you must trust to your conversational powers to get you out of the scrape.

Volantes are capricious and too exotic a vehicle to trifle with; moreover, they turn corners with difficulty, and corners in Havana are the things you meet the most of.

The streets are narrow; so that if you wish to avoid adventures you must be careful to give your coachman the correct address before starting off. The porter of the hotel did this for us to-day, as our Spanish has not reached *perfection* yet.

All the streets are labeled *subida*, which means, "go up this street," or *bajado*, "down this street." If, by chance, you want to go to 27 *subida*, and you amble on to 29, it takes you hours to go *bajado* and get back to *subida* again, going round in a *cercle vicieux*. We spent a whole broiling afternoon buying two spools of thread, my parasol being mightier than my tongue, as the poor coachman's back can vouch for. When everything else failed we shouted in unison, "Hotel San Carlos," and the black coachman grinned with delight. Seeing *bajado* so often at different points, Laura thought it was the sign of an assurance company; when I saw it on the same house as Maria Jesus Street I thought it was some kind of charitable institution.

A *volante*, as I have said, is a unique and delightful vehicle, which one requires to know to appreciate. There are two huge wheels behind and none in front; the animal, secured between the shafts, supports the weight of the carriage. The seat is very low, so that you recline, more than sit; your feet are unpleasantly near the horse's tail; a small seat can be pulled out between

you and your companion if there is a child in the
party. A dusky postilion decked out in high top-boots,
with enormous spurs of real silver, sits astride the horse
between the shafts, and a huge *sombrero* covers his woolly
head.

The harness, spurs, buckles, and a good deal of the
carriage trimmings are silver; the horse's tail is braided
once a week and tied to the saddle. No frisky fright-
ening off the flies from his perspiring and appetizing
body! Sometimes (in fact, usually) there is an extra
horse outside of the traces, so that labor is thus divided.
The *volante* drags the people; the horse in the shafts
drags the *volante*, and the extra horse drags everything;
the coachman does the spurring, whipping, and shouting, and the inmates do the lolling.

I forgot to say that my friend, Lola Maddon, whom I
used to know in Paris, is here, married to Marquis
San Carlos, who was a fascinating widower with several
children, whom Lola, like the dear creature she is, had
taken under her youthful wing. She rushed to see me
the moment she heard that I had come, and has already
begun to "turn the stones" which are to be turned for
me to make my "visit illustrious" here. She has invited us to the opera to-morrow, and gives a *soirée* for
me on the following evening. I confess I am rather
curious to see a *soirée* in Havana. I hope they have ice-
chests to sit on and cool conversation. I shall not talk
politics; in the first place I can't, and in the second place
because it is heating to the blood.

Lola says her husband is a rabid Spaniard. "A rabid
Spaniard!" Could anything be more alarming? No;
I will not be the innocent means to bring about dis-

cussions, and precipitate a conflict between the Cubans and the Spaniards! I have pinned upon the bed-curtains, next to the precautions for preserving health and the washing-list, the words, "Never talk politics, nor be led into listening to them." I can always, if pushed into a corner, assume an air of profundity and say, "Is the crisis—" and then stop and look for a word. The politician, if he is anything of a politician, will finish the phrase for me, with the conviction that I know all about it but am diplomatic.

To see the cows in Havana is enough to break your heart. I weep over them in a sort of milky way. I have always seen cows in comfortable stables, with nice, clean straw under their feet and pails full of succulent food placed within easy reach, while at certain intervals a tidy, tender-hearted young milkmaid appears with a three-legged stool and a roomy pail, and extracts what the cow chooses to give her. But here the wiry creatures roam from door to door, and drop a pint or so at each call. It is pitiful to see the poor, degraded things, with their offspring following behind. The latter are graciously allowed to accompany them; but no calls on Nature are permitted, the poor little things are even muzzled!

Whenever I wish to go into the public parlor, where there is a piano, I meet the Countess C——, who has evidently just been singing to her son and her husband.

The first day I met her I approached her with the intention to talk music; but she swept by with a look which withered me up to an autumn leaf and left the room, followed by her music, son, and husband; but afterward, when she saw the Captain of the Port in full gala offering me "Cuba et ses dépendances," she changed her manner, and *then it was my turn!* When she asked me if I also knew Count Ceballos, the Governor-General, I answered, with a sweet smile, "Of course I do." "And many other people here?" she asked. "All I think that are worth knowing," I replied, getting up and leaving the room as abruptly as she had done. It was great fun, though L—— thought I was rude.

We went to the theater with Marquise San Carlos. "All the world is here," said she. Certainly it looked as if all Havana filled the Tacon, which is a very large theater. Every box was full, and the parquet, as Lola told me, contained the *haute volée* of the town; the open balconies were sacred to the middle-class, while in the upper gallery were the nobodies, with their children, poor things! decked out with flowers and trying to keep awake through the very tiresome and *démodé* performance of "Macbeth." Tamberlik sang. What a glorious voice he has! And when he took the high C (which, if I dare make the joke, did not at all resemble the one Laura and I encountered coming out of New York Harbor) it was all I could do to sit quiet. I wanted to wave something. The prima-donna was *assoluta*, and must have been pickled in some academy in Italy years ago, for she was not preserved. She acted as stupidly as she sang.

Each box has six seats and are all open, with the eternal lattice-door at the back, and separated from its neighbor by a small partition. It was very cozy, I thought; one could talk right and left, and when the gentlemen circulated about in the *entr'actes* smoking the inevitable cigarette, which never leaves a Cuban's lips (except to light a fresh one), all the lattice-doors are eagerly opened to them. Lola presented all the *haute volée* to us; the unpresented just stared. I never realized how much staring a man can do till I saw the Cuban. I mentioned this to Lola, to which she responded, "It is but natural; you are a stranger."

"Dear friend," said I, "I have been a stranger in other lands, but I have never seen the like of this. If I was an orang-outang there might be some reason; but to a simple mortal, or two simple mortals, like my sister and myself, their stares seem either too flattering or the reverse."

"Why, my dear," she replied, "they mean it as the greatest compliment, you may believe me." And she appealed to her husband, who confirmed what she said. All the gentlemen carry fans and use them with vigor; the ladies are so covered with powder (*cascarilla*) that you can't tell a pretty one from an ugly one. If one of them happens to sneeze, there is an avalanche of powder.

Lola showed us her establishment and explained the architecture of a Cuban house. If chance has put a chimney somewhere, they place the kitchen near it. Light and size are of no account, neither is cooking of any importance.

CUBA, *February, 1873.*

We make such crowds of acquaintances it would be useless to tell you the names. The Marquise San Carlos sent her carriage for us the evening of her *soirée.* All the company was assembled when we arrived: the Marquis, the Dean of Havana, and two abbés were playing *tresillo*, a Spanish game of cards.

A group of men stood in the corner and seemed to be talking politics, as far as I could judge from their gesticulations. A few ladies in sweeping trains, and very *décolletées*, sat looking on listlessly. The daughter of the house was nearing the piano. The Dean said to me, with a sly smile, "Now is the *coup de grâce!*"—his little joke. She sang, "Robert, toi que j'aime. Grâce! Grâce!" etc. Also she sang the waltz of "Pardon de Ploërmel, a familiar *cheval de bataille* of my own, which I was glad to see cantering on the war-path again. In the mean time conversation was at low ebb for poor Laura. She told me some fragments which certainly were peculiar. For instance, she understood the gentleman who had last been talking to her to say that he had been married five times, had twenty-eight children, and had married his eldest son's daughter as his fifth wife. I afterward ascertained that what he had intended to convey was that he was twenty-eight when he married and had fifteen children. That was bad enough, I thought.

I sang two or three times. The gaiety was brought to rather an abrupt close, as the Marquis received a telegram of his brother's death. The Abbé went on playing his game, not at all disturbed (such is the force of habit); but we folded our tents and departed.

The hours are sung out in the streets at night, with a little flourish at the end of each verse. I fancy the watchman trusts a good deal to inspiration about this, as my clock—an excellent one—did not at all chime in with his hours. Perhaps he composes his little verse, in which case a margin ought to be allowed him. . . .

The bells in the churches are old and cracked and decrepit.

All the fleet, and any other boat that wants to join in, fire off salutes, to wake you up in the morning.

I bought to-day the eighth part of a lottery-ticket.

The Captain of the Port thinks his English is better than his French, but sometimes it is very funny. He says: "Don't take care," instead of "Never mind"—"The *volante* is to the door"—"Look to me, I am all proudness"—"You are all my anxiousness."

The houses are generally not more than one story high, built around an open court, on which all rooms open. In the middle of this is a fountain; no home is complete without a fountain, and no fountain is complete without its surroundings of palms, plants, and flowers. In one of the rooms you can see where the *volante* reposes for the night. You only see these glories at night. When the heavy bolts are drawn back you and everybody can look in from the street on the family gathering, basking in rocking-chairs around the fountain, and in oriental, somnolent conversation.

Cuba, *February*.

The annual *soirée* of the Governor and his wife took place last night. The Captain of the Port came to fetch us. The palace is, like all other official buildings, magnificent on the outside, but simple and severe within. There was a fine staircase, and all the rooms were brilliantly lighted, but very scantily furnished, according to our ideas. We must have gone through at least six rooms before we reached the host and hostess. Every room was exactly alike: in each was a red strip of carpet, half a dozen rocking-chairs placed opposite one another, a cane-bottomed sofa, a table with nothing on it, and walls ditto. There are never any curtains, and nothing is upholstered. This is the typical Cuban salon.

There was an upright piano and a pianist at it when we entered, but the resonance was so overpowering that I could not hear what he was playing. Laura and I (after having been presented to a great many people) were invited to sit in the rocking-chairs. The gentlemen either stood out in the corridor or else behind the chair of a lady and fanned her. *Dulces* and ices were passed round, and every one partook of them, delighted to have the opportunity to do something else than talk.

When the pianist had finished his Chopin a lady sang, accompanied by her son, who had brought a whole pile of music. She courageously attacked the *Cavatina* of "Ernani." The son filled up the places in her vocalization which were weak by playing a dashing chord. She was a stout lady and very warm from her exertions, and the more she exerted herself the more frequently the vacancies occurred; and the son, perspiring at every pore, had difficulty to fill them up with the chords, which became louder and more dashing.

Countess Ceballos, with much hemming and hawing, begged me to sing. I felt all eyes fixed on me; but my eyes were riveted to the little, low piano-stool on which I should have to sit. It seemed miles below the piano-keys. "How could I play on it?" Evidently none but long-bodied performers had been before me, for when I asked for a cushion, in order to raise myself a little, nothing could be found but a very bulgy bed-pillow, which was brought, I think, from the mother country. There was a sort of Andalusian swagger about it.

The dream "that I dwelt in marble halls" was no longer a dream. Here I was singing in one. I sang "Ma Mère était Bohémienne," and another song which had an easy accompaniment. It took me a little moment to temper my voice to these shorn rooms.

The charge of musketry which followed was deafening, though only gentlemen clapped their hands; ladies don't rise to such exertion in Cuba. I sang "Beware!" as a parting salute. The Captain of the Port came up, flushed with pride, and said, in his best English, "I am all proudness!"

Panelas (large pieces of frosted sugar, to be melted in water) and other sweets were passed about at intervals.

Shaking hands is a great institution here. No one wears gloves except at the opera, so that one's hands are in a perpetual state of fermentation, especially after one of these functions, when making acquaintances, expressing thanks, and everything else are done through the medium of the hands. One can literally say that one wrings one's hands.

We, as the distinguished guests, were led into the supper-room very ceremoniously, and put among the higher strata of society. The buffet was overflowing with Cuban delicacies and *dulces*. I reveled in the fruit and left the viands severely alone.

After supper we went into the ball-room, and saw for the first time the Cuban waltz, otherwise called *Habanera*, a curious dance something between a shuffle and a languid glide. The dancers hardly move from the same spot, or at most keep in a very small circle, probably on account of the heat and exertion; and then the dispersing of so much powder, with which every lady covers herself and gets rid of when she moves, has to be considered.

The music has a peculiar measure; I have never heard anything like it before. The instruments seemed mostly to be violins, flutes, clarinets, and a small drum. The bass is very rhythmical and deep, whereas the thin tones of the other instruments are on the very highest notes, which leaves a gap between the upper and lower tones, making such a peculiar effect that the music pursues and haunts you even in your dreams.

We bade our host and hostess good night and, followed by the Captain of the Port, who now was not only "all proudness," but full of "responsibilitiveness," left the palace. In passing the music-room I took a farewell look at the bulgy bed-pillow, which was still reposing on the music-stool.

CUBA, *February.*

DEAR MAMA,—You have no idea of the heat here. I never felt anything so scorching as it was to-day. Let me tell you what happened.

General Lliano came in the morning to ask what Havana could show me. I answered that above all things I wanted to see Morro Castle. He replied that Morro Castle was mine, and that I had only to fix the time and he would take us there.

I did fix it, and fixed it at two o'clock, as a fit hour to visit the *Cabaña.* I noticed the look of blank despair on our friend's face, but, not knowing that all Cuba slept between the hours of two and five, I did not realize the piteousness of it. General Lliano begged the Captain of the Port, Señor Català, to accompany us, and both of these gentlemen came in full uniform, as well as their aides-de-camp.

The Captain's trim little boat was at the wharf near our hotel, and we were rowed over by the governmental crew to the opposite shore, and were met by the Governor of Morro Castle at the landing in the most sweltering heat. I had not forgotten to take the precaution, which anywhere else would have been appropriate, to carry extra wraps, as I told Laura that they were necessary for every water excursion. You may imagine the *de-trop*ness of these articles when the thermometer was up at one hundred and twenty in the shade.

We were taken about conscientiously and shown all that there was to be seen: all the dungeon-cells and subterranean passages, and up the hill to see the view, which was very extended and very beautiful. From there we went to the Governor's house, where we were greeted by his wife and daughter, the wife stiff in black moiré (I mean the moiré was stiff, not she). He placed himself, his wife and daughter, and his mansion at my disposal. I would not have minded taking the old gentleman; but I absolutely refused the lady and the moiré dress.

Dulces were served and some unappetizing-looking ices, which tasted better than they looked. Cakes also were offered us, of which I picked out those which had the least mauve and yellow coatings. When we were presented with some stiff little bouquets we thought it was a signal for departure, and bade adieu to the black moiré and the fast-melting ices.

From the *Cabaña* we walked along the macadamized road to the Morro Castle, a long distance it seemed to me in the heat; but we left the hard and glaring road and walked over the grass, following the line of the subterranean passage, which made a sort of mound, and finally reached Morro Castle. Here there were more officials, more presentations and more ceremonies, and more *dulces* and more bouquets.

The view from the ramparts, on which stood the lighthouse, was sublime: the blue sea underneath us, Havana on the left, and the purple mountains in the far distance.

One of the officials asked us whether we wanted to go to the top of the lighthouse. I declined, much to the relief of the assembled company. They say that fish have been thrown up by the spray over the lighthouse; but this seems almost as incredible as the majority of fishy stories. The castle is very high, the ramparts are higher, and the lighthouse crowns everything. The water dashes up through narrow crevices in the rocks, which gives it great force, and possibly might account for the fish story, but I doubt it.

By this time (six o'clock) we were utterly exhausted. Even at this hour the heat was intolerable. We had hoped for a little breeze on the water; but, alas! there was none. Poor Señor Herreras held his foot incased in tight patent - leather boots in his lap, moaning, "Comme je souffre!"

How they all must have blessed me for this idea of mine! I felt ashamed to look them in the face.

IN THE COURTS OF MEMORY

I could not tell you all the things we were taken to see. We visited the German and Spanish men-of-war. As we were in the company of the Governor-General, the Commander, and the Captain-General, we were not spared the proper salutes. The tour of the war-ships had to be made, and in place of the eternal *dulces* international refreshments were offered us. We departed in the Captain of the Port's steam-launch, and drove to the Carreo, where the pretty villas are.

The Governor-General drove us out to his *quinta* in great style: English horses and carriage and an American coachman. The roads were pretty bad, and we were considerably jostled going through the *Paseo*. The coachman careered from side to side to avoid ruts and tracks, and the dust was overpowering. No conversation was possible, as our throats were filled with dust and our lives hanging on a thread. I waved my hand in the direction of anything I thought pretty, and silence followed.

At the *quinta* all was ready and waiting for us. Fountains were playing, servants in red and yellow gorgeous liveries, with white stockings, were flitting about; various Cuban delicacies were offered to us, and we admired everything that was to be admired. The return drive was delightful, through the long avenues of stately palms and graceful date-trees.

The carnival is a great event and very amusing. I am not spoiled in the way of carnivals, only having seen that of Paris (the *Bœuf gras*) and the Battle of Flowers at Nice. The populace turn out in great force, every one is gay and happy, and the Cubans high and low join in the sport.

We were invited to drive in a four-in-hand. In this way we had a kind of bird's-eye view of the whole. No lady thinks herself too fine to join in the carnival. The procession, which defiles up and down the *Paseo* during the fray, begins at four in the hot, broiling afternoon, and ladies, decked out as Diana, Minerva, or other celebrities, powdered *à l'outrance*, smiling and proud of their success, recline in their *volantes*. Their own servants, with false noses or otherwise disguised, have their fun, too. I never saw such an orderly crowd; no pushing, no quarreling, no drunkenness, and yet every one was enjoying himself. There were two rows of carriages, one going up, one going down, with a place in the middle for the four-in-hands and the *chars*, some of which were very ingenious. There was a steamship with sailors, who kept firing off the whistle every time they saw a skittish horse. On another car were men dressed as skeletons with death's-heads instead of masks, and Shylock-looking Jews riding with their backs to the horses' heads, holding on to their tails.

A Punch and Judy were acting on a little stage during the procession, surrounded by children of all sizes and ages decked out in costumes, their tinselly flowers showing off their thin and sallow faces. There was a tremendous tooting of horns, and, with the music in the square and the music on the *chars*, made a perfect Bedlam. People nudged one another as we hove in sight in our four-in-hand.

The G——s did not relish the carnival as much as we did, and thought it a dismal affair. They captured a victoria by force, the coachman refusing to take them until they said "Paseo," upon which he started off on a trot. He had a dilapidated old horse, who had to be beaten all the way there, and when there, what do you think the coachman did? Simply pulled out a false nose and put it on and lighted a cigarette, stuck his hat on the lamp, and jeered at all the other vehicles, being on jeering terms with all the other cabmen; and as the *Paseo* is a mile long, it meant a mile of mortification. They came home disgusted and voted the carnival a "disgraceful affair."

MATANZAS, CUBA.

DEAR M.,—In my last letter I told you of our invitation to the *bal poudré* and *masqué* here. Count Ceballos, thinking it would amuse us to see it, arranged that we should stay at the palace, where the ball was to take place.

The Captain of the Port, with his aide-de-camp, accompanied us on our trip, and as he was going there in some official capacity, we shared his honors.

We had no adventures except that of traveling in company with a rather rough-looking set of men, who were on their way to a cock-fight. The cocks were tied up in bags; but as I wanted to see one the man opened the bag and took it out, and also showed me the spurs they strap on them when they fight.

We arrived in Matanzas about six o'clock, to find the Mayor's carriage waiting for us. We drove to the palace, and after dinner dressed for the ball. We did not attempt anything in the way of mask or costume, as being unknown and *unpowdered* was a sufficient disguise.

The Captain of the Port knew every one there, and presented many of his friends. We went out and stood on the balcony, looking at the sea of upturned heads. It seemed as if every Matanzois who was not inside was outside gazing at the windows, and listening to the band which was playing in the square. The night was glorious with a full moon.

I think that I have described in a former letter the Cuban dance, the languid tropical shuffle they call the *Habanera*. The music is so monotonous, always the same over and over again, and only ceases when it is convenient to the musicians.

The ladies had *cascarilla* (a powder made of egg-shells) an inch thick on their faces. I doubt if the officers ever saw so much powder as they did at this *bal poudré*.

There was a sit-down supper, consisting of sandwiches smelling strong of bad butter, ham and chicken salads, *dulces* of all sorts, but, alas! no fruit. The dancing continued long after we had retired for the night.

The Marquis Aldamar invited us to a *déjeûner* for the following day; the *volantes* were again "to the door," and we started off in grand style and great spirits and drove to the top of the mountain, from which we enjoyed a perfectly glorious view of the Yumiri Valley. The winding river looked like a silver thread as it wound in and out through the grassy meadows.

Our *déjeûner* was of a more European character than any that we had yet had in Cuba; the menu was in French—evidently the cook was also French—and the servants looked imported. In fact, everything was in very good style. The hostess was charming and musical; she sang some very pretty Cuban songs, and after a while asked me if I were musical, and if I would play something.

The Captain, in an undertone and in all "proudness," said, "Ask Madame to sing." And she did so in a rather condescending manner.

I accepted and went timidly to the piano, and as I hesitated as to what I should sing, she said, "Oh! just sing any little thing." With an amused glance at Laura I sang Chopin's waltz, which is the most difficult thing I sing, and the astonishment depicted on the countenance of my patronizing hostess was highly diverting.

"I wonder if you are any relation of a Mrs. Moulton whom my cousin knew in Paris," she said. "He was very intimate with a family of your name, and often talked to me about a Mrs. Moulton who sang so beautifully."

"Can it be that I am the same person? I have lived in Paris. What was your cousin's name?" I inquired.

"Jules Alphonso."

"What!" I cried. "Jules Alphonso your cousin? I have not seen him for years. I used to know him so well. Where is he?"

"He lives here in Cuba," she answered.

"Where in Cuba?" I interrupted. "How extraordinary! How much I should like to see him again!"

"And he, I am sure, would like to see you, he has so often talked about you to me. I felt directly last night that I knew you; it must have been intuition."

I think, Mama, you must remember Jules. He was

like a second son in our house, and was an intimate friend of my brother-in-law, and would have liked to have been a brother-in-law himself if he had been accepted. We all loved him. How strange to find him here! The last place in the world I should have dreamed of! I am not sure that I ever knew that he was a Cuban.

My new friend was wild with joy. "You are the one person that I have wanted to know all my life, and, fancy, here you are!"

Was it not a curious coincidence to meet *here*, in this out-of-the-way place, some one who knew all about me?

I repeated, "I must see Jules, and if he is anywhere near I shall certainly try to find him." "Let us go together," she said. "I will drive you there, and we will take him by surprise." Two *volantes* were immediately before the door, and the Marquise Aldamar, the Captain of the Port, Laura, and I started for La Rosa, Jules's plantation. It was an enchanting drive, though a long one, leading, as it did, through avenues of royal palms, and it was quite six o'clock before we reached Jules's house. I said to the Marquise Aldamar, "As Jules has no idea that I am in this part of the world, let me go in alone and surprise him."

We drove up to the entrance of his pretty villa, and the others accompanied me to the door of the salon with a finger on their lips, so that the servant should not announce us. We saw Jules sitting at a table reading. I entered softly and went behind him, and laying my hand on his shoulder said, "Jules!"

He turned quickly about, and when he saw me he thought I was an apparition or a dream. "What! What!" he cried, trembling with astonishment.

"It is I—Lillie Moulton," I said, quietly.

"You! you! No, it can't be possible!" And he took hold of my hands as if to see if they were flesh and blood. "Where did you come from? How did you get here? What brought you here?" followed in quick succession. The others pushed aside the curtain and came in. Then followed explanations. I was obliged to answer thousands of questions, and go into thousands of details, concerning the family, Paris, the war, and so forth. He ordered champagne, improvised a little supper for us, and did not seem to be able to do enough to show his delight at seeing me. But the Captain of the Port soon reminded us that it was time to be on our way back to Matanzas, as it was a long drive, and I bade a tearful farewell to lonely Jules. Our comet-like visit must have seemed to him like a vision, and he watched us, with eyes full of tears, drive away out of his life. Poor Jules!

MATANZAS, CUBA.

We spent the following morning in driving about the city. At half-past two crossed the ferry to Yuananabocca, where we found the amiable director and the rest of the party. The cars, with their cane-bottomed seats, were cool. The scenery was exquisite. On both sides of the road were real jungles of tropical growth, with the purple mountains as a background. We passed many *ingenios* (plantations), with their tall, smoking chimneys, all in full blast.

On reaching our destination we were met by *volantes* and saddle-horses. The former were for the ladies, the latter for the gentlemen of the party, and we made our way through the narrow, dirty streets, passed the walls of the city, and came out on to the beautiful road, where a gang of chained prisoners were breaking stones.

We passed many villas and well-kept gardens, and arrived at the bottom of the hill, where we were obliged to get out and walk, for the roads became impassable. It was a stiff climb; but when we reached the summit we were rewarded by a most magnificent view. We descended and reached the *volantes*, the drivers whipped up their horses, and away we went over rocks and ruts, but feeling nothing of them. That is the charm of a *volante;* only the wheels, which are behind you, get the jerks and jolts.

After a half-hour's drive we reached the famous cave, Laura and I were supplied with garments looking like mackintoshes, and, provided with torches, we began to descend. We first came to a large, vaulted hall, where miles of stalactites in every form and shape twinkled in the light of the torches.

We had to crawl through a small opening to get into another vaulted room which boasted of an echo. The guide struck a note and I sang a cadenza, which resounded like a thousand voices.

There never could have been a thermometer made that could register such heat as we felt here; the air was frightfully oppressive and almost intolerable.

They pointed out the Pope's Miter, the Virgin's Veil, the Altar, the Boat—all looking about as much like their names as an apple looks like a pack of cards. After being shown the lake I begged for fresh air, and we mounted the steep wooden stairs. The hot air outside seemed like a wintry breeze when we came into it, and we were told that we must cool off before venturing into the hot sun. Then we *volanted* back to Matanzas.

Our next visit was to the well-known *ingenio* (sugar-plantation) belonging to the cousin of the Marquis San Carlos. The sugar-mill stood in front of the master's house, so that the master could watch from his broad balcony the bringing in of the sugar-cane, which was hauled by huge cart-loads drawn by oxen. The sugar-cane, on its arrival, was put between great crushing wheels before it was thrown into the vats. The sturdy negresses, up to their elbows, stirred the foaming syrup after it had boiled. Then it was skimmed and boiled again to purify it. It went through a centrifugal process to crystallize it, and afterward was packed in boxes and stamped in less time than it takes to relate this. I liked to breathe the hot vapors coming from the huge tanks. What remains of the sugar is used as fuel; so nothing is wasted.

All the slaves seemed gay and well-fed. The Chinese, I believe, are liked better than the natives, they are so clean and adroit. We visited the houses of the slaves and found them all well kept. The master threw silver pieces (ten cents) to the children, who seemed content in their bare nakedness and clamored for more pennies. We drank *querap* (molasses) from the tanks mixed with whiskey. It was very good; but a little went very far. Two small children fanned us with palmettos during dinner. We passed the night there in the *ingenio;* but we saw no tarantulas, as was predicted. The next morning, when our coffee was brought, there was an assortment of delicious fruits—pineapples, guavas, bananas, cocoanuts, mangos, etc., which we enjoyed immensely. There was a little excitement before we started: the gardener, a bridegroom of eighty-five summers, was married to a blooming young person of eighty, both slaves and black as ink. We arrived at Havana that evening.

You can't tell how grieved I was to hear of the kind and good Emperor Napoleon's death. He was only sixty-five years old. I thought he was older. What an eventful life he had—tragical would be the right word. What did he not endure? When he was a child he was an exile, and since then, until he became first President and then Emperor, he was knocking about the world, sometimes hidden and sometimes pursued. However, he had fifteen years of glory, for there was not in all Europe a man more considered than he was, and he had until the last four years of his reign more prestige than any other sovereign. I think after the tragedy of Mexico his star began to pale.

The Emperor Napoleon was certainly the kindest-hearted and best-intentioned man in the world, so full of life, fun, and appreciation. I can see him now shaking with laughter when anything amused him, as was often the case at Compiègne.

The papers say that he had once been a policeman in London. I do not believe this is true, though the Emperor told me himself that he had lived very humbly at times; still, that is very different from being a policeman. I wonder if the Prince will try to get back the throne. He does not look as if he had a strong character, nor does he look as if he had the energy of the Emperor, which enabled him to go through so many hardships to gain his ends.

How sad it is! I am sure the Empress's only consolation is the thought that her son can recover the position the father lost.

We returned to Havana quite tired out with our little journey, and glad to rest in the quiet of our cool rooms, and I looked across the water, crowded with boats of every description, and gazed with delight at the distant mountains, with their clouds dragging themselves from one summit to the other.

How hot it is! I never thought that the sun, which is so high up, could pour down so; but it does pour down. I think it is hotter here than in Matanzas.

We shall be leaving here in a few days, and I suppose we shall find ice and snow in New York, and return to india-rubbers and umbrellas — things unknown here. During our absence some German men-of-war have arrived here, and stationed themselves right in front of our windows.

It must be their wash-day, for all the sailors' clothes are hanging out to dry.

Lola San Carlos is in light gray—the mourning one wears for a brother-in-law is not heavy in this warm country. She has invited us to a card-party for to-morrow; card-parties are evidently not gay enough to interfere with tears.

CUBA, *February*.

DEAR MAMA,—Well, we are really going to return! As usual, I have no more clothes, and I certainly will not be bothered to have anything made here. My black tulle dress has become brown and gray in its efforts to keep up to the mark; and as for Laura's white lace, it has become gray and brown, so you see we must go home.

We went to Lola's card-party. There was the bereaved brother, looking very chirpy, and the Dean, and the Abbé. They kindly proposed to teach me their favorite game of *tresillo*. They took a lively interest in my ignorance. They told me the rules and the names of the extraordinary cards; for instance, hearts were represented by coins, for clubs there were clubs, while trees and swords served for diamonds and spades. Every card is something else than what you have called it before. The value of each is changed according to the trump. What you have considered always as a low card, such as the two of spades, suddenly becomes the best card in the pack.

All the cards have Spanish names—Spadilla, Manilla, Basta, Ponto, and Matadores—which sound very romantic. A simple seven of hearts becomes suddenly top card and is called Manilla, which is the second best when hearts are trumps, and then the two of clubs, which was miles high the last hand, is at the tail of all the other cards now. It is a dreadful game. I thought that I should have brain fever while learning it. They went on playing it for hours; there never seemed any end to it; they counted in the weirdest way, making ciphers and tit-tat-toes on the green baize table with chalk, and wiped out with a little brush. Every trick of the adversary was deducted, and all the heads met over the chalk-marks to find out mistakes.

CUBA.

DEAR M.,—A dance was given at the Captain-General's, where all the officers of the German and Spanish men-of-war were present. It was a very brilliant sight, and we made many delightful acquaintances: Commodore Werner of the German *Friedrich Wilhelm*, Commodore Livonius of the *Elizabeth*, besides many other charming officers, as well as many Spanish officers from the *Gerona*. The Germans danced with more energy than the Cubans are accustomed to, and they stared at the unusual vigor displayed, and accounted for it, saying it was because they were new-comers. In fact, the officers, in their trim uniforms, looked very hot and wilted at the end of the evening. Commodore Werner was a most gallant gentleman, and as we did not dance, he had the leisure to tell me all about his family, his literary tastes, and his admiration for pretty ladies; and he finished by asking if we would do him the honor to lunch on his ship the next day. A handsome young lieutenant (Tirpitz) came to ask me to dance, but Commodore Werner gave him what in other less tropical countries might be called a freezing look, remarking that no one ought to dance in such heat as this. The young lieutenant left us quite subdued; but the heat did not prevent his dancing with many ladies, if not with me.

The next day we went to lunch on the *Friedrich Wilhelm*, and it was with delight that we sat on the awning-covered deck. The Commodore asked me to give him an idea for some occupation for the sailors, who had so much time on their hands, and, as I happened to know how to plait straw, I proposed showing them how to do it.

The Commodore sent a launch to Havana to get the straw, and we passed the afternoon dividing the time between listening to the music of the ship's band and tasting different beverages and eating German pretzels and teaching the sailors how to plait.

At five o'clock we were rowed ashore, and welcomed a little fresh breeze which had sprung up.

The following morning the inmates of the hotel were awakened at an early hour by the soelmn hymn which belongs to a German serenade. The kind Commodore had sent his band to play for me, and it filled the whole hall.

The early breakfasters were dreadfully put out about it; the brass instruments sounded like a double orchestra, and resounded in these marble halls like volleys of musketry; and as for the hotel-keeper, he has not got over his surprise yet.

We had many pleasant days after this. Each one, we said, would be the last; still we stayed on. One of the German men-of-war gave a ball, the Spanish gave another; each vied with the other to give the finest entertainment. It was a pleasure to go on board the German boats, everything was so spick and span, the sailors so neat and trim, the deck so beautifully kept, and the brasses glistened red-hot in the sun.

I cannot tell you all we did these last days. I was glad to hear that the German sailors had profited by my lessons, and had in a short time plaited straw enough to make some hats for themselves. I shall always feel proud when I see a German sailor with a straw hat, for I shall feel that I laid the foundation of this industry.

One of the afternoons we spent on the Commodore's boat. I sang for the officers in the cabin, and then, when I was on deck, I sang some of the songs from

25   373

"Pinafore" for the sailors, whom the Commodore called together to hear me. They grinned from ear to ear when I sang "What, never?" "Hardly ever," and "Never used a big, big D," in the captain's song in "Pinafore." This was the last time we visited our amiable German host.

I shall post this letter in New York. It will probably reach you before we do.

Our departure was a triumphal procession. The Captain of the Port, devoted to the last, took us in his official steam-launch to our steamer. Flowers, fruit, and souvenirs of all kinds filled our cabin to overflowing, and when we passed the German boats, hats and handkerchiefs were waved aloft, and the bands on the decks played with all their Teutonic might until we were out of hearing distance.

We noticed our tall, handsome lieutenant standing alone on the fore part of the deck. He made a fine naval salute, while the good Commodore waved his handkerchief frantically.

The Captain of the Port accompanied us down the harbor as far as Morro Castle in his steam-launch.

Adieu, dear Havana!

WASHINGTON, *April, 1873*.

DEAR LAURA,—The weather was atrociously bad when we returned to New York, and as for Boston—it was simply impossible. I began coughing and sneezing as soon as I reached home. So I decided to go to Washington on a visit to Mrs. Robeson, wife of the Secretary of the Navy. She had often asked me; this was an excellent opportunity to accept.

Mrs. Robeson is a fine woman, built on ministerial lines, and looks like a war-ship in review rig. They have an amusing house. Their Sunday evenings are the rendezvous of clever people; the men are particularly entertaining—Mr. Blaine, Mr. Bayard, and other shining lights.

She is musical, and sings with pleasure. She has a luscious mezzo-soprano. She sang "Robin Adair" on one of these occasions with so much conviction that it seemed as though she was routing Robin from his first sleep. Then she sang a French song in a childish voice (she thought it was a *backfisch* song); but I think it was anything but that, for I noticed some Scandi-knavish glances between the Danish and Swedish Ministers, which made me suspicious.

There is a delightful German Minister (Mr. Schlözer) here, who is very musical; though he does not know a note of music, he can improvise for hours.

. . . .

SOMMERBERG, *July, 1874.*

DEAR MAMA,—My last letter was from Dinard, where I was nestling in the bosom of my family and enjoying the repose and the rest that family bosoms alone can give. I told you of my intention to visit Helen at her place on the Rhine, and here I am enjoying another kind of rest: the rest of my income.

Paul is at present Minister in Madrid; Helen and I lead a very quiet life. Driving to Wiesbaden to see the Nassaus and other friends is our favorite occupation. We linger in the shady walks of the park, look in at the gambling-rooms, sometimes we go to the races, and always come home tired. And then, how we enjoy the garden and the beautiful view over the Rhine! Some days we go out riding in the lovely forest, which leads to the most prettily situated little "bad" place in the world—Schlangenbad.

Helen has in her stables three horses, two of which are the "fat ponies," and the third is the war-horse that Paul used in the French-German campaign. We take the war-horse in turn, as he has to be exercised. When it is my day I shudder at the thought of it. Riding is not my strong point; in fact, it is my weakest point, and I feel that I am not at all in my element; and when I see the tall beast being led up to the door, and I know that at a given moment I am to be fired up on to his back, my heart sinks. He has a gentle way with him which makes the process of getting on him extremely difficult. Just as my foot is in the groom's hand, and I say one—two—three, and am in midair, the horse moves gently to one side, and I either land on the hard pommel or, more often, I fill an empty space between the horse and the groom, which is awkward. However, when, after repeated efforts, I *do* manage to hit the saddle on the right place I stick there.

He is full of fancies—this horse—and reminiscences, and sometimes gets the idea into his head that he hears the bugle-call to arms. Then off he goes to join his imaginary companions, and charges the trees or anything that occurs to him, and nothing on earth can stop him, certainly nothing on his back can. My hair comes down and my hat flies off, and I feel I am not doing the *haute école* in proper style. Fortunately Helen and I are alone, and as the war-horse is miles in front of the "fat pony," she does not see the *école* I am doing, and I rather enjoy the wild way we career over space. I do not attempt to guide his martial steps, but let him come into camp when he feels inclined.

The groom is never surprised if I come an hour too late. I fancy he knows what I have gone through: brambles, branches, and—agony.

SOMMERBERG, *July, 1874.*

I have just returned from a delightful visit to the Prince and Princess Metternich. It was very hot the day I left here, and the sun poured down on the broad, white roads which lead from Sommerberg to the station. On my arrival at Johannisberg Prince Metternich was waiting for me with a *calèche à la Daumont.*

Our jaunty postilion blew his little horn incessantly as we galloped through the village and up the long, steep hill which leads to the château. The walls on both sides of the badly paved, narrow road were high and unpicturesque—not a tree to be seen; vineyards, vineyards everywhere—nothing but vineyards.

The château is a very ugly building, of no particular kind of architecture, looking more like a barn than a castle. It is shaped like an enormous E, without towers or ornamentation of any kind.

The Princess was at the door, and welcomed me most affectionately, and with her were the other guests: the handsome Duchess d'Ossuna, Count Zichy, Count Kevenhüller, Count Fitz-James, and Commandant Duperré.

The immense hall, which occupies the entire center of the house, has five windows giving out on the courtyard and five on the terrace, and is comfortably furnished with all kinds of arm-chairs, rugs, and so forth. A grand piano stood in one corner near the window, and over this window was an awning (an original idea of the Princess, to put an awning inside, instead of outside of the window). An unusually large table, covered with quaint books, periodicals, and the latest novels, stood in the middle of the room, and there were plants, palms, and flowers everywhere.

The Princess showed me the different rooms. Her boudoir was hung with embroidered satin. One room I liked particularly; the walls were covered with the coarsest kind of écru linen, on which were sewed pink pigeons cut out of cretonne; even the ceiling had its pigeons flying away in the distance. Another room was entirely furnished in cashmere shawls—a present from the Shah himself. There must have been a great many, to have covered the walls and all the divans.

Nowhere could the Princess have had such a chance to show what she could do as here, in the transforming of this barrack into a livable place. I admired everything immensely. She told me that she thought she was very practical, because, when they leave here, all the hangings can be taken down and folded and put away, so that the next year they are just as good as new.

They only stay here two months every year (July and August); the enormous display of flowers on the long terrace before the château is also temporary. There are at least four to five hundred pots of flowers,

mostly geraniums, which make a brilliant effect for the
time being, as long as the family are here; then they go
back to the greenhouse.

Tea was served in the hall; every one was in the gayest of spirits, and crowded around the piano to hear
Prince Metternich's last waltz, which was very inspiring. After the music was finished and the tea-table
removed, I was shown to my rooms; I reached them
by a tiny winding staircase, the walls of which were
hung with Adrianople (turkey red), and covered with
miniatures and fine engravings.

Dinner was served very sumptuously; the servants
were in plush breeches and had powdered hair. I sat
on the left of Prince Metternich and next to Count
Kevenhüller, who is a Knight of Malta. I said to the
Prince, "A Knight of Malta always suggests to my
mind romance and the Middle Ages."

"It shows," the Prince replied, "how naïve you are.
It is true that he is middle-aged, but he has not a ray
of romance in him. Don't trust him! Maltese Knights
and Maltese cats do their killing on the sly."

During the dinner delicious Johannisberg was served
alternately with ordinary beer. Conversation alternated with laughter, and after dinner albums and music
alternated with flirtations. The Prince played some of
his charming new songs. On the piano was a beautifully bound book containing them. He pointed to it,
saying, "I have had this made for you," and showed
me the title-page, where he had written, "À l'Inspira-
trice!" I was tremendously pleased and sang all the
songs, one after the other. The Prince has had leisure
to compose a great deal since he retired into private

life. He is wonderfully talented—not only for music, but for painting. Everything he does he does better than any one else.

He said that during the war, when he was obliged to stay in Bordeaux, he would have died of ennui if he had not had his music and drawing to occupy him, especially as the Princess and the children were not with him, and he was dreadfully lonely.

It was a lovely night, and we walked till very late on the terrace and gazed at the view across the Rhine, over the miles of vineyards and little villages sparkling with lights.

The Prince told me all about the Empress's flight from the Tuileries after the catastrophe of Sedan. He said that when the news came to the Embassy that the mob was about to enter the Tuileries he communicated with Count Nigra (the Italian Ambassador), and they decided to go there instantly, to offer their services to the Empress.

When they arrived there they saw the mob already before the gates. They left their carriages on the quay, and entered by a door into the gallery of the Louvre, and hurried to the apartment of the Empress. There they found her with Madame Le Breton. She was very calm and collected, already dressed in a black-silk gown, and evidently prepared for flight. She had in her hand a small traveling-bag, which contained some papers and a few jewels.

Seeing them, she exclaimed, "Tell me, what shall I do?"

The Prince said, "What does General Trochu advise, your Majesty?"

"Trochu!" she repeated. "I have sent for him twice, but he does not trouble himself to answer or to come to me."

Then the Prince said, "Count Nigra and I are here to put ourselves entirely at your Majesty's service."

The Empress thanked them and said: "What do you think best for me to do? You see how helpless I am."

The Prince answered that, according to their judgment, the wisest thing for her Majesty to do would be to leave Paris at once, and added that his carriage was there and she could make use of it.

She then put on her hat and cloak and said, "I am ready to follow you."

They went through the Pavillon de Flore and through the Galerie du Louvre until they reached a small door leading out on to the quay, where the two coupés were waiting. The Prince had already thought of one or two friends to whom the Empress could go and remain until they joined her, to help her to devise some means for leaving Paris. He said that during the long walk through the gallery the Empress remained calm and self-possessed, though one could see that she was suffering intensely.

They reached the quay without hindrance and found the carriages. The Prince opened the door of his and gave his orders to his coachman; but the Empress suddenly refused, saying that she preferred to go in a cab, and begged them not to follow her.

There was a cab-stand directly opposite where they stood. They hailed one, and she and Madame Le Breton were about to get in when a little boy cried out,

"Voilà l'Impératrice!" Count Nigra, quick as thought, turned on the boy and said in a loud voice, "Comment! tu cries 'Vive la Prusse!'" and boxed his ears, so that attention should be diverted from the Empress.

The Prince gave the names of the streets and the numbers of the houses to the cabman where he had proposed to the Empress to go, and the ladies drove away.

"Did you not follow her?" I asked.

"Yes," he answered. "In spite of the Empress's wishes, after allowing enough time for her to get well on her way, we drove to the two addresses given, but did not find her at either of them. We could not imagine what had happened to her."

"What *had* happened to her?" I asked.

"It was only after hours of the greatest anxiety that we ourselves knew. About six o'clock I received a note from the Empress saying that she had gone to the two houses we had named, but that no one was there, and then, not knowing what to do, had in despair thought of Dr. Evans, the dentist, and had driven to his house, where she was in safety for the moment."

"What a dreadful moment for the Empress! How did she dare to send the note to you?"

"It was imprudent," said the Prince; "but she intrusted it to Dr. Crane, who happened to be dining with Dr. Evans. He brought it to me and gave it into my own hands."

"Did you go to see her?"

"Yes, I went to see her; but strict orders had been given not to let any one enter, not even me."

The Prince showed me this letter, which he kept

locked up in a desk. Seeing the tears in my eyes, he said, giving me the envelope, "I know you will value this, and I beg you will keep it."

Prépé

A Son Altesse

Le Prince de Metternich

L'Impératrice

I told him that I would value it more than any one possibly could, and did not know how to thank him enough.

He told me a great deal more about the Empress, her hardships and trials, and how brave she had been through them all. She never uttered a word of reproach against any one, except against Trochu, whom she called an arch-traitor. He told me also of the last time he had seen her Majesty at Chiselhurst, and how sad this interview had been. The beautiful and adored Empress of France now a widow and an exile! I was sorry that our conversation was interrupted—I could have listened for hours; but tea was announced, and we were obliged to leave the library.

The next day the Prince and his friends were deeply

engaged in making a kite; they tried everything imaginable to coax it to fly, but it refused. The Prince even mounted a ladder, hoping to catch the wind by holding it higher; but all in vain. The moment he let go, down flapped the kite with almost human spitefulness.

After the Prince had said *saperlotte!* twenty times, they gave up the kite and played tennis, a new game, over which he is as enthusiastic as he used to be over croquet, until the blast of a horn announced the arrival of the archducal four-in-hand, which they were expecting.

Then there was a hurried putting on of coats and wiping of perspiring brows, and they all went forward to receive the Archduke Louis, who had driven over from Wiesbaden to spend the day, bringing with him some younger gentlemen.

Prince Metternich immediately proposed their playing tennis. Some of them were eager to do so, but the Archduke, being fatigued by his long drive, begged to go to his room until luncheon.

Then, while the gentlemen were playing tennis, the Princess took me to the kitchen-garden to show me the American green-corn, planted from seeds which we had given to her at Petit Val four years ago. She told me, with great joy, that we were to have some for dinner.

After luncheon we were invited to visit the famous wine-vaults. The intendant appeared with the keys, and, accompanied by a subordinate, we followed him down the stairs to the heavily bolted oak door, which he opened with a flourish. The first thing we saw, on entering, was *Willkommen* in transparencies in front of the entrance.

These cellars had the same dimensions as the castle, one hundred feet each way. Rows and rows of large casks placed close together lined the walls, and each cask had a lighted candle upon it embedded in plaster. Lamps hung at intervals from the vaulted ceiling, giving a weird look to the long alleys, which seemed to stretch out for miles through the dim vista.

We walked on. Every little while we came to what the Prince called a *cabaret*, and what the Princess called more poetically a *bosquet*, but which literally was a table and chairs surrounded by plants. The smell of the wine was overpowering. When we reached *bosquet* No. 1 the intendant handed each of us a full glass of Johannisberg, the same that was served at the table; at *bosquet* No. 2 we received only half a glass of a finer quality. At *bosquet* No. 3, on the walls of which were the initials of the Duchess d'Ossuna (E. O., formed by candles), we only got a liqueur glassful.

The farther we went the older, and therefore the more valuable, the wine was, and the less we were given. When we reached *bosquet* No. 6, the last stop, we were allowed a discreet sip from a sherry glass, which was passed on from one to the other like a loving-cup.

We were told that the wines from the years 1862 and 1863 are considered to be the best. It is strange that they are entirely different from each other; the first is very sweet and the second is very dry.

What was my surprise to see here, "I know a Lillie fair to see," against the walls designed in candles. The Princess told me that the Prince had been a long time making this, and I hope I showed due appreciation of the compliment. I was immensely flattered.

The wine is the color of amber, or pale yellow, according to the year, and tastes delicious; the aroma reminds one of sandalwood.

The wines of the best years are only sold in bottles bearing the cachet of the Prince's arms, and the autograph of the intendant; the color of the seal denotes the quality. *Cabinet bleu* is the best that can be bought; the less fine qualities are sold in barrels.

You will be interested to hear how they gather the grapes. It is very carefully done: each bunch is picked like a flower, and each grape is selected with the greatest care; any grape with the slightest imperfection is discarded. They remain longer on the vines here than anywhere else, so that the sweetness of the grape is doubly concentrated.

A good year will produce from sixty to eighty thousand bottles, and bring in an income of one hundred and fifty thousand marks.

The company which built the railroad through the grounds had to pay an enormous sum for the land, every inch of which is worth its weight in gold.

You may imagine the despair of the intendant when he sees so much of this valuable land taken for the croquet and tennis games; but the last straw is—the corn!

One of the guests here, Duchess d'Ossuna, is a very striking and handsome lady who has been a great beauty and is still, though now about forty years old. Her husband is one of the richest men in Spain, but is in such wretched health that she has expected hourly to be a widow for many years.

Coming away from the insidious fumes of the wine

into the hot air, and leaving the dark cellars for the glaring broad daylight, made us all feel a little light-headed. I noticed that the Archduke had to be gently and with due discretion aided up the steps.

He dropped into the first available bench and said, solemnly and with conviction: "To see this wine makes one want to taste it; to taste it makes one want to drink it; to drink it makes one want to dream."

I hope that you appreciate this profound saying; it ought not to be lost to posterity.

We left him, thinking he would prefer the society of his adjutant to ours. I knew that I preferred mine to any one else's, and went to my room, mounting its winding staircase, which I thought wound more than was necessary. Taking guests into wine-cellars is the great joke here, and it never fails.

Every one was in exuberant spirits at dinner. I wish I could remember half of the clever things that were said. The corn came on amid screams of delight. Our hostess ate thirteen ears, which, if reduced to kernels, would have made about one ordinary ear, there was so much cob and so little corn. The Princess enjoyed them hugely.

Coffee was served on the terrace. Later we had music in the hall, and before the departure of the Archduke there was a fine display of fireworks sent off from the terrace, which must have looked splendid from a distance.

SOMMERBERG, *August, 1874.*

DEAR M.,—Prince Emil Wittgenstein and his wife have a pretty villa at Walhuf, directly on the Rhine, and they invited Helen and me to dine and spend the night there. Prince Wittgenstein promised to show us some wonderful manifestations from spiritland. Helen is not a believer, neither am I, but the Prince thinks I am, and, as Helen could not leave her guests, I went alone.

The Prince wrote that he had induced, with great difficulty (and probably with a great deal of expense), the much-talked-of Miss Cook to come with her sister to pay them a visit at their villa. Miss Cook is the medium through whom the Empress Josephine and Katie King (a lady unknown to the world, except as being the daughter of a certain old sea-captain, called John King, who roamed the seas a hundred years ago and pirated) manifest themselves.

I was delighted to have this chance of seeing Miss Cook, because I had read in the English papers that she had lately been shown up as a gigantic fraud. At one of her séances in London, just as she was in the act of materializing in conjunction with the Empress Josephine, a gentleman, disregarding all rules of etiquette, sprang from the audience and seized her in his arms; but instead of melting, as a proper spirit would have done, the incensed Empress screamed and scratched and tore herself away, actually leaving bits of her raiment in his hands. This rude gentleman swears that the imperial nails seemed wholly of earthly texture, and that the scratches were as thorough and lasted as well as if made by any common mortal.

Since this incident Miss Cook had thought it wiser to retire into private life, and has secured a husband calling himself Corner. Prince Wittgenstein found her, and, wishing to convert his wife, could think of no better way than to let her see Miss Cook materialize. The wife and her friend, Princess Croy, are avowed disbelievers.

Our dinner was dull beyond words. There were the Prince Nicholas-Nassau and his wife; the Duke Esslingen, who is nearly blind, without a wife but with convictions; Count and Countess de Vay, and the two English ladies already mentioned. Miss Cook, *alias* Mrs. Corner, is a washed-out blond, rather barmaidish-looking English girl of medium (oh dear! I really did not mean to) height and apparently very anemic.

After dinner we were led into the room in which the séance was to take place, and were seated round a large table, and told to hold our tongues and one another's hands; the gas was turned down to the lowest point, the lamps screwed down, and there we sat and waited and waited.

The poor host was chagrined beyond utterance; something was the matter with the magnetic current. Sometimes he would tap on the table to attract the attention of the spirit underneath, but nothing helped; the spirits were obstinate and remained silent.

I ventured to ask the Duke, by the side of whom I sat and held on to, in what manner the spirits made known their answers. He said that one knock meant "yes," no knock meant "no," and two knocks meant "doubtful." At last we heard a timid knock in the direction of Mrs. Corner. Then every one was alert. Prince Wittgenstein addressed the spot and whispered in his most seductive tones, "Dear spirit, will you not manifest yourself?" Two knocks (doubtful).

26

"Is the company seated right?" (Silence, meaning "no.")

"Is the company congenial?" (Silence.)

To find out who the uncongenial person was, every one asked, in turn, "Is it I?" until Princess Wittgenstein put the question, upon which came a vigorous single knock.

"My dear," said the Prince, "I am sorry to say it, but you must go."

So she left, nothing loath. We all thought for sure something would happen now, but nothing did.

Prince Wittgenstein commenced the same inquiries, whether the company was now congenial; but it seemed that Princess de Croy was *de trop*, and she was also obliged to leave the room. (You see, the spirits did not like to single out the hostess alone.) Now we were reduced to nine believers with moist hands.

Would the Empress not now appear? We waited long enough for her to make up her mind; but it seemed that neither her mind nor anything else was ready to be made up. The spirits were perhaps willing, but the flesh was too weak. Then Mrs. Corner remembered that at the last sitting the Empress had declared that she would never appear on German soil (her feelings having been wounded during the Franco-German War).

There still remained Katie King. We had not heard from her yet. Prince Wittgenstein addressed the table under his fingers: "Oh, dear spirits, do do something! Anything would be acceptable!" How could he or she resist such humble pleadings?

Then some one felt a cold wind pass over his face. Surely something was happening now!

"It must be Katie King about to materialize," said the hopeful Prince.

Then we saw a dim light. We strained our eyes to the utmost to discover what it was. I should have said, if I had been truthful, that to me it looked like a carefully shaded candle; but I held my tongue. The hand of my neighbor was fast becoming jelly in mine, and I would have given worlds to have got my hand out of the current; but I did not dare to interfere with it, and I continued to hold on to the jelly. Whoever was being materialized was doing it so slowly, and without any kind of system, that we hardly had the patience to sit it out. Then a tambourine walked up some one's arm, Prince Nassau's spectacles were pulled off his august nose by invisible hands (of course, who else would have dared?), thus making him more near-sighted than ever. His wife's necklace of turquoises was unclasped from her neck and hooked on to the neck of the acolyte sister; but on anxious and repeated demands to have it returned, it was replaced, much to the owner's relief. Prince Wittgenstein thought it silly of her to have so little confidence. Suddenly, while necklaces were changing necks, we saw what looked like a cloud of gauze. We held our breaths, the raps under the table redoubled, and there were all sorts of by-play, such as hair-pulling and arm-pinching, but no Katie. The gauze which was going to be her gave up trying and disappeared altogether. "Never mind," said the Prince. "It does not matter [I thought so, too.] She will come to-morrow night."

This was very depressing; even Prince Wittgenstein was utterly discouraged and decided to break up the séance, and, groping his way to the nearest lamp, turned it up. We went into the other salon, where we found the two discarded ladies sitting peacefully before a samovar and playing a game of two-handed poker.

Miss Cook told Prince Wittgenstein that Katie King would probably materialize if she had the promise of getting a sapphire ring which he wore (a beautiful sapphire). Miss Cook suggested that if this ring could be hung up on a certain tree in the garden Katie King would come and get it, and would certainly materialize the next evening. Prince Wittgenstein was credulous enough to pander to this modest wish, and hung up the desired ring, hoping Katie King would return it when she was in the flesh. But Miss Cook had a succession of fainting fits which necessitated her sudden departure for England, so we never saw Katie King, neither did Prince Wittgenstein ever get his ring back, as far as I know.

September, 1874.

Last Tuesday we three—Count and Countess Westphal and I—left Wiesbaden, slept at Frankfort, and starting the next morning at eleven o'clock, we arrived at our destination at 5.00 P.M. We found three carriages; one for us and two for the maids and luggage. Halfway to the castle we met, driving the lightest and prettiest of basket-wagons, our host and hostess, Count and Countess W—; the latter got into the carriage with us and one of us took her place by the side of the host. We passed through the village, which had but one street, irregular and narrow, and we were in constant danger of running over the shoals of little

392

children who stood stupidly in the middle of it, gazing at us with open eyes and mouth.

The Schloss is a very large, square building, with rounded towers in the four corners. It has been remodeled, added to, and adorned so many times that it is difficult to tell to which style of architecture it belongs. The chapel is in an angle and opens on to the paved courtyard.

Our first evening was spent quietly making acquaintance with the other guests. The next morning we lunched at eleven o'clock, the gentlemen in knickerbockers and shooting attire, the ladies in sensible gowns of light material over silk petticoats. Simplicity is the order of the day. Our lunch consists of many courses, and we might have lingered for hours if the sight of the postman coming up the avenue had not given us the excuse to leave the table and devote ourselves to our correspondence, which had to be done in double-quick time, as the postman only waited a short fifteen minutes, long enough to imbibe the welcome cup of coffee or the glass of beer which he found waiting him in the kitchen. The Countess, although the mother of a young man twenty-four years of age, has a pink-and-white complexion and a fine, statuesque figure. She is a Russian lady by birth, and does a lot of kissing, as seems to be the custom in Russia. She told me that when a gentleman of a certain position kisses your hand you must kiss his forehead.

"Isn't this rather cruel toward the ladies?" I said.

"Why," she asked, "do you think it is cruel?"

"Ladies sometimes have on gloves when they give their hands to be kissed, whereas there are some foreheads which ought to have gloves on before they are kissed."

The young Count, when he returned from the races at Wiesbaden, brought with him a young American who had been presented to him by a friend of his, who said that Mr. Brent, of Colorado (that was his name), was very "original" and *ausserordenlich charmant*. And he *was* both charming and (especially) original; but not the type one meets in society.

He was a big, tall, splendidly built fellow with the sweetest face and the liquidest blue eyes one can imagine. He had a soft, melodious voice and the most fascinating manner, in spite of his far-Western language. Every one liked him; my American heart warmed to him instantly, and even the austere *grande dame*, our hostess, was visibly captivated, and the prim German governess drank in every word he said, intending, no doubt, to improve her English, which otherwise she never got a chance to speak.

The two young men arrived yesterday just in time for tea. When the Countess asked him, in her most velvety tones, "Do you take sugar, Mr. Brent?" "Yes, ma'am, I do—three lumps, and if it's beety I take four." (I trembled! What would he say next?) "I've got a real sweet tooth," he said, with an alluring smile, to which we all succumbed. The governess, remembering what hers had been before acquiring her expensive false set, probably wondered how teeth could ever be sweet.

While dressing for dinner I shuddered at the thought of what his dinner toilet might be; but I cannot say how relieved I was when I saw him appear (he was the last to appear) dressed in perfect evening dress, in the latest fashion, except his tie, which was of white satin and very badly tied. The salon in which we met before dinner is a real museum of rare pictures, old furniture, and curiosities. The walls are hung with old Italian faïences and porcelains. A huge buffet, reaching to the ceiling, is filled with Venetian goblets and majolica vases.

A vast chimneypiece, under which one can stand with ease, is ornamented with a fine iron bas-relief of the family arms, and a ponderous pair of andirons which support a heavy iron bar big enough to roast a wild boar on. Count G—— called Mr. Brent's attention to it, and Mr. Brent said, pleasantly, "I suppose this is where the ancestors toasted their patriarchal toes."

At dinner he sat next to the governess, and I could see her trying to digest his "original" language; and I was near enough to overhear some of their conversation. For instance, she asked him what his occupation was in his native land. "Oh," he said, "I do a little of everything, mostly farming. I've paddled my own canoe since I was a small kid."

"Is there much water in your country-place?" she inquired.

"Don't you mean country? Well, yes, we have quite a few pailfuls over there, and we don't have to pull a string to let our waterfalls down."

My neighbor must have thought me very inattentive; but I felt that I could not lose a word of Mr. Brent's conversation. The vestibule (or "Halle," as they called it), where we went after dinner, used to be occupied by the *Corps du Garde*. It had vaulted ceilings and great oak beams, and was filled with hunting implements of

all ages arranged in groups on the walls very artistically; there were cross-bows, fencing-swords, masks,
guns (old and new), pistols, etc. Mr. Brent was very
much impressed by this collection, gazed at the speci-
mens with sparkling admiration, and remarked to the
governess, who was always at his elbow, "I never saw
such a lot of things [meaning the weapons] outside of
a shindy."

"What is a shindy?" inquired the governess, always
anxious to improve her knowledge of the language.

"Why, don't you know what a shindy is? No?
Well, it's a free fight, where you kill promiscuous."

"Gott im Himmel!" almost screamed the terrified
damsel. "Do you mean to say that you have killed
any one otherwise than in a duel?"

"I can't deny that I have killed a few," Mr. Brent
said, cordially, "but never in cold blood."

"How dreadful!" his listener cried.

"But you see, over there," pointing with his cigar
into the vague (toward Colorado), "if a man insults
you, you must kill him then and there, and you must
always be heeled."

"Heeled!" she repeated, puzzled. "Do they always
get well?"

Neither understood.

Probably she thinks to this day that a shindy is an
exceptionally good hospital.

The Count said, "This room is a very good specimen
of Renaissance style."

Mr. Brent replied, "I don't know what 'renny-
saunce' means, but this room is the style I like"; and
added, "It's bully; and to-morrow I'd like to take a

snap-shot of it and of all the company to show mother, if [with his charming smile] you will let me."

"You shall take that and any other thing you like," said the Count. "How long do you intend staying in Europe?"

"That depends," answered Mr. Brent. "I came across the pond because the doctor said I needed rest and change."

"I hope that you have had them both," the Count said, kindly.

"I got the change, all right; but the hotel-keepers got the rest, as the story goes."

Every one laughed and voted the young and clever American perfectly delightful.

The Countess extended her jeweled hand when she bade him good night, the hand that always had been held with reverence and pressed gently to lips, and felt it seized in a grip which made her wince.

"Madame, you are just as sweet as you can be. I cottoned to you right off the minute I saw you, just as I did to 'sonny,' over there," pointing to the noble scion of the house. The governess made a note of the word "cotton." The Countess was dumfounded; but our young friend seeming so unconscious of having said or done anything out of the way, she simply, instead of resenting what in another would have been most offensive, looked at him with a lovely, motherly smile, and I am sure she wanted to imprint a kiss on his forehead *à la Russe*.

The next morning the Countess mentioned that she had a quantity of old tapestries somewhere about in the house. "Where are they?" we all exclaimed. "Can we not see them?"

"Certainly, but I do not know where they are," answered the Countess. "They may be in the stables."

We went there, and sure enough we found, after rummaging about in the large attic, a quantity of old tapestries: three complete subjects (biblical and pastoral), all of them more or less spoiled by rats and indiscriminate cutting.

It amused me to see in the servants' dining-room some good old pictures, while in ours the walls were covered with modern engravings.

We were about thirty at table, and in the servants' hall there were nearly sixty persons. Lenchen, my old-maid maid, puts on her best and only black-silk dress every day and spends hours over her toilette for dinner.

Mr. Tweed, the English trainer, says that the stables here are among the finest in Germany, and that the Count owns the best race-horses in the land, and is a connoisseur of everything connected with horses.

Our Colorado friend did not seem at all overwhelmed with the splendor of the stables, but with a knowing eye, examining the horses (feet, fetlocks, and all), and without further preliminaries, said, "This one is not worth much, and that one I would not give two cents for, but this fellow," pointing to the Count's best racer, "is a beauty."

Mr. Tweed's amazement at this amateur (as he supposed him to be) was turned into admiration when Mr. Brent walked into the paddock, asked for a rope, and proceeded to show us how they lasso horses in America. Every one was delighted at this exhibition.

Then Mr. Tweed brought out the most unruly horse he had, which none of the English or German grooms could mount. Mr. Brent advanced cautiously, and with a few coaxing words got the horse to stand quiet long enough for him to pass his hand caressingly over his neck. But putting the saddle on him was another matter; the horse absolutely refused to be saddled. So what did our American friend do but give one mighty spring and land on the horse's bare back. He dug his strong legs into the sides of the horse, and though the horse kicked and plunged for a while, it succumbed finally and was brought in tame and meek.

Nothing could have pleased the Count more than this, and the rest of us were lost in admiration.

Mr. Brent invited all the stable-boys *en bloc* to come over to America to see him; he guessed he "and the boys could teach them a trick or two."

After luncheon Mr. Brent wanted us all to come out on the lawn to be photographed, particularly the Countess, and said to the young Count, "You tackle the missis [meaning the Countess], and I'll get the others."

Of course no one refused. How could we resist such a charmer? Who could ever have believed that this simple, unaffected youth could have so completely won all hearts?

He said to the Countess while "fixing" her for the group, "I wanted you, because you remind me so of my dear old mother." The Countess actually purred with ecstasy; but I don't think she would have liked to be compared to any "old" thing (mother or not) by anybody else. In this case she merely looked up at him and smiled sweetly, and as for the *blasé*, stately Count, he simply would not let him out of his sight.

At last the group was arranged according to Mr.

Brent's ideas; the host and hostess in the center, while the others clustered around them.

"Now, ladies and gentlemen, please look pleasant," said Mr. Brent, and we all took the attitude we remembered to have looked well in on some former occasion, and hoped we looked "pleasant," and that "mother," when contemplating us, would approve of us.

The Count's birthday happened to be on one of these days. Mr. Brent, who had intended to leave, was urged by both him and the Countess to stay. The young Count said, "Papa would be really unhappy if you went away." "That's real nice of him; you bet I'll stay, then." On the day itself he was all-pervading. It was he who hung the heavy garlands and wreaths on the highest poles, agile as a cat, and draped the flags about the escutcheons placed everywhere. He helped the ladies arrange the flowers in the innumerable vases in the salons. He it was who led the applause when the deputation of young people from the village made their speech, and when the Count responded, in his most dignified and courtly manner, Mr. Brent cried out, in a most enthusiastic voice, "Good for you!"

In the evening there were visits from all the surrounding neighborhood; the ladies wore tiaras and all their jewels, and the gentlemen all their decorations; there was a grand supper in the state dining-room. Although I suppose it was the first time Mr. Brent had ever seen such a sight, he did not seem in the least astonished. He circulated about the distinguished company and made himself most agreeable indiscriminately to young and old. He was in full glory, and certainly was the life of the evening, which finished brilliantly with a grand display of fireworks set off from the tower, so that they could be seen from far and near.

The next day Mr. Brent left. When he bade me good-by he said: "Good-by, ma'am. If I have had a good time here, I owe it all to you." "Oh no, you don't!" I said. "You owe it all to yourself, and you may say to your mother, from me, that you won all hearts."

He sighed and turned away his head, giving my hand an extra squeeze. "If you ever come to Colorado, just ask any one for Johnny Brent, and if I don't stand on my head for you it 'll be because I've lost it."

His leave-taking of the Countess was almost pathetic. He held her hand long and tenderly, and said, "I can't find any word, ma'am—I mean, Countess—but —thank you, thank you, that's all I can say."

And the Countess (we thought she would faint) put her hand on his shoulder. He bent his head, and she kissed him on his forehead; and he (were the heavens going to fall?) stooped down and kissed her cheek.

The Count said: "Good-by, my boy. Come again to see us"—and going to the walls where his collection of pistols hung, took one of them and handed it to him. "This will remind you of us, but don't kill any one with it."

"Never," said Mr. Brent. "I will hang it round my neck."

Thus departed our American hero, for who but a hero could have stormed such a fortress and broken down all the traditional barriers?

A day or two later we received a visit from royalty, in the person of Prince Frederick Charles of Prussia. In the evening we played a wonderful game called *taroc*, which was very intricate and almost impossible to learn. Old Baron Kessler, who undertook to teach it to me, got so sleepy that he actually yawned in my face.

This Baron Kessler is quite a character—very clever, very artistic, very musical, and, strange to say, very superstitious. For instance, he wears an old waist-coat which has certain magical grease-spots on Fridays; on Mondays his purse must be in the left pocket of his coat, on Thursdays in his right pocket. He drinks nine times before twelve o'clock on special days, and has a cigar-case for each different day of the week. He hates losing at cards, and when he does it is quite an affair; and I am not sure that prayers are not offered up for him by his family in the chapel on his baronial estates.

The last thing I saw was a vision of Herr Lenning (the head butler), who is sometimes a little shaky himself, helping the Baron up the stairs. Possibly it was the evening of the nine-drink morning.

Next day we all left, except the old Baron, who for reasons of his own remained.

WEIMAR, *September, 1874.*

DEAR M.,—I thought it would be a good idea to go to Weimar, the place *par excellence* to study German, the Germans, and their literature; and, moreover, my boy might go to school there. Mrs. Kingsland had given me a letter to the Grand Duke of Saxe-Weimar, and recommended the place, not because she knew the town, but because she knew the Grand Duke. Besides, had I not a dear cousin who had written a most attractive book about Weimar, combined with Liszt and his enchantments?

I was all enthusiasm.

I decided to go to the hotel which Liszt honored. The proprietor put me into Liszt's very room, where a framed letter of his hung on the wall. . . . This did not in the least overcome me, as I had several of Liszt's letters at home. But what did overcome me was that I was charged four times the price of any other hotel, on Liszt's account!

Weimar may be very pleasant in the season when the little Court sheds its mild light about; but out of the season, especially at this time of the year, when there is nothing but dried and fluttering leaves, students, and dogs in the streets, I found it woeful. It was reeking of Schiller and Goethe. For two marks you can have a pretty good idea of how these great men lived and had their being. Everywhere we turned, and we turned everywhere, there were statues, busts, autographs, writing-desks, beds, and wash-stands which had belonged to them. I admired everything until my vocabulary of exclamations was exhausted and my head whirled.

I told Howard, as young as he was, I would not have him Goethed and Schillered, as he certainly would be if he stayed here; so I changed my plans and made up my mind to accept the invitation of my friend the Countess Westphal to make her a visit at her château in Westphalia. We took a train which dropped us at her station, where she met us and drove us to Fürstenberg.

Westphalia is renowned for its hams. Perhaps you don't know this, therefore I tell you. It is also renowned for the independent spirit of the Westphalians.

FÜRSTENBERG, *1874.*

DEAR M.,—This château is a fine old castle, with rounded towers and mysterious passages, and has a village tucked on to it. The family consists of the Countess, the Count, and three children, a tutor, a governess, and everything which belongs to the old families and their traditions. The mysterious passages possessed no ghosts, for which I was sorry, though my maid (a timid and naïve old German maiden) thought that she heard "things" at night when she came up the dark, winding stone staircase which led to my room.

Life passed quietly at Fürstenberg. Countess Westphal and I amused ourselves with music and embroidery and listening to the Count's report of his hunting expeditions.

One day, in a spasm of energy, she proposed to take me to see a friend of hers, Countess B——, who, she said, lived quite near. We would spend the night, returning the next day. She thought it would be a very pleasant and entertaining little excursion for us.

She telegraphed to Countess B—— that we were coming without maids, and with only necessary baggage; and my maid immediately went to work to pack what she considered necessary for this visit. She put a dinner-dress, with high and low waists, as the occasion might require, an extra day-dress, and all kinds of accessories, filling a good-sized trunk.

We started early the next morning. Countess Westphal was full of happy expectations; so was I. We were four hours on the way before we reached our destination;

but Countess Westphal cheerfully remarked that time was of no consequence.

On our arrival at the forlorn little station I looked in vain for the lordly chariot I thought would be waiting for us. Countess Westphal seemed astonished also, but with her usual good-nature accounted for the absence of the chariot by saying that her friend could not possibly have received the telegram. We lingered about, hoping that some vehicle would appear; but as none did so, Countess Westphal started off to find one, and she finally succeeded in tempting a man, for the vast sum of four marks, to drive us to the *schloss*.

After the coachman had gathered the reins off the back of the old, rickety horse, I leaned back in my seat and pictured to myself what this beautiful *schloss* we were going to would be like.

Of course, it would have a moat around it (all old castles do); it would have all the modern comforts combined with the traditions of past glories; it would have avenues of grand old trees and marble statues, and terraces leading into Italian gardens, and so forth. In fact, my imagination got so riotous that I forgot to look at the treeless, muddy roads, and I never noticed the wrenching of the ancient landau in which we were.

As we were jolted over the desolate landscape, Countess Westphal tried to tell me the family history of the B——s, but I only gathered bits of it here and there; such as that he was the fourth son of a very distinguished father and mother, and had no prospect worth speaking of, except the prospect of the dreary place we were careering over; that they never left their native heath and had no children, and that they lived on their

27   405

estate (being the only thing they had to live on), and so forth and so forth, all of which went in at the ear next the Countess and went out at the ear next the road.

Finally we spied the *schloss*. It had been a convent in some former century, and still had iron bars on the windows. We drove through a muddy lane, passing a sort of barn with grated loopholes, and stopped before a courtyard filled with chickens and geese; on the left was a pigsty, smelling not at all like Westphalian hams, and on the other side a cow-stable. In front was the *schloss* and the lady of the manor, the honorable Countess herself, on the steps, quite by chance, so it seemed. She led us proudly into the salon. A large bunch of keys hung at her girdle. I wondered why she needed so many! After the coal-bin, wine-vault, and sugar-bowl, and linen-closet had been locked up, what more did she need to lock up? There was no mention that the telegram had been received. Strange!

Count B—— was not there, "but would be coming soon." I felt that I could wait. The salon was of the kind that one often sees in houses where the mistress, having no children and plenty of time, embroiders things. Every possible object had a coat of arms and huge crowns embroidered on it, so that you could never forget that you were in the house of ancient nobility, which had the right to impose its crowns on you. All the chairs, tables, sideboards, and things on the walls were made out of the horns of stags and other animals the Count had shot. Sometimes the chairs were covered with the skin of the same, minus the hair, which was missing and moth-eaten in spots.

I was taken up-stairs to my bedroom, and I was

thankful to see that the horns and crowns had nearly given out before they finished furnishing the first story, and that I had an ordinary middle-class chair to sit on. There were many pictures of Madonnas and saints, from which I inferred that our hosts were Catholics, and a *prie-dieu*, which, strange to say, was made of horns; and the mat in front of my bed was a blaze of the united coats of arms and *two* crowns! So she was a Countess born, which accounted for the doubleness.

We were obliged to make *le tour du propriétaire*, and, of course, as there was no other place to take us to, we went to the stables. There we admired the two cows (Stella and Bella) with horns. They had their names painted in blue and white over their respective heads, but they had no crowns.

Then the Count appeared in very nice clothes. I fancy, while we had been admiring Stella and Bella, he had been changing his boots. Owing to these fresh boots we were spared the pigsties. On our return to the house Countess B—— said, "You know, we don't dress for dinner." I thought with dismay of my trunk laden with all its superfluous contents, and what a bore the bringing of it had been, and the opinion my maid would pass on our noble hosts, who "don't dress for dinner," when she unpacked the undisturbed finery which she had thought indispensable.

After dinner the conversation was chiefly pastoral, of the kind I do not join in because I hate it. How many chickens had died, how Bella and Stella had borne last winter's cold, how many sacks of potatoes had been spoiled, etc. My Countess enjoyed it immensely, and sat on a horny chair and sympathized. Our host took pity on me and taught me a patience. I had known it all my life as "the idiot's delight," but I pretended I had never heard of it before, and he had the satisfaction of thinking he was entertaining me—which he wasn't! On the contrary, Job's patience never could have equaled this one; the Count talked French fluently. The dinner was not good, nor was it frugal.

The Count said, "Nous n'avons que le stricte nécessaire, rien de plus."

The Countess said, in English, "One can't have in the country all that one wants."

I could not help feeling that one could not have even the half of what one wanted, and more than once I caught myself thinking, "None but the brave deserve this fare." They noticed if you took a second helping, and you felt that they made a mental note if your glass was filled more than once with wine. However, it was all very nice, and they were very kind, good people. It was not the Count's fault if the stags he killed had too many horns, neither was it the Countess's fault that time hung heavy on her hands and embroidery occupied them.

Fortunately we would go away next day, so what did it matter? But getting away was a very different thing from coming. When the Countess Westphal suggested it, and said that we intended to take a certain train, the faces of our hosts presented a blank look of apprehension! Their horses were plowing! What should we do? The doctor, they said, who lived in the village, had a carriage, but the horse was sick; there was, however, the *schimmel* of the baker, which, fortunately, was in good health, and perhaps, in conjunction with the wagon of the doctor, one could manage. It sounded like a gigantic exercise of Ollendorff:

"Avez-vous le cheval du boulanger?"

"Non, mais j'ai le soulier du boucher," etc.

After what seemed an eternity, the wagon of the doctor appeared, so did the *schimmel*. The wagon of the doctor, usually dragged by two animals, had a pole in the middle, to which the *schimmel* was attached, giving him a very sidelong gait. The question now was, who was to drive the *schimmel* attached to the pole?

The young man who milked the cows, killed the pigs, dressed the Count, picked the fruit, drove the Countess, waited at table, served everybody, did everything, and smelled *awfully* of the stables—could he be spared?

Well, he was spared, and off we started majestically, but sideways, waving a courtly adieu. We reached home in a drenching rain, wondering what on earth ever possessed us to want to go to visit the noble B——s. I don't think I ever want to see that establishment again, and I don't think I ever shall.

FÜRSTENBERG, *December*.

DEAR M.,—The Duke of Nassau had promised to come here to shoot wild boars, for which this forest is celebrated. Count Westphal sent invitations far and wide to call his hunting friends together. Before the arrival of the Duke, carriage after carriage entered the courtyard; oceans of fur-coats, gun-cases, valises, bags, and fur-lined rugs were thrown about in the hall, to be sorted out afterward. Then the Duke drove up in a sleigh with four horses, his aide-de-camp, two postilions, and a friend, both of them so wrapped up in *pelisses* and immense fur-caps that you could only see the tips of their red noses, like danger signals on railroads. No wonder! They had had three hours of this cold sleigh-ride!

The quiet old *schloss* was transformed. Each guest had his own servant and *chasseur*. The servants helped to wait at dinner. The *chasseurs* cleaned the guns, lounged about smoking their pipes, and looking most picturesque in their Tyrolean hats, with their leather gaiters, short green jackets, and leather belts, in which they carried their hunting-knives and cartridges.

His Highness (who is very short and what one calls thick-set) was accompanied by a secretary, a *chasseur*, a valet, two postilions, two grooms, and four horses. He had six guns, six trunks, and endless coats of different warmth. In the twinkling of an eye cigar-cases, pipes, photographs, writing-paper (of his own monogram), and masses of *etceteras* were spread about in his salon, as if he could not even look in his mirror without having these familiar objects before his eyes.

At twelve o'clock, high—very high—lunch was served. The servants brought in the eatables in monstrous quantities, and disappeared; the guests helped themselves and one another, and when without occupation fed the fire, where logs smoldered all day.

At a reasonable hour, after cigars and cigarettes had been smoked, the sleighs were ordered to be in readiness in the courtyard. Thirty or forty *treibers* (beaters) had been out since early morn. The Count has fourteen thousand acres to be beaten, therefore an early start was necessary.

The hunters swallowed a bitter pill when they asked us ladies to accompany them; but they knew their hostess would not let them go without her at least, so why not take the tame bores while shooting the wild ones?

They portioned off one lady and one gentleman to each sleigh. These sleighs are very small, and contrived for the confusion of mankind. You sit in a bag of sheep's skin, or perhaps the bag is simply two whole skinned sheep sewed together. You must stretch your legs, thus pinioned on the sides, out as far as they reach; then the driver puts a board over them, on which he perches himself, nearly over the horse's tail, and off you go. I cannot imagine what a man does with his legs if he has very long ones.

The poor horses are so dressed up that, if they could see themselves, they would not know if they were toy rabbits or Chinese pagodas. Over the horse is a huge net, which not only covers him from head to tail, but protects those in the sleigh from the snow flying in their faces. I should think that this net would be excellent in summer to keep the flies off; it does certainly suggest mosquito-netted beds and summer heat. Over the net is an arrangement which looks like a brass lyre, adorned with innumerable brass bells, which jingle and tinkle as we trot along, and make noise enough to awake all the echoes in the forest. On each side of the horse's head hang long, white, horse-hair tails.

What did we look like as we proceeded on our way? A procession of eight sleighs, combining a *ranz des vaches*, a summer bed, and an antiquary shop!

Arrived at the rendezvous, Count Westphal placed

his guests by different trees. The best place, of course, fell to the Duke, and I had the honor to stand behind him and his gun. I hoped that neither would go off! The Duke is very near-sighted and wears double-barreled spectacles, which have windows on the sides, so that he can look around the corner without turning his head.

Every one was requested to be perfectly quiet, otherwise there would be disaster all along the line. I could keep quiet very well, *for a time;* but the back view of a man crowned with a Tyrolean hat, and terminating in a monstrous pair of overshoes lined with straw, lost its interest after a while, and I began to look at the scenery. It must be lovely here in the summer. The valley, where a little brook meandered gracefully through the meadow (now ice and snow), bordered on both sides by high pine woods, must then be covered with flowers and fresh green grass, and full of light and shadow.

His Highness and I were under a splendid oak, and there we stood waiting for something to happen. The Duke, the oak, and I were silence personified. A dead branch would crack, or the trunks of smaller and ignorant pines would knock together, and the Duke would look around the corner and say "Chut!" in a low voice, thinking I was playing a tattoo on the tree.

"Now the beaters are on the scent!" he said. After this I hardly dared to breathe.

"They have to drive the boar with the wind," he whispered.

"I thought they did it with sticks," I answered in a low tone.

To this remark he did not pay the slightest attention. Between a sneeze and a cough—we were rapidly catching our deaths—he said, under his breath, "If they smell us they go away."

The *treibers* work in couples, Count Westphal leading them. It is not etiquette for the host to shoot; he must leave all the chances of glory to his guests. Among the *treibers* were various servants and *chasseurs* carrying extra guns and short daggers for the final despatch (*le coup de grâce*). We heard them coming nearer and nearer, but we saw no boar. Many other animals came wonderingly forward: some foxes, trailing their long tails gracefully over the snow, looked about them and trotted off; a furtive deer cautiously peered around with ears erect and trotted off also; but it is not for such as these we stand ankle-deep in the snow, shivering with cold and half frozen. A shot now would spoil all the sport. One has a longing to talk when one is told to be quiet. I can't remember ever having thought of so many clever things I wanted to say as when I stood behind the ducal back—things that would be forever lost! And I tried to enter them and fix them in my brain, to be produced later; but, alas!

The Duke (being, as I said, very short-sighted) came near shooting one of his own servants. The man who carried his extra gun had tied the two ends of a sack in which he carried various things, and put it over his head to keep his ears warm. Just as the Duke was raising his gun, thinking that if it was not a boar it was something else, I ventured a gentle whisper, "C'est votre domestique, Monseigneur." "Merci!" he whispered back, in much the same tone he would have used had I restored him a dropped pocket-handkerchief.

Finally (there must be an end to everything) we saw

beneath us, on the plains, three wild boars leaping in the snow, followed by a great many more. They had the movements of a porpoise as he dives in and out of the water, and of an ungraceful and hideous pig when hopping along.

The Duke fired his two shots, and let us hope two boars fell. The others flew to right and left, except one ugly beast, who came straight toward our own tree. I must say that in that moment my little heart was in my throat, and I realized that the tree was too high to climb and too small to hide behind. The Duke said, in a husky voice, "Don't move, for God's sake, even if they come toward us!"

This was cheery! Abraham's blind obedience was nothing to mine! Here was I, a stranger in a foreign land, about to sacrifice my life on the shrine of a wild boar! Count Metternich, behind the next tree, fired and killed the brute, so I was none the worse save for a good fright. It was high time to kill him, for he began charging at the beaters, and threatened to make it lively for us; and if Count Metternich had not, in the nick of time, sent a bullet into him, I doubt whether I should be writing this little account to you at this moment.

There was a great deal of shouting, and the hounds were baying at the top of their lungs, and every one was talking at the same time and explaining things which every one knew. Counting the guests, the servants, the trackers, the dilettantes, there were seventy people on the spot; and I must say, though we were *transis de froid*, it was an exhilarating sight—the snow is such a beautiful *mise en scène*. However, we were glad to get back into the sheep-skin bags and draw the fur rugs up to our noses, and though I had so many brilliant things to say under the tree I could not think of one of them on our way home.

Fourteen big, ugly boars were brought and laid to rest in the large hall, on biers of pine branches, with a pine branch artistically in the mouth of each. They weighed from one to three hundred pounds and smelled abominably; but they were immensely admired by their slayers, who pretended to recognize their own booty (don't read "beauty," for they were anything but beautiful) and to claim them for their own. Each hunter has the right to the jaws and teeth, which they have mounted and hang on their walls as trophies.

Count Westphal has his smoking-room filled to overflowing with jaws, teeth, and chamois heads, etc. They make a most imposing display, and add feathers to his already well-garnished cap.

Howard said, in French, to the Duke, in his sweet little voice, looking up into his face, "I am so sorry for you!"

"Why?" inquired the Duke.

"Because the Prussians have taken your country."

We all trembled, not knowing how the Duke would take this; but he took it very kindly, and, patting Howard on the back, said: "Thank you, my little friend. I am sorry also, but there is nothing to be done; but thank you all the same." And his eyes filled with tears.

The next day he gave Howard his portrait, with, "Pour mon petit ami, Howard, d'un pauvre chassé.—Adolf, Duc de Nassau." Very nice of him, wasn't it?

In the evening they played cards, with interruptions

such as "Der verfluchte Kerl," meaning "a boar that refused to be shot," or "I could easily have killed him if my gun," etc., till every one, sleepy and tired, had no more conversation to exchange, and the Duke left, as he said, to write letters, and we simpler mortals did not mind saying that we were dead beat and went to bed.

The next day being Sunday, I sang in the little church (Catholic, of course, as Westphalia is of that religion). The organist and I had many rehearsals in the *schloss*, but none in the church, so I had never made acquaintance with the village organ. If I had, I don't think I should have chosen the *Ave Maria* of Cherubini, which has a final amble with the organ, sounding well enough on the piano; but on that particular organ it sounded like two hens cackling and chasing each other. I had to mount the spiral staircase behind the belfry and wobble over the rickety planks before reaching the organ-loft. Fortunately, Count Metternich went with me and promised to stay with me till the bitter end; at any rate, he piloted me to the loft. The organ was put up in the church when the church was built, in the year Westphalia asserted herself, whenever that was; I should say B.C. some time. It was probably good at that time, but it must have deteriorated steadily ever since; and now, in this year of grace, owns only one row of keys, of which several notes don't work. There are several pipes which don't pipe, and an octave of useless pedals, which the organist does not pretend to work, as he does not know how. However, there is no use describing a village organ; every one knows what it is. Suffice to say that I sang my *Ave Maria* to it, and the Duke and my hosts, miles below me, said it was very fine, and that the church had never heard the like before, and never would again. Certainly *not from me!* . . .

The village itself is a pretty little village and very quaint; it has belonged to the *schloss*, as the *schloss* has to it, for centuries. The houses are painted white, and the beams of oak are painted black.

On the principal cross-beams are inscriptions from the Bible, cut in the oak, and the names of the people who built the house. There is one: "Joseph and Katinka, worthy of the grace of God, on whom He cannot fail to shower blessings. For they believe in Him." The date of their marriage and their virtues are carved also (fortunately they don't add the names of all their descendants). Sometimes the sentences are too long for the beam over the door, and you have to follow their virtues all down the next beam.

This is perplexing on account of the German verb (which is like dessert at dinner—the best thing, but at the end), and *gehabt* or *geworden* is sometimes as far down as the foot-scraper. Some houses are like barns: one roof shelters many families, having their little booths under one covering, and they sit peacefully at their work in front of their homes smoking the pipe of peace, and at the same time cure the celebrated hams which hang from the ceiling. I won't say all hams are cured in this way, because, I suppose, there are regular establishments which cure professionally. But I have seen many family hams curing in these barns.

The costumes of the women are wonderful, full of complexities; you have to turn them around before you can tell if she is a man or a woman; they wear hats like

a coal-carrier in England, pantaloons, an apron, and—
well! the Countess had a woman brought to the *schloss*
and undressed, so that we could see how she was dressed.
I ought to send a photograph, because I can never describe her. There is a bodice of black satin, short in
the back, over a plastron of pasteboard of the same,
and a huge black-satin cravat sticking out on both sides
of her cheeks, a wadded skirt of blue alpaca, and pink
leg-of-mutton sleeves. I can make nothing of this description when I read it. I hope you can!

Count Metternich entertained us all the afternoon
talking about himself. He has fought with the Emperor
Maximilian in Mexico, and when he speaks of him the
tears roll down his bronzed cheeks. He has fought in
all Don Carlos's battles, and is a strong partisan of the
Carlist party. His description of Don Carlos makes
one quite like him (I mean Don Carlos). He said that
Don Carlos goes about in a simple black uniform and
béret (the red cap of the Pyrenees), with the gold tassels
and the Order of the Golden Fleece on his neck (I call
that fantastic, don't you?). During his campaign he
suddenly swoops down upon people, no matter what
their condition is, and immediately there is a sentinel
placed before the door. The *consigne* is not strict: any
one can come and go as he pleases: photographers,
autographers, reporters, without hindrance, and there
is a general invitation to tea at headquarters. He has
an army of volunteers, of whom the Count is one. The
rations are one-half pound of meat, one-half pound of
bread, and three-quarters liter of Navarre wine, which
the Count says is more fit to eat than to drink, "it is
so fat." Navarre furnishes the wine gratis, and prom-

ises to furnish twenty-four thousand rations daily as long as the war lasts. The artillery is "not good," Count Metternich added, but the officers are "colossal," a word in German that expresses everything.

Count Metternich is the greatest gentleman jockey in the world; he has not got a whole bone in his body. They call him *der Mexicano*, as he is so bronzed and dark-skinned and has been in Mexico.

But he cannot rival Count Westphal, who, in his time, was not only the greatest gentleman jockey, but a hero. At a famous race, where he was to ride the horse of Count Fürstenberg, he fell, breaking his collar-bone and his left arm; he picked himself up and managed to re-mount his horse. He held the reins in his mouth, and with the unbroken arm walloped the horse, got in first, and then fainted away.

It was the pluckiest thing ever seen, and won for him not only the race, but the greatest fame and his Count-ess, who made him promise never to ride in a race again, and he never has. She told me that many ladies fainted and men wept, so great was the excitement and enthu-siasm! Count Fürstenberg had a bronze statue made of the horse, and it stands on Count Westphal's table now, and is an everlasting subject of conversation.

The Duke invited us all to come to Lippspringe. He and all the hunting-men have clubbed together and have hired the estate from the Baron B——, who owns both house and country and is fabulously rich, so people say. Here these gentlemen (I think there are twenty of them) go to pass two months every year to hunt foxes. There are forty couples of foxhounds, which have been im-ported from England.

There were eight of us, and we quite filled the four-horse break; servants and baggage followed later. We arrived at Paderborn, a thriving and interesting town of historical renown (see Baedeker). A two hours' drive left us rather cold and stiff, but we lunched on the carriage to save time. At the hotel we found a relay of four fresh horses harnessed in the principal street, the English grooms exciting great admiration by their neat get-up and their well-polished boots, and by the masterful manner they swore in English.

After racing through the quiet streets at a tearing pace, we arrived at the villa (*alias* club-house) at six o'clock, in time to dress for dinner at eight. The gentlemen appeared in regular hunting-dress: red evening coats, white buckskin trousers, top-boots, white cravats, and white vests; the ladies were *décolletées en grande toilette*.

Our dinner lasted till ten o'clock. The French chef served a delicious repast; everything was faultless even to the minutest details; the servants were powdered, plushed, and shod to perfection. Then we went to the drawing-room, where cards, smoking, billiards, and flirtation went on simultaneously until the small hour of one, when we retired to our rooms.

Countess Westphal and I had adjoining rooms, very prettily furnished in chintz. Everything was in the most English style.

It is the correct thing here to affect awful clothes in the daytime. The Baron (*der alte Herr*), when not hunting, wears an Italian brigand costume (short breeches, tight leggings, stout boots) and some animal's front teeth sewed on his Tyrolean hat to hold the little feathers. But in the evening, oh, dear me! nothing is equal to his elegance.

The next day the gentlemen (twenty in number), all splendidly mounted on English hunters, rode off at eleven o'clock, masses of grooms and *piqueurs*, with lots of hunting-horns and the dogs. We ladies followed in the break. The masters of the hounds were already at the rendezvous on the hill. They soon started a fox, and then the dogs tore off yelping and barking, and the riders riding like mad; and we waited in the carriages, sorry not to be with them. The red coats looked well against the background; the dogs, all of the same pattern, were rushing about in groups with their tails in the air; but while our eyes were following them the fox ran right under our noses, within a hair's-breadth of our wheels. Of course the dogs lost the scent, and there was a general standstill until another fox was routed out, and off they flew again. *Der alte Herr* is very much thought of in these parts; he was the only one who dared oppose the House of Peers in Berlin in the question of war with Austria in 1866, and made such an astounding speech that he was obliged to retire from politics and take to fox-hunting. He gave the speech to me to read, and—I—well!—I didn't read it!

The Westphalians seem to go on the let-us-alone principle; they seem to be anti-everything—from Bismarck and Protestantism downward. I sang the last evening of our stay here. The piano belonging to this hunting-lodge is as old as the *alte Herr*, and must have been here for years, and even at that must be an heirloom. The keys were yellow with age and misuse, and if it had ever been in tune it had forgotten all about

28 421

it now and was out of it altogether. I picked the notes out which were still good, and by singing Gounod's "Biondina" in a loud voice and playing its dashing accompaniment with gusto, I managed to keep myself awake. As for the tired hunters who had been in the saddle all day, they were so worn out that nothing short of a brass band could rouse them long enough for them to keep their eyes open.

The next day we bade our hosts good-by and, thanking them for our delightful visit, we departed. I wonder if the gentlemen liked being trespassed upon as much as we did who did the trespassing. However, they were polite enough to say that they had never enjoyed anything so much as our visit, and especially my singing. What humbugs! I was polite enough not to say that I had *never* enjoyed anything so *little* as singing for sleepy fox-hunters.

ROME, *January, 1875.*

DEAR MOTHER,—I am here in Rome, staying with my friends the Haseltines, who have a beautiful apartment that they have arranged in the most sumptuous and artistic manner in the Palazzo Altieri. Mr. Haseltine has two enormous rooms for his studio and has filled them with his faultless pictures, which are immensely admired and appreciated. His water-colors are perfection.

I have met many of your friends whom you will be glad to hear about: to begin with, the Richard Greenoughs, our cousins. We had much to talk about, as we had not seen each other since Paris, when he made that bust of me. They are the most delightful people, so talented in their different ways, and are full of interest in everything which concerns me. She has just published a book called *Mary Magdalene*, which I think is perfectly wonderful.

I have made the acquaintance of William Story (the sculptor). He spoke of you and Aunt Maria as his oldest and dearest friends, and therefore claimed the right to call me Lillie.

I have not only seen him, but I have seen Mrs. Story, Miss Story, and the third story in the Palazzo Barberini, where they live, and I have already counted many times the tiresome one hundred and twenty-two steps which lead to their apartment, and have dined frequently with them in their chilly Roman dining-room. This room is only warmed by the little apparatus which in Rome passes for a stove. It has a thin leg that sticks out of a hole in the side of the house and could warm a flea at a pinch.

The hay on the stone floor made the thin carpet warmer to my cold toes, which, in their evening shoes, were away down below zero, but my cold and bare shoulders shivered in this Greenland icy-mountain temperature which belongs to Roman palaces. This was before I was an *habituée;* but after I had become one I wore, like the other jewel-bedecked dames, woolen stockings and fur-lined overshoes. The contrast must be funny, if one could see above board and under board at the same time.

The Storys generally have a lion for dinner and for their evening entertainments. My invitations to their dinners always read thus: "Dear Mrs. Moulton,—We are going to have (mentioning the lion) to dinner. Will you not join us, and if you would kindly bring a little music it would be such a," etc. No beating about the bush there! The other evening Miss Hosmer—female rival of Mr. Story in the sculpturing line—was the lion of the occasion, and was three-quarters of an hour late, her excuse being that she was studying the problem of perpetual motion. Mr. Story, who is a wit, said he wished the motion had been perpetuated in a *botta* (which is Italian for cab).

February 1st.

Last Thursday, at nine o'clock in the morning, a card was brought to my bedroom. Imagine my astonishment when I read the name of Baroness de C——, the wife of the French Ambassador to the Vatican. What could she want at that early hour? I had heard many stories of her absent-mindedness. I thought that nothing less than being very absent-minded, or else the wish to secure my help for some charity concert, could account for this matutinal visit, especially as I knew her so slightly.

To my great surprise she had only come to invite me to dinner, and never mentioned the word charity concert or music. I thought this very strange; but as she is so *distraite* she probably did not know what time of day it was, and imagined she was making an afternoon visit.

One of the stories about her is that once she went to pay a formal call on one of her colleagues, and stayed on and on until the poor hostess was in despair, as it was getting late. Suddenly the ambassadress got up and said, "Pardon, dear Madame, I am very much engaged, and if you have nothing further to say to me I should be very grateful if you would leave me." The Baroness had been under the impression that she was in her own salon. They say that, one day, when she was walking in the Vatican gardens with the Pope, and they were talking politics, she said to him, "Oh, all this will be arranged as soon as the Pope dies!"

Well, we went to the dinner, which was quite a large one, and among the guests was Signor Tosti, which would seem to denote that there *was*, after all, "music in the air"; and sure enough, shortly after dinner the ambassadress begged me to sing some *petite chose*, and asked Tosti to accompany me. Neither of us refused, and I sang some of his songs which I happened to know, and some of my own, which I could play for myself.

However, I felt myself recompensed, for when she thanked me she asked if I had ever been present at any of the Pope's receptions.

I told her that I had not had the opportunity since I had been here.

"The Pope has a reception to-morrow morning," said she. "Would you care to go? If so, I should be delighted to take you."

"Oh," I said, "that is the thing of all others I should like to do!"

"Then," said she, "I will call for you and take you in my carriage."

This function requires a black dress, black veil, and a general funereal appearance and gloveless hands. Happily she did not forget, but came in her coupé at the appointed time to fetch me, and we drove to the Vatican.

The ambassadress was received at the entrance with bows and smiles of recognition by the numerous *ca-*

merieri and other splendidly dressed persons, and we were led through endless beautiful rooms before arriving at the gallery where we were to wait. It was not long before his Holiness (Pius IX.) appeared, followed by his suite of monsignors and prelates. I never was so impressed in my life as when I saw him. He wore a white-cloth *soutane* and white-embroidered *calotte* and red slippers, and looked so kind and full of benevolence that he seemed goodness personified. I knelt down almost with pleasure on the cold floor when he addressed me, and I kissed the emerald ring which he wore on his third finger as if I had been a born Catholic and had done such things all my life.

He asked me in English from which country I came, and when I answered, "America, your Holiness," he said, "What part of America?" I replied, "From Boston, Holy Father."

"It is a gallant town," the Pope remarked; "I have been there myself."

Having finished speaking with the men (all the ladies stood together on one side of the room and the men on the other), the Pope went to the end of the gallery. We all noticed that he seemed much agitated, and wondered why, and what could have happened to ruffle his benign face. It soon became known that there was an Englishman present who refused to kneel, although ordered to do so by the irate chamberlain, and who stood stolidly with arms folded, looking down with a sneer upon his better-behaved companions.

His Holiness made a rather lengthy discourse, and did not conceal his displeasure, alluding very pointedly to the unpardonable attitude of the stranger.

On leaving the gallery he turned around a last time, made the sign of the cross, giving us his blessing, and left us very much impressed. I looked about for my companion, but could not see her anywhere. Had she forgotten me and left me there to my fate? It would not be unlike her to do so.

I saw myself, in my mind's eye, being led out of the Vatican by the striped yellow and black legs and halberded guards, and obliged to find my way home alone; but on peering about in all the corners I caught sight of her seated on a bench fervently saying her prayers, evidently under the impression that she was in church during mass. As we were about to enter the coupé she hesitated before giving any orders to the servant, possibly not remembering where I had lived. But the footman, being accustomed to her vagaries, did not wait, and as he knew where to deposit me, I was landed safely at the Palazzo Altieri.

February 15th.

The Storys gave "The Merchant of Venice" the other evening. They had put up in one of the salons a very pretty little stage; the fashionable world was *au complet*, and, after having made our bows to Mrs. Story, we took our places in the theater. Mr. Story was Shylock, and acted extremely well. Edith was very good as Portia. Waldo and Julian both took part. Mr. and Mrs. Frank Lascelles, of the English Embassy, both dressed in black velvet, played the married couple to the life, but did not look at all Italian. The whole performance was really wonderfully well done and most successful; the enthusiasm was sincere and warmed the cold hands by the frequent clapping. We were so glad to be enthusiastic!

Mr. Story gave me his book called *Roba di Roma*, which I will tell you does *not* mean Italian robes—you might think so; it means things about Rome. I will also tell you, in case that your Italian does not go so far, that when I say that the Storys live in the third *piano*. I do not mean an upright or a grand—*piano* is the Italian for story.

Madame Minghetti—the wife of the famous statesman —receives every Sunday twilight. Rome flocks there to hear music and to admire the artistic manner in which the rooms are arranged; flirtations are rife in the twilit corners, in which the salon abounds. As Madame Minghetti is very musical and appreciative, all the people one meets there pretend to be musical and appreciative, and do not talk or flirt during the music; so when I sing "Medjé" in the growing crepuscule I feel in perfect sympathy with my audience. Tosti and I alternate at the piano when there is nothing better. If no one else enjoys us, we enjoy each other.

I have always wanted very much to see the famous Garibaldi, and knowing he was in Rome I was determined to get a glimpse of him. But how could it be done? I had been told that he was almost unapproachable, and that he disliked strangers above all.

However, where there is a will there seems to come a way; at any rate, there did come one, and this is how it came:

At dinner at the French Embassy I sat next to Prince Odescalchi, and told him of my desire to see Garibaldi. He said: "Perhaps I can manage it for you. I have a friend who knows a friend of Garibaldi, and it might be arranged through him."

"Then," I said, "your friend who is a friend of Garibaldi's will let you know, and as you are a friend of my friend you will let *her* know, and she will let *me* know."

"It sounds very complicated," he answered, laughing, "and is perhaps impossible; but we will do our best."

No more than two days after this dinner there came a message from the Prince to say that, if Mrs. Haseltine and I would drive out to Garibaldi's villa, the friend and the friend of the friend would be there to meet us and present us. This we did, and found the two gentlemen awaiting us at the gate. I felt my heart beat a little faster at the thought of seeing the great hero.

Garibaldi was sitting in his garden, in a big, easy, wicker chair, and looked rather grumpy, I thought (probably he was annoyed at being disturbed). But he apparently made up his mind to accept the inevitable, and, rising, came toward us, and on our being presented stretched out a welcoming hand.

He had on a rather soiled cape, and a *foulard*, the worse for wear, around his neck, where the historical red shirt was visible. His head, with its long hair, was covered with a velvet *calotte*. He looked more like an invalid basking in the sun with a shawl over his legs than he did like the hero of my imagination, and the only time he did look at all military was when he turned sharply to his parrot, who kept up an incessant chattering, and said, in a voice full of command, "Taci!" which the parrot did not in the least seem to mind (I hope Garibaldi's soldiers obeyed him better).

Garibaldi apologized for the parrot's bad manners by

saying, "He is very unruly, but he talks well"; and added, with a rusty smile, "Better than his master."

"I don't agree with you," I said. "I can understand you, whereas I can't even tell what language he is speaking."

"He comes from Brazil, and was given to me by a lady."

"Does he only speak Brazilian?" I asked.

"Oh no, he can speak a little Italian; he can say 'Io t'amo' and 'Caro mio'."

"That shows how well the lady educated him. Will he not say 'Io t'amo' for me? I should so love to hear him."

But, in spite of tender pleadings, the parrot refused to do anything but scream in his native tongue.

Garibaldi talked Italian in a soft voice with his friend and French to us. He asked a few questions as to our nationality, and made some other commonplace remarks. When I told him I was an American he seemed to unbend a little, and said, "I like the Americans; they are an honorable, just, and intelligent people."

He must have read admiration in my eyes, for he "laid himself out" (so his friend said) to be amiable. Amiability toward strangers was evidently not his customary attitude.

He went so far as to give me his photograph, and wrote "Miss Moulton" on it with a hand far from clean; but it was the hand of a brave man, and I liked it all the better for being dirty. It seemed somehow to belong to a hero. I think that I would have been disappointed if he had had clean hands and well-trimmed finger-nails. On our taking leave of him he conjured

GIUSEPPE GARIBALDI

up a wan smile and said, very pleasantly, giving us his ink-stained hand, "A rivederci."

I wondered if he really meant that he wanted to see us again; I doubt it, and did not take his remark seriously. On the contrary, I had the feeling that he was more than indifferent to the pleasure our visit had given him.

When we were driving back to Rome the horses took fright and began running away. They careered like wildfire through the gates of the Porta del Popolo, and bumped into a cart drawn by oxen and overloaded with wine-casks. Fortunately one of the horses fell down, and we came to a standstill. The coachman got down from the box and discovered that one of the wheels was twisted, the pole broken, and other damage done. We were obliged to leave the carriage and walk down the Corso to find a cab.

Just as we were getting into one we saw on the opposite side of the street a man who, while he was cleaning the windows in the third story of a house, lost his balance and fell into the street.

We dreaded to know what had happened, and avoided the crowd which quickly collected, thus shutting out whatever had happened from our view. We hurried home, trembling from our different emotions.

The next morning I awoke from my sleep, having had a most vivid dream. I thought I was in a shop, and the man serving me said, "If you take any numbers in the next lottery, take numbers 2, 18, and 9. This was extraordinary, and I immediately told the family about it: 2, 18, 9 (three numbers meant a *terno*, in other words, a *fortune*). Mr. H—— said, "Let us look out these numbers in the *Libro di Sogni* (the Book of Dreams)," and sent out to buy the book. Imagine our feelings! Number 2 meant *caduta d'una finestra* (fall from a window); number 18 meant *morte subito* (sudden death), and number 9 meant *ospedale* (hospital).

Just what had happened; the man had fallen from the window and had been carried dead to the hospital!

Perhaps you don't know what a tremendous part the lottery plays in Italy; it is to an Italian what sausages and beer are to a German. An Italian will spend his last *soldo* to buy a ticket. He simply cannot live without it. The numbers are drawn every Saturday morning at twelve o'clock, and are instantly exposed in all the tobacco-shops in the town.

An hour after, whether lucky or unlucky, the Italian buys a new ticket for the following week, and lives on hope and dreams until the next Saturday; and when any event happens or any dream comes to him he searches in the dream-book for a number corresponding to them, and he is off like lightning to buy a ticket. I was told that the Marquis Rudini, on hearing that his mother had met her death in a railroad accident, sought in the dream-book for the number attached to "railroad accident," and bought a ticket before going to get her remains.

A winning *terno* brings its lucky owner I don't know exactly how much—but I know it is something enormous.

Well, this would be a *terno* worth having. My dream, coming as it did straight from the blue, must be infallibility itself, and we felt perfectly sure that the three magical numbers would bring a fortune for every one of us, and we all sent out and bought tickets with all the money we could spare.

This was on Thursday, and we should have to wait two whole days before we became the roaring millionaires we certainly were going to be, and we strutted about thinking what presents we would make, what jewels we would buy; in fact, how we would use our fortunes! We sat up late at night discussing the wisest and best way to invest our money, and I could not sleep for fear of a *contre-coup* in the shape of another dream. For instance, if I should dream of a cat miauling on a roof, it would mean disappointment. It would never do to give fate a chance like that!

Imagine with what feverish excitement we awoke on that Saturday, and how we watched the numbers, gazing from the carriage-windows, at the tobacco-shop! Well, not one of those numbers came out! We drove home in silence, with our feathers all drooping. However, we had had the sensation of being millionaires for those two days (ecstatic but short!), and felt that we had been defrauded by an unjust and cruel fate.

Unsympathetic Mr. Marshal said, mockingly: "How could you expect anything else, when you go on excursions with the Marquis Maurriti [that was the name of Garibaldi's friend]? You might have known that you would come to grief."

"Unfeeling man! Why should we come to grief?" we cried with impatience.

"Because, did you not know that he has the *mal' occhio* [the evil eye]? I thought every one knew it," said he, making signs with his fingers to counteract the effect of the devil and all his works. We said indignantly,

"If every one knows it, why were we not told?" Our tormentor continued: "There is no doubt about it, and nothing can better prove that people are afraid of him than that when, the other evening, he gave a *soirée* and invited all Rome, only half a dozen people out of some five hundred ventured to go. The mountains of sandwiches, the cart-loads of cakes, the seas of lemonade, set forth on the supper-table, were attacked only by the courageous few."

"How dreadful to have such a thing said about you! Who can prove that he or any one else has got the evil eye?"

"Sometimes there is no foundation for the report; perhaps some one, out of spite or jealousy, spreads the rumor, and there you are."

"Does it not need more than a rumor?" I asked.

"Not much; but we must not talk about him, or something dreadful will happen to us."

"Do you also believe in such rank nonsense?" I asked.

"Of course I do!" Mr. Marshal replied. "You can see for yourself. If you had not gone with him your horses would not have run away, and you would surely have got your million."

"Well, we have escaped death and destruction and the million; perhaps we ought to be thankful. But in his case I would go and shut myself up in a monastery and have done with it."

"No monastery would take him. No brotherhood would brother *him*."

"You can't make me believe in the evil eye. Neither shall I ever believe in dreams again."

You will hardly believe how many acquaintances I have made here. I think I know all Rome, from the Quirinal and the Vatican down. The Haseltines know nearly every one, and whom they don't know I *do*.

We were invited to see the Colosseum and the Forum illuminations, and were asked to go to the Villino, which stands in the gardens of the Palace of the Cæsars, just over the Forum.

That there would be a very select company we had been told; but we did not expect to see King Victor Emanuel, Prince Umberto, and Princess Margherita, who, with their numerous suites and many invited guests, quite filled the small rooms of the Villino. I was presented to them all.

I found the Princess perfectly bewitching and charming beyond words; the Prince was very amiable, and the King royally indifferent and visibly bored. That sums up my impressions.

At the risk of committing *lèse majesté*, I must say that the King is more than plain. He has the most enormous mustaches, wide-open eyes, and a very gruff, military voice, speaking little, but staring much. The Prince, whom I had seen in Paris during the Exposition, talked mostly about Paris and of his admiration of the Emperor and Empress. The Princess was fascinating, and captivated me on the spot by her affability and her natural and sweet manner.

The Colosseum looked rather theatrical in the glare of the red and green Bengal lights, and I think it lost a great deal of its dignity and grandeur by this cheap method of illumination.

I met there a Spanish gentleman whom I used to

know in Paris years ago. He was at that time the Marquis de Lema, a middle-aged beau, who was always ready to fill any gap in society where a noble marquis was needed.

He began life, strange to say, as a journalist, and as such made himself so useful to the ex-King of Naples that the King, to reward him, hired the famous Farnesina Palace for ninety-nine years. Here the former Marquis, who is now Duke di Ripalda, lives very much aggrandized as a descendant of the Cid, glorying in his ancestorship.

He was very glad to see me again, he said, and to prove it came often to dine with us.

One day he asked Mrs. Lawrence, Miss Chapman, and myself to take tea with him in the romantic garden of the Farnesina. Mrs. Lawrence said it was like a dream, walking under the orange-trees and looking down on the old Tiber, which makes a sudden turn at the bottom of the broad terrace.

Her dream came suddenly to an end when she saw the stale cakes and the weak and watery tea and oily chocolate which, out of politeness, we felt obliged to swallow; and the nightmare set in when she saw his apartment on the first floor, furnished by himself with his own individual taste, which was simply awful. But who cares for the mother-of-pearl inlaid furniture covered with hideous modern blue brocade and the multicolored carpets in which his coat of arms were woven, when one can look at his Sodomas and Correggios and Raphaels? His coat of arms, which is a sword with "Si, si, no, no," is displayed everywhere throughout the palace.

The "*cid-evant*" Marquis told us that the Cid had given the sword to one of his ancestors, and remarked that it signified that his forefathers had very decided characters, and that it was either yes or no with them. I thought it might work the other way; it might just as well mean that the ancestors did not know their own minds, and that first it was *yes* and then it was *no* with them. The Duke, in a truly grandiose manner, lays no restriction on the public, but throws his whole palace open every first and fifteenth of the month, and allows people to roam at their pleasure through all the rooms; they can even sit on the blue brocade furniture if they like, and there is no officious guide ordering people about with their, "This way, Madame," or "Don't sit down," "Don't walk on the carpet," or "Don't spit on the floor."

On the ground floor are the celebrated frescoes of "Psyche," painted by Raphael, and in the large gallery there is a little design on the walls to which the Duke called our attention, saying it was Michelangelo's visiting-card, and told us that Michelangelo came one day, and, finding Raphael absent, took up his palette and painted this little picture, which still remains on the walls, framed and with a glass over it.

Mrs. Lawrence told us of a new acquaintance she had made, a Baron Montenaro, who said he was the last (the very last) of the Rienzis, a descendant of Cola di. The last tribune left! "Is it not romantic?" cried Mrs. Lawrence, and was all eyes and ears. But prosaic Duke di Ripalda said, "How can he say he is the last of the Rienzis, when he has a married brother who has prospects of a small tribune of his own?"

ROME, *April, 1875.*

Mrs. Polk (widow of the former President Polk) and her two daughters are very much liked here. I call Miss Polk *la maîtresse demoiselle,* because she rules every one with a high and masterful hand.

They had some wonderful tableaux recently at their palace (Salviati), which were most beautiful and artistically arranged by different artists. They had turned a long gallery which had once served as a ballroom into the theater. I was asked to sing in a tableau representing a Bohemian hall, where, as a background, Bohemian peasants in brilliant costumes sat and stood about. I was also dressed in a Bohemian dress, and leaned against a pillar and held a tambourine in my hand. Tosti played the accompaniment of "Ma Mère était Bohémienne," which was most appropriate to the occasion.

The Princess Margherita sat in the front row, and a more sympathetic and lovelier face could never have inspired a singer. She insisted upon my repeating my song, which rather bored the other performers, as they had to stand quiet while the song was going on. Tosti made the accompaniment wonderfully well, considering that I had only played it once for him.

After the tableaux, and when the Princess had retired to a little salon placed at her disposal, she sent word to ask me to come to her, as she wished to speak with me. I was overjoyed to see her again, as the short interview at the Villino could hardly be called an interview.

The Princess said: "I have heard a great deal about

438

your singing; but I did not believe any amateur could sing as you do. Your phrasing and expression are quite perfect!" She finished by asking me to come to the Quirinal to see her, "and perhaps have a little music"; and added, "The Marquis Villamarina sings beautifully, and you shall hear him." The Princess is so lovely, no words can describe her charm and the sweet expression of her face. Her smile is a dream.

I had intended leaving Rome the very day she fixed for my going to her, but of course I postponed my departure and I went, and had a most delightful afternoon. It was the first time that I had seen the Quirinal and I was very much interested. One of the numerous *laquais* who were standing about in the antechamber when I arrived preceded me into a salon where I found the Marquise Villamarina (first lady-in-waiting of the Princess). She came toward me, saying that the Princess was looking forward with pleasure to seeing me, and added that she hoped that I had thought to bring some music. I followed her through several very spacious salons until we reached a salon which evidently was the music-room, as there were two grand pianos and a quantity of music-books placed on shelves. Here I found the Princess waiting for me, and she received me with much cordiality.

The Marquis Villamarina has a most enchanting voice, liquid and velvety, the kind that one only hears in Italy. Signor Tosti (the composer) was already at the piano and accompanied the Marquis in "Ti rapirei, mio ben," a song he composed and dedicated to him. The Princess sang a very charming old Italian song. She has a mezzo-soprano voice and sings with great taste and sweetness. She, the Marquis, and I sang a trio of Gordigiani; then the Princess asked me to sing the "Ma Mère était Bohémienne," which I had sung at the tableaux. I also sang "Beware!" which she had never heard and which she was perfectly delighted with, and I promised to send her the music. It was a great pleasure to sing in this intimate and *sans façon* way, with the most sympathetic and charming of Princesses. Chocolate, tea, and little cakes were served, which I supposed was the signal for departure. The Princess, on bidding me good-by, gave me her hand and said, "I hope to see you soon again."

"Alas!" I replied, "I am leaving Rome to-morrow," and as I stooped down to kiss her hand she drew me to her and said, "I am sorry that you are going, I hoped that you were staying longer," and kissed me on both cheeks.

PARIS, *May, 1875.*

I have had a lazy month. Mrs. Moulton was delighted to have me back again, and I was glad to rest after all my junketing. Just think, I was almost a year in Germany!

Nina has had the measles, fortunately lightly; I was *garde malade,* and stayed with her in her sick-room.

Howard goes to a day-school not far from the Rue de Courcelles every morning, and comes home at two o'clock and shows with pride the book the teacher gives him to show. They must mean it to be shown, otherwise so much trouble would not be taken to make such lengthy and marvelous accounts of his prowess, the numbers running up in the thousands, and notations all through, such as *très bien, verbes sans faute,* and *dictés parfaits.* He can repeat all the departments of France backward and forward, and goes through the verbs, regular and irregular, like a machine. The French love these irregular verbs, so irregular sometimes that they border on frivolity. He has learned some rather inane patriotic poetry, which he recites with a childish dramatic swagger.

This is about all they teach in this school; but the *rapports* are worth the money: they deceive the parents, making them believe their geese are swans of the first water.

PARIS, *May.*

We have had real pleasure in hearing a young *pianiste* from Venezuela called Teresa Careño. She is a *wunderkind.* Her mother says she is nine years old; she looks twelve, but may be sixteen. No one can ever tell how old a *wunderkind* really is. Her playing is marvelous, her technic perfect. She knows about two hundred pieces by heart, is extremely pretty and attractive, and performs whenever she is asked. I think she has a great career before her, and she has already got the toss-back of her black hair in the most approved pianist manner. "Elle ne manque rien," the great Saint-Saëns said. One can't imagine that she could play better than she does; but *she* thinks that she is by no means perfect.

Though I said that I had led a *dolce-far-niente* existence, and had been lazy, I have been dreadfully busy and have been on the go from morning till night: I might call it a *dolce-far-molto* existence. I spend hours, which ought to be better spent, in shops. I simply revel in them.

You have heard of the famous actress Sarah Bernhardt. Well, she is not only an actress, but she is a sculptress, and is a very good one. She is now playing at the Vaudeville. But I must begin at the beginning, the whole thing was so amusing.

You remember Mrs. Bradley? You used to scold me for calling her "the Omelette." They are living now in Paris; her hair and complexion are just as yellow as they used to be; but her dresses are yellower. Beaumont said that she was "Une étude en jaune."

The other evening she had a box at the theater, and asked me to go to hear Sarah Bernhardt in "Le fils Giboyer." Her son, the immaculate Bostonian, went with us. He is a duplicate of his mother's yellowness. I took Nina, who looked extremely pretty: she was beaming with excitement; her cheeks were flushed, and her curly, golden hair made a halo about her delicate features. Every one stared at her when we entered the box. During the second act I let her take my place in front, and, observe how virtue is rewarded! In the following *entr'acte* the *ouvreuse* came in suddenly without knocking (*ouvreuses* never knock! that is one of their many privileges) and begged to *parler à* Monsieur. Imagine the chaste George's feelings when he was told that the famous Sarah wished to speak with him, and, moreover, desired him to come behind the scenes to her dressing-room. What a situation! His red hair blushed to the very roots, and his yellow face became a sunset. However, one is or one is not a man. He proved himself to be one who could face danger when the time came.

Trembling at the thought of Boston, the virtuous, hearing of it, he saw in his mind's eye the height the Puritan brows of his most distinguished family would reach when the news would be spread over the town, and a certain biblical scene passed before his mental vision.

He gave his lemon-colored mustache a final fascinating twist, and, humming to himself "Hail, the conquering hero comes!" he buckled on his sword and went—all his colors flying.

We waited breathlessly for his return, which was much sooner than we expected, and the smile he wore was not that of a conquering hero; it was another kind of a smile. Well, what do you think Madame Sarah wanted? Merely to know if the child in the box was his! His! His unmarried hair stood on end; he was so taken aback that he only had breath to mutter, "I am not married, Madame."

Then in her most dramatic tones she demanded, "Who is the child, then?"

He told her.

"Where does this Madame Moulton live?" she asked.

He told her that also. Then, with a dismissing wave of the hand, Sarah bade him farewell. It was all over. He had survived! Boston would never know.

The next day I received a note from Sarah Bernhardt, asking me if I would allow her to make a bust of *la charmante petite fille*. I answered that I should be delighted. Then came another note telling me at what time *l'enfant* should come for the first sitting.

I took Nina to the studio, which was beyond the Boulevard de Courcelles in a courtyard. It was enchanting to watch the artist at work. She was dressed like a man: she wore white trousers and jacket, and a white *foulard* tied artistically about her head. She had short and frizzly hair, and she showed us how she did it, gathering the four corners as if it were a handkerchief, with the ends sticking up on the top of her head. She smoked cigarettes all the time she was working.

She posed Nina in the attitude she thought interesting, with head down and eyes up—a rather tiring position. And to keep *l'enfant* quiet she devised all sorts of things. Sometimes she would rehearse her rôles in the voice they speak of as golden; because it coins gold for her, I suppose. The rehearsing of her rôles was not so amusing, as there were no *répliques;* but what kept Nina most quiet was when Sarah told her of the album she was making for her. Every artist she knew was working at some offering, and when it would be finished Nina was to have it. She would expatiate for hours on the smallest details. Meissonier, for instance, was painting a water-color, a scene of the war: a German regiment attacking a French inn, which was being defended by French soldiers. Then Gounod was writing a bit of music dedicated to *la charmante modèle*, and so forth. Nina would listen with open mouth and glistening eyes, and at every sitting she would say, "Et mon album?" expecting each time to see it forthcoming. But it never came forth. It only existed in Madame Bernhardt's fertile brain. It had no other object than to keep the model still. It seemed cruel to deceive the child. Even to the last, when Nina had said for the last time, "And shall I have my album to-day?" Sarah answered that it was not *quite* ready, as the binding was not satisfactory, and other tales, which, if not true, had the desired effect, and she finished the bust. It was not a very good likeness, but a very pretty artistic effort, and was sent to the next Exposition, receiving "honorable mention," perhaps more honorable than we mentioned her at home. She gave me a duplicate of it made of terra-cotta.

Don't expect any more letters, for I shall be very busy before my departure for America, which is next week, and then I shall. . . . Well, wait!

Good-by.

INDEX

IN THE COURTS OF MEMORY

dame, 364; discovers and visits Jules Alphonso, 365; news of Napoleon's death, 369; a German serenade, 373; "Pinafore" for the sailors, 374; a triumphal departure, 374.

Curls from the "Magasin du Bon Dieu" cause a sensation, 51.

D'AOUST'S, Marquis, operetta, 191, 198, 222, 227.

De Bassano, Duchess, *grande maîtresse*, 100.

Delle Sedie, music-teacher, and his theories, 38.

Delsarte and his emotion diagrams, 77; his "tabac," 145; the Emperor's joke, 150; Madame visits him during the siege, 287; his evening dress, 308.

De Morny, Duke (Queen Hortense's son), and his protégé, 31; as a librettist, with music by Offenbach, 36; his death, 76.

Doré caricatures nobility, 151.

EMERALDS from the Khedive, 171.

Eugénie, Empress, skates with Madame, 24; "a beautiful apparition," 28; in collision with an American, 30; at the play in Compiègne, 127; her flight from the Tuileries after Sedan assisted by Prince Metternich, 380; takes refuge with Dr. Evans, 382; widow and exile at Chiselhurst, 383.

Evans, Dr., American dentist, shelters the fleeing Empress after Sedan, 382.

Exposition of 1867, 154.

GALLIFET, Marquis de, tells of his silver plate, 142; criticizes English idioms, 212.

Garcia, Manuel, teacher of singing, engaged, 11; first impressions and lessons, 13; "Bel raggio" the first song, 14.

Garibaldi in retirement, 429; autographs his portrait, 430.

Gautier, Théophile, dinner companion, tells of his educated cats, 111; his poetical tribute to Madame, 131.

Germans in Versailles, 256.

Germany and the Rhineland, 375; visit to the Metternichs' château, Johannisberg, 377; reminiscences of the war, 380; famous Johannisberg wine, 384; a gentlemanly American broncobuster captures the Westphals, 394; at Weimar, 402; calling on a noble farmer, 404; boar-hunting in Westphalia, 409.

Gold button of the Imperial Hunt, a gift from Napoleon, 122; worn at a *chasse-à-tir*, 123; at a mock battle, 133.

Gounod "hums" deliciously, 159.

Green corn and a clay pipe at Fontainebleau, 93.

Green, Joshua, and his Creator, 6.

Gudin, William, artist, and his collection of cigars and cigarettes, 45.

HATZFELDT, Count, married to Madame's sister Helen, 248; Bismarck's secretary, 256; his opinion of Napoleon, 257; German minister to Madrid, 375.

Hegermann - Lindencrone, Madame Lillie de, prefatory note, i, iii.

IN London society, 236.

Imperial gifts, 76, 105, 122, 150, 171.

Imperial hunt fashions and cruelty to animals, 123, 146; the dog's share, 149, 220.

"LA DIVA DU MONDE"—Strakosch tempts Madame to sing in concert, 335; an immediate success, 337; story of a floral harp, 338; a trying moment in oratorio, 339; news of Mr. Moulton's illness and sudden death, 339, 340.

Lincoln, President, at the Sanitary Fair, 64; compliments Madame,

448